I0062992

The Heart and Brain of Your Business

The Role of Architecture and Engineering in Business Operations

An Architectural Approach to Business Planning, Analysis, Management, Monitoring, and Modernization

Anthony Insolia
Russell Boyd
David Rice

Copyrights © 2004-2020 by
Anthony Insolia,
Russell Boyd, and
David Rice

Self-published by Anthony Insolia, Russell Boyd, and David Rice

Hardcover and Softcover are distributed worldwide by
IngramSpark.COM

Printed in the United States of America

All rights reserved. No part of this publication may be reproduced,
distributed, or transmitted in any form or by any means, including
photocopying, recording, or other electronic or mechanical methods,
without the prior written permission of the publisher, except in the case
of brief quotations embodied in critical reviews and certain other
noncommercial uses permitted by copyright law. For permission
requests, write to the publishers, addressed "Attention Permissions
Coordinator," at TheHeartAndBrainOfYourBusiness@gmail.com.

Library of Congress Control Number: 2020908181

Hardcover ISBN: 978-1-7350022-0-0

Softcover ISBN: 978-1-7350022-1-7

TABLE OF CONTENTS

FIGURE LIST

PREFACE

Do you think of your business as having a heart and brain? It isn't often, even in the business world, that we hear this. The closest we got to this sort of thinking was in the early 2000's when, according to a Wikipedia® article, IBM®[1] initiated the concept of Autonomic Computing and the idea of computer systems being capable of self-management and facilitating systems management[2]. But what about a business capable of some level of self-management? Companies like SAP®[3] get us close with the advent of Enterprise Resource Planning (ERP) systems and their holistic approach to looking at and managing a business. This book is about an added component and discipline which has been around for a while but is typically not integrated into the business. We are referring to the Architecture or design of your business.

The integrated approach to documenting both business and Information Technology is referred to as Enterprise Architecture (EA). But in the digital era that we are in, that approach has been considered a discretionary Information Technology (IT) discipline placed within IT organizations where the architecture is used to define the structure and components of an IT System or a Computer Application, and (at best) to modernize IT. At present, and if produced, these architectures as descriptions of IT Systems are more often than not informal and they are too focused on the technical solution and not business itself. The architectures rarely provide an unambiguous specification of what is to be built, they don't describe the business, the data is not used in day to day business operations, and they don't result in effective and cost-efficient modernization. This is some of what is happening within the IT side of the organization.

Simultaneously, people on the business side of the organization say, "what is Architecture and why do I need that?". Some understand what a

---

1 IBM® is a registered trademark of the International Business Machines (IBM) Corporation

2 The Wikipedia® article on Autonomic Computing is found at:
   https://en.wikipedia.org/wiki/Autonomic_computing

3 SAP® is a trademark or registered trademark of SAP AG® in Germany and in other countries

business plan[4,5,6,7] is and why it is important, why not an architecture? Like a business plan the architecture documents and includes, among other things, goals, objectives, and performance expectations for each planning cycle and then acts as a baseline against which one measures and monitors performance. It also includes Business Scenarios that the business may need to be prepared for. In this case, the Architecture documents what is needed, what to avoid, the direction to head in, and the intended business outcomes.

> This form of architecture is a more complete and unambiguous business plan that is developed using formal methods. We are referring to the architecture of a business but refrain from calling it Business Architecture straight away because Business Architecture as practiced today does not result in a complete and holistic view of the business.

There are issues on both sides of the business and the issues are compounded by the fact that people seem to be on the "fast path to enlightenment", so much so that some people will forgo or minimize the architecture and others are even forgoing the development of business plans. While this might feel good to higher-ups in the organization, it places the business at risk and if the organization has launched an

---

4 Ernst & Young, LLP has an outline for a business plan online at https://bizplan.mgt.unm.edu/assets/pdf/ey-plan.pdf. We've cited this outline for the opening sentence which says that a business plan is: "*a written representation of where a company is going, how it will get there, and what it will look like once it arrives*". This is exactly what a Business Architecture is intended to do.

5 The Investopedia has a good writeup entitled "*Business Plan*", on what a business plan is and why it is important. See https://www.investopedia.com/terms/b/business-plan.asp. At this time, the article is "Reviewed by Will Kenton" and "Updated on June 25th, 2019

6 Given that most businesses start out small and given that they are grown organically, you may also want to refer to the Investopedia on "The 4 Most Common Reasons a Small Business Fails". One of reasons cited is business plan issues. See https://www.investopedia.com/articles/personal-finance/120815/4-most-common-reasons-small-business-fails.asp. At this time, the article shows the author as Melissa Horton and that the article was updated on August 12th, 2019.

7 We cite yet another Investopedia article entitled "*Business Startup Costs: It's in the Details*" written by Chizoba Morah and last updated on August 12th, 2019. We cite this article given that an Architectural approach to documenting a business provides details that might otherwise be overlooked. The Architectural approach also provides both the owner and the venture capitalist with a better understanding of the funding required to start and sustain the business. See https://www.investopedia.com/articles/pf/09/business-startup-costs.asp We like the opening line: "*There's more to a business than furnishings and office space*".

architecture initiative, it risks turning the architecture team into a collection of talented first responders rather than strategic contributors. Business leaders will view the architecture initiative as tactical and ad hoc, and stakeholders in the wider organization won't see it as something that adds value.

Without formal documentation (Architecture) on target operating models and without plans for establishing the target operating model, a business startup or transformation initiative can be quite ineffective. Without this documentation, plans, and an eye towards the future, these initiatives tend to:

- **Create reactive initiatives that hinder business engagement -** today's business environment faces increasingly high levels of uncertainty and change. This often leads to evolving business demands that seem to require immediate attention. Architecture and engineering teams that are set up purely to react to these demands will become ineffective as they become pulled in many different directions at once. In this environment, if the architecture and business teams do not operate from a shared set of principles and guidelines, it becomes impossible to coordinate efforts

- **Establish technology-driven priorities with no business context -** many technology management leaders are under immense pressure to control technology costs while supporting the business agenda. Frequently, however, architecture and engineering teams are set up as owners of the application inventory and pictorial representations of the IT applications and shared software services that comprise those applications. In this role, the architecture team struggles to balance the needs of the business technology agenda with the technology management agenda. As a result, the architecture organization typically loses the attention of the business executives because there is no business context to the architecture and engineering mandates.

- **Remain mired in the past** trying to justify their existence to people that don't understand what architecture is and why it is important

Even in articles published by the U.S. Government's General Accountability Office (GAO) there is an equal emphasis on the applicability of architecture to organizational transformation and system modernization. The GAO knows that one must consider both operational and IT aspects of a business and its' mission. As an example, consider the GAO report published in August of 2010: GAO-10-846g Organizational Transformation Series and article[8] by Randolph Hite which states:

> "*Effective use of well-defined Enterprise Architecture (EA) is a hallmark of successful organizations and a basic tenet of <u>organizational transformation</u> <u>and</u> <u>systems</u> <u>modernization</u>. Since the early 1990's, GAO has promoted federal department and agency EA adoption as an essential means to achieving a desired end: having <u>operational</u> <u>and</u> <u>technology</u> <u>environments</u> that maximize institutional mission performance and outcomes. Among other things, this includes realizing cost savings through consolidation and reuse of shared services and elimination of antiquated and redundant mission operations, enhancing information sharing through data standardization and system integration, and optimizing service delivery through streamlining and normalization of business processes and mission operations. The alternative, as GAO has reported, is department and agency operations and supporting information technology (IT) infrastructures and systems that are duplicative, poorly integrated, unnecessarily costly to maintain and interface, and unable to respond quickly to shifting environmental factors.*"[9]

Why the myopia and obsession with IT and why the malaise when one talks about Architecture? We are in the midst of the digital revolution and information technology is important in that respect, but architecture plays a more important role and architecture focused on applications and systems alone is inadequate. One must understand and apply the complete architecture metaphor and the architecture must provide a holistic view of the business. This holistic view incudes where the business is going, and how it will get there.

This architectural approach provides industry with a standard framework for practitioners and individuals who wish to address business challenges and adopt architecture as a form of business planning. This book comes in the form of best practices, a "how-to" guide, and lessons learned by the three authors who have been leading the practice of business architecture within organizations for nearly 60 years combined. As a "how-to" guide, the book is intended to help a government agency or company understand this architectural approach to documenting the composition of their business and the inter-relationships between investments. Since the architectural approach entails both business and IT, it also helps the IT side

---

[8] GAO Report from the Organizational Transformation Series can be found here: https://www.gao.gov/assets/80/77233.pdf

[9] Note that the terms "federal" and "agency" in this quote refer to the U.S. Federal Government and U.S. Federal Government Agency's

of the business minimize duplication of systems and to improve interoperability and compatibility between systems.

In this book, we emphasize the importance of the architecture and engineering disciplines to business operations. We also attempt to address challenges associated with launching an architecture and engineering initiative and getting the disciplines engrained in existing processes. To do this, we've broken the book down into parts as follows:

- In **Part I – Setting the Stage**, we introduce the architecture metaphor and provide a formal definition of this form of architecture being discussed. We also introduce the concept of a business or operating model where the architecture is viewed as the rationale behind the chosen Business / Operating Models and how those models create, deliver, and capture value.
- In **Part II – Success Factors,** you will discover that architecture and engineering methods are the tools for creating formal descriptions of a business, and that the architecture also includes a tool agnostic[10] repository for maintaining the data / information that the methods yield. In this section, we discuss the architecture framework and how it is used to position and stage the gathering of the information that comprise formal descriptions of the business and the underlying IT. We also share some of the more important building blocks of a business to provide a clear and concise understanding of what the business does and how it operates.
- In **Part III – Architecture in Business Operations** we touch on the uses of architecture and how to fully embrace the architecture metaphor. Before wrapping up, we share some lesson learned in **Part IV – Case Studies** and discuss some foundational matters in **Part V – Foundations** and then we wrap up with **Part VI – Closing**.

There has never been a better time than today to become the Chief Architect of your business with an architecture focus and tools at your side. Tools and data that are essential to any business and their need to modernize and remain competitive and vibrant.

---

10 With one exception that the authors are aware of, EA Tools at this time are typically standalone tools designed to support one or two forms of modeling and they have unique formats. Large businesses, more than likely, employ multiple tools. For these reasons and because the architecture information needs to come together (warehoused), one needs a repository that is tool agnostic.

PART I – SETTING THE STAGE

INTRODUCTION

This book presents an architectural approach to documenting a business[11] and it presents the resulting architecture as the heart and brain of the business as an autonomic[12] system. Certain functions of the body are referred to as autonomic because they are involuntary and they are performed unconsciously. Like the body breathes without us thinking about it, so should architecture be part of the life of a business, without it being forced and without it being a planned event. As involuntary functions, there is no need to mention agility and as you will see, having architecture data on hand makes for an agile business.

To establish this understanding of the role of architecture in business, we discuss the traditional architectural approach to documenting business operations and documenting how Information Technology supports and automates business operations. We present that architectural approach in a new light where the subject of the architecture is a business and where the business is typically a company or government agency. Also, where the emphasis is on the importance of architecture and engineering data in day to day operations. We show what information is in the architecture and how the information is used to monitor the health and well-being of the business and make adjustments accordingly. We also present some of the important business applications of this form of this architecture.

The architecture of a business or government agency is a living part of the organization, one that documents what the organization is intended to be, how it is to operate, and where actual performance measures are established, monitored, and acted upon. As such, the architecture serves as both the heart and brain of the business or agency as an autonomic system. This is depicted in *Figure 1: The Architecture of an organization as the Heart and Brain*. The center boxes and repositories in that figure represent architecture or plans and the IT environment / automation. In this notional view (an architectural view is provided later in *Figure 27 on*

---

11 There are businesses that are sometimes referred to as an Enterprise. In the simple case, an Enterprise is an organizational unit within a company or the company itself. On the complex end an Enterprise might be a government where the Enterprise Architecture is "federated" based on the architecture of each agency/authority that comprises the governmental body. Two examples of an Enterprise that is larger than one business include (A) the U.S. Department of Defense, and (B) the U.S. Federal Government.

12 The word Autonomic alone means "involuntary or unconscious". It is used specifically in the medical field relating to the autonomic nervous system. The autonomic nervous system in the body regulates and balances two competing parts of the nervous system.

page 122), the Architecture Repository is representative of the heart and brain of the business. The three boxes across the top are a notional representation of the activities performed, and the boxes across the bottom are representative of some internal and external sources informing the architecture.

Note that there are specialty data sources like the American Productivity

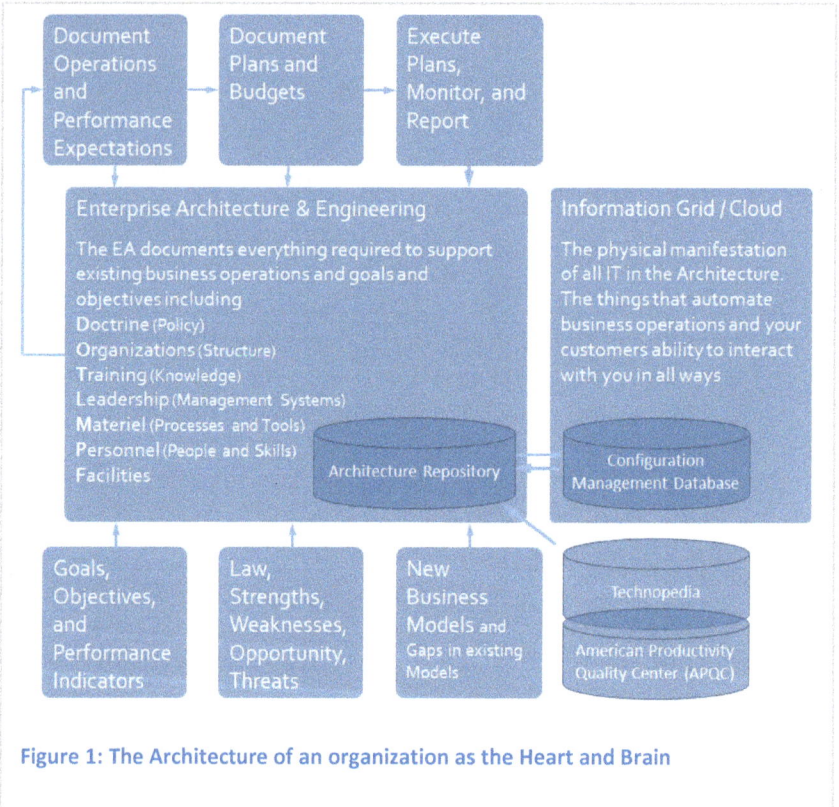

Figure 1: The Architecture of an organization as the Heart and Brain

Quality Center (APQC®) for business process data and the FLEXERA®[13] Technopedia® for product data. Each of these (and other potential sources) are important in and of themselves but they don't provide a complete picture. This is one example of where the Architects and Engineers come in. Using the Technopedia® as an example, Architects and Engineers document where in the business certain products are being used and assess the efficacy of those products. Also note in this figure that,

---

[13] Flexera acquired BDNA. See https://www.linkedin.com/company/bdna-corporation/
was recently acquired by Flexera Corporation

some of that architecture and engineering data feeds the IT Configuration Management Database (CMDB)[14].

By positioning the architecture in this manner and by focusing on the business, performance indicators and cost, one caters to the business community, customers, and suppliers. One of the first steps in positioning the architecture in this way is to fully embrace the architecture metaphor and to replace discussions about frameworks and tools with discussions on the Business Areas / Lines, Business Models, Capabilities, Performance Measures, and Best Practices. These are some of the more important building blocks of a business. They are documented in the architecture to provide a clear and concise understanding of how the business is structured, what the business does, and how it operates.

Generally speaking, the architecture metaphor is understood to mean that, if one creates blueprints for the planning, costing, construction and maintenance of a building then one can and should do the same for an entire business or government agency. The metaphor is more encompassing though, and the architecture of a business is more than just a set of blueprints. The architecture of a business is the source of knowledge about the constituent parts and capabilities of the business, the underlying Doctrine, Organization, Training, Materiel, Leadership, Personnel, and Facilities (DOTMLPF)[15] and the expectations and performance of each.

---

14 The authors have implemented such a feed / interface and they have experienced both the benefits of having this interface and the woes of not. In one client engagement, the authors established a formal architecture repository and an interface from the repository to the client's service management system. This made for a very smooth transition to production and enables support / operational readiness. In another engagement, the client did little formal architecture, what they did have in the way of data was individually owned spreadsheets and no though was put into data needed for support until the system was deployed. In this engagement, the client paid several million dollars, after the fact, to load the Configuration Management Database.

15 DOTMLPF is Doctrine, Organization, Training, Materiel, Leadership, Training, Personnel, and Facilities from The Chairman of the Joint Chiefs of Staff Instruction (CJCSI) 3170.01H, "Joint Capabilities Integration and Development System" (JCIDS)

Cutting to the chase, the complete architecture metaphor is comprised of three simple verbs and three nouns:

1. Zone the Business / Organization
2. Architect Capabilities, and
3. Engineer DOTMLPF

and there are three tools, commonly referred to as frameworks, that the authors use to do this. They are the:

1. Zachman Framework®
2. Federal Enterprise Architecture Framework (FEAF), and
3. Department of Defense Architecture Framework (DODAF)

While there are other frameworks like the Open Group® Architecture Framework® (TOGAF®) this book and our discussion is based on the above-mentioned frameworks. You may choose another framework or even create a hybrid as we have done.

The concept of the architecture as the heart and brain of a business is rooted then, in the need to understand what the business does, how it is structured, how it operates, and how well the business is performing. With an architecture in place[16], one can then readily answer questions like "Have the performance expectations for the various parts of the business been set and is each part of the business performing as expected?".

Given the importance of this focus on the business, we introduce a synonym and definition which does not use the 'E' word (Enterprise), the 'A' word (Architecture), and it certainly doesn't use the 'F' word (Framework). A Business or Operating Model is a suitable alternative:

> "A **Business / Operating Model** describes the rationale of how an organization creates, delivers, and captures economic, social, and other forms of value. The term business model is thus used for a broad range of informal and formal descriptions to represent core aspects of a business, including purpose, offerings, strategies, infrastructure, organizational structures, trading practices, and operational processes and policies"[17]

Architecture frameworks and the supporting engineering methods are the tools for creating the formal descriptions of a business, where the

---

16 One can do this with some Enterprise Resource Planning (ERP) systems, but ERP systems do not typically cover all aspects of the architecture and engineering discipline being discussed.

17 For an overview of what a Business Model is, refer to the Wikipedia® at http://en.wikipedia.org/wiki/Business_model

architecture includes a tool agnostic repository for maintaining the data / information that the methods yield. The Architecture Framework is used to position and stage the gathering of the information that comprise those formal descriptions.

Informally, we have introduced architecture as documentation and the idea that there are activities that produce and / or consume that documentation. We've introduced both the noun and verb forms of the term. The Architecture (noun), as information in a tool agnostic repository, being a broad yet thin view of the business best described in Zachman Framework®[18],[19] terms as a *Planner's View* of the business[20].

We mentioned the Zachman Framework® but the authors leverage three architecture frameworks that when combined, almost completely, enable this Architecture and Engineering as a discipline. The gaps are covered in the section entitled: *Methods, Languages, and Notations*. The frameworks are the:

- o   Zachman Framework®[21],
- o   Federal Enterprise Architecture Framework (FEAF)[22], and
- o   Department of Defense Architecture Framework (DODAF)[23].

We count three frameworks because the originators of those frameworks refer to them as such, but taking a "forest for the trees" view of the discipline, we see the Zachman Framework® as the framework proper. We view the FEAF as a specification for the development of a "Planner's View" of the business. We view the DODAF as a specification for architecting and blueprinting each capability that comprise the business. The DODAF being a specification which is already unified in its' adoption of the architecture constructs originally found in the UK Ministry of Defense Architecture

---

18 Information on the Zachman Framework can be found at
   https://www.zachman.com/
19 Zachman®, Zachman Framework® and Zachman International® are trademarks or registered trademarks of Zachman International, Inc.
20 A Planner's View of a business may contain some owner level detail. That is, the demarcating line between the Planner and Owner Views of a Business, Capability, or System is somewhat arbitrary and up to you as to where the line should be drawn.
21 The Zachman Framework® is introduced by the Zachman Institute® here:
   https://www.zachman.com/about-the-zachman-framework
22 The FEAF is documented here:
   https://obamawhitehouse.archives.gov/sites/default/files/omb/assets/egov_docs/fea_v2.pdf
23 The DODAF is documented here: https://dodcio.defense.gov/Library/DoD-Architecture-Framework/dodaf20_all_view/

Framework (MODAF), the NATO Architecture Framework (NAF), and the Open Group Architecture Framework (TOGAF).

The Zachman Framework® is the framework that we apply, and we apply it recursively in documenting the business and the Capabilities of the business. It is through this recursive approach that we first create a FEAF-based Planner's View of the business in the form of FEAF Reference Models[24] and then create DODAF-based blueprints for each Capability found in the Planner's View.

> Please note that, our choice of frameworks and specifications is based on repeated successes that the authors have had with these frameworks and on our unbiased approach. While two of the frameworks come from the government / public sector, they have served the authors well in the private sector too.
>
> Our successes are also premised, at this point in time, on the need for a hybrid framework taking piece parts from other frameworks. It is our view that this book should help with the creation of a unified framework that all organizations can apply.

The framework is also used for the care and feeding of the architecture repository. With the idea that the architecture requires maintenance in mind, the framework and specifications comprise an approach and a set of activities for assuring that the architecture repository is up to date and correct.

Today the architecture metaphor, the role of architecture in business operations, the frameworks, and the engineering methods do not appear to be fully understood. This include a lack of focus on the portfolio management aspects of this form of architecture and a dearth of business involvement. The issue is exacerbated by people not taking the time to look at their respective disciplines and observing that they are really trying to do the same thing: document the business in a complete and systematic way. Symptoms of this are:

   o   Business Analysts and Requirements Management folks thinking that they are not practicing architecture, or that they are

---

24 According to the OASIS (Organization for the Advancement of Structured Information Standards) a reference model is "*a framework for understanding significant relationships among the entities of some environment, and for the development of consistent standards or specifications supporting that environment*"

practicing "Business Architecture" while other folks are tending to the IT.

- o Advisory firms skipping very important steps and, in some cases, launching straight away into detailed workflows without having first applied any IDEFo® methods to document what the business does
- o Placement of the architecture function in a technology organization re-enforcing a perceived separation of business and IT. People speak of the need for a "bridge" between Business and IT. These are not islands; no bridge is required.
- o The relegation of the CIO to IT operations and assuring that common / enterprise-wide systems like the EMAIL system is up and working
- o The placement of roles like the Chief Data Officer (CDO) outside the of the architecture and engineering organization
- o Placing the Chief Architect below the CIO or CTO
- o Little to no coordination between the CIO, COO, CTO, CDO, and CFO
- o Staffing the architecture and engineering function with a single person when in fact the function is an Initiative with an embedded Program

Another symptom, is the overloading of the architecture term. In spite of the architecture malaise, people seem to make casual use of the 'A' word (Architecture) and talk about:

- o Business Architecture,
- o Data Architecture,
- o Application Architecture,
- o System Architecture
- o Computer Architecture,
- o Technical Architecture,
- o Network Architecture,
- o Infrastructure Architecture,
- o Integration Architecture,
- o Etc.

The list goes on and on but, aside from "Business Architecture" these are forms of engineering, and the architecture and engineering discipline being discussed is a holistic and integrated approach to doing what people refer to as "Business Architecture".

Where are we then? We have a set of activities and an architecture repository but what do we do with them, how are they put to use?

Architecture is used in *strategic planning* and *investment management, contract management, risk management, supplier management,* and *the maturation and optimization of business operations*[25]. The Architecture provides an integrated view of the information required for these disciplines. This is why the architecture is so central to business operations and why it serves as the heart and brain of the business.

We elaborate on each of these uses later but first emphasize *Strategic Planning*. In particular, we elaborate on the role of the architect in facilitating that process and the information gathering required to get the business from the early stages of the planning process to the final stages[26]. This information gathering is done so that investment decisions made in the later phases of the planning process are informed. Engineering is the thing that happens in the mid-stages of strategic planning to assure that proposed investments have a positive net-present value.

The architects then, are organizationally neutral: they are not a member of either the IT organization or the Business Area / Line that has to realize some capability or facet of the business. Ideally, architects are part of the strategy and planning organization. The business Areas / Lines do require architects and the strategy and planning organization can provision trained architects and engineers with tools. Having the strategy group as a service provider assures that policy is adhered to and that the architecture comes together as a whole.

Architecture in business operations and optimization is analogous then, to the set of master plans that towns and cities establish to assure that growth is planned, organized, and geared towards desired outcomes. While we have introduced the concept of a business or operating model and whereas the architecture content can be viewed as the 'rational' behind how a particular Business / Operating Model creates, delivers, and captures value, there is more to it than that as a business may employ multiple operating models, especially conglomerates, where each business line (some wholly owned subsidiaries) have a unique operating model and their own Architecture.

---

25 You might argue that these are the business functions that your company uses an Enterprise Resource Planning (ERP) System for, and you are correct, but ERP systems at this time do not cover all the elements and building blocks of a business.
26 Your organization may have an annual planning cycle with spring and fall stages or something more complex like the Department of Defense's Five-Year Development Plan or FYDP cycle, it doesn't matter. Zoning/Planning, Architecture, and Engineering are practiced throughout the cycle and leveraged throughout.

Whether architecting a capability or a house; architecture, plans, and costing models are needed to understand what is being proposed and built / acquired. The discipline and products are key in understanding the reasons for constructing and making the acquisitions. The architecture and plans articulate what is required at any one point in time for the realization of business goals and business scenarios. Architecture plays a key role in optimizing the developmental and operational aspects of the capabilities of a business. It optimizes cost of the delivery against mission / business needs, revenue / appropriations[27], goals, and investment money at hand.

Before moving on then, it is important to understand the context of this discipline and to dispel some misconceptions. It has been asserted that **(A)** there is an "Architecture Process" and **(B)** that this discipline is a subset or part of Service Management and the Information Technology Infrastructure Library (ITIL) Framework.

We view this architecture and engineering discipline, not as a process but rather, as a set of activities that comprise the Strategic Planning and Program / Project Management Processes. It is these activities, as parts of these processes, that result in **(A)** a strategic plan and budget, and **(B)** formally documented Capabilities.

By embedding architecture and engineering activities into these processes, the business reduces risk with a more complete understanding of the investment being made and the associated net-present value.

While the ITIL is maturing and while ITIL is recasting itself as IT Service Management (ITSM) it remains an IT discipline that focuses on *"aligning IT services with the needs of business"* (see https://en.wikipedia.org/wiki/ITIL).

---

27 This applies to 'for-profit' companies. In the case of governments, one uses architecture to balance mission and public needs against appropriations

ARCHITECTURE DEFINED

According to a definition found on the worldwide web, Architecture is "the conceptual structure and logical organization of a computer or computer-based system"[28]. Definitions vary though; the Merriam Webster Dictionary® adds to this: "the manner in which the components of a computer or computer system are organized and integrated"[29] Interestingly, both are computer and IT focused.

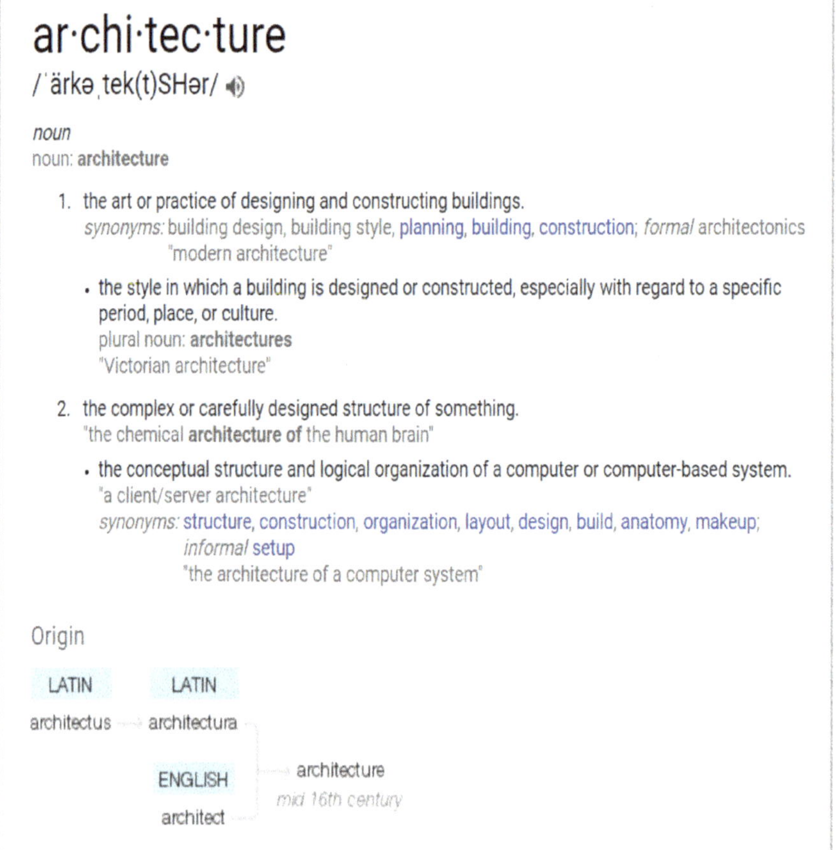

ar·chi·tec·ture
/ˈärkəˌtek(t)SHər/ ◄))

noun
noun: **architecture**

1. the art or practice of designing and constructing buildings.
   synonyms: building design, building style, planning, building, construction; *formal* architectonics
   "modern architecture"

   - the style in which a building is designed or constructed, especially with regard to a specific period, place, or culture.
     plural noun: **architectures**
     "Victorian architecture"

2. the complex or carefully designed structure of something.
   "the chemical **architecture of** the human brain"

   - the conceptual structure and logical organization of a computer or computer-based system.
     "a client/server architecture"
     synonyms: structure, construction, organization, layout, design, build, anatomy, makeup; *informal* setup
     "the architecture of a computer system"

Origin

LATIN	LATIN
architectus	architectura

ENGLISH — architecture
mid 16th century
architect

Figure 2: Architecture as Defined in the Dictionary

---

28 This definition is the result of a google.com search for "Architecture Definition".
29 The Merriam Webster Dictionary provides a definition for Architecture at
  http://www.merriam-webster.com/dictionary/architecture

The application of the architecture concept to information systems can be traced back to, among other sources, an article by John Zachman[30] in the IBM® Systems Journal where John discussed the need for "*information systems architecture*". Implicit in this is the idea that the information system[31,32] can be a business. In that case the business is viewed as a system of systems and the associated IT piece parts as components. Using the term *system* loosely, a business is an information system that produces product and information for consumers and interested parties. The system consumes information about how its' products and services are doing in the market. This applies to both companies and governments.

We are dealing with the Architecture and Engineering of organizations where an organization can be an entire company, a single organizational unit within a company, a collection of companies, or a federation of legal entities like governmental agencies and authorities[33]. With the above definition and our introductory material in mind then, one would say that this architecture and engineering discipline is a tool for documenting the logical and physical structure of a business / organization and that the architecture is used to document the manner in which the components of the business are organized and integrated.

This form of architecture does entail documenting the manner in which the components of the business are organized and integrated, but there needs to be some consensus on the primary components (Building Blocks) of a business. A preview of some large grained and high order building blocks is depicted in *Figure 3: Key Building Blocks of a Business*. As depicted, a business is composed of Functional Areas which are either a Business Line (operating unit) or a Business Area (non-operating unit). Also depicted is Capability, where Capabilities are large grained activities performed by and germane to a Business Area / Line. We are getting slightly ahead of

---

30 John A. Zachman (1987). "A Framework for Information Systems Architecture"; IBM® Systems Journal, volume 26; no 3; IBM® Publication G321-5298

31 A working definition for what a System of Systems is can be found in the Wikipedia® at https://en.wikipedia.org/wiki/System_of_systems. Additional background and discussion can be found on the IEEE website at https://rs.ieee.org/tech-activities/77-systems-of-systems

32 Note that in the Zachman article, John Zachman states "*discussion is limited to architecture and does not include a strategic planning methodology*". Architecture and strategic planning apply the same framework recursively.

33 The term Federation is typically used in governments where the federation may be comprised of some logical collection of governmental agencies or organizational units that comprise one agency. In particular, the concept of federation is applied when the owner of the architecture does not have complete control over the architecture. That is, the architecture is a collection of architectures.

ourselves though, and need to get back to our definition and the metaphor.

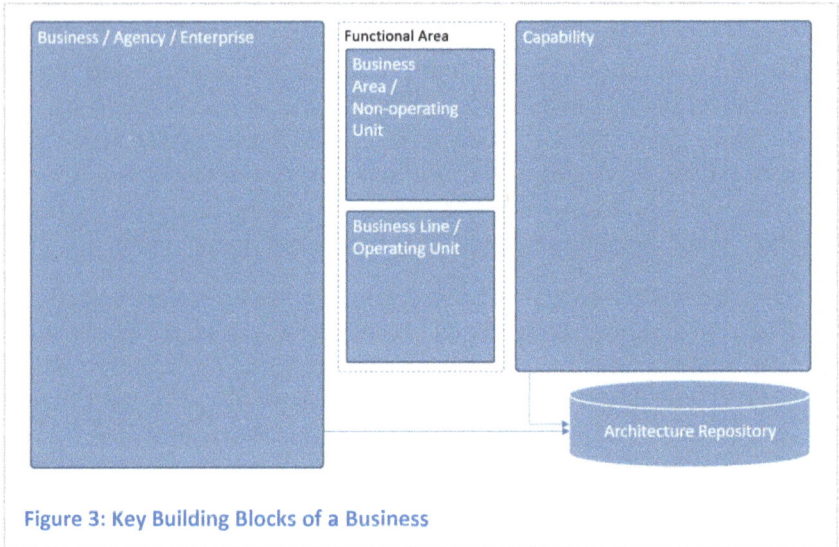

Figure 3: Key Building Blocks of a Business

To be clear and to avoid overloading the word "Architecture", we use different terms to describe what is being done. The need for different terms is apparent in looking at this architecture discipline[34] and realizing that one is planning the future and modernization of a business. The complete metaphor is comprised of three verbs and three nouns:

- o   Zone the Business,
- o   Architect the Capabilities that comprise the Business, and
- o   Engineer the underlying details (DOTMLPF) of each Capability

Just as one architects a building within a city, we architect the capabilities of a business. Applying formal methods, one documents the rationale behind how the Business is segmented or Zoned and the placement of Capabilities within each segment of the business. Whether one is Zoning the Business, Architecting a Capability, or Engineering the underpinnings

---

34 Architecture is not developed outside the context of the Strategic Planning and the Program and Project Management Processes. The authors view Architecture as a set of activities that are embedded in those processes. This does not mean that an Architecture Program doesn't have processes associated with it, an Architecture Program has processes for the delivery of services, or engagement processes. Having said this, the architecture and engineering activities are still embedded in the clients planning and program management processes.

of the Capability, one focuses on value in the form of monies saved, costs avoided, appropriations realized or revenues generated[35].

In this Architecture and Engineering discipline then, the Business is analogous to the City and a Capability is analogous to the Building. Zoning the Business entails segmenting the business into Business Areas[36], and customer facing Business Lines. One then documents the Capabilities that each Business Area / Line requires to realize its' mission. One does this with an eye towards common operating models and shared services. Each

> Through the application of the complete metaphor and practice, one ultimately shows, that there is a positive net-present value over the life span of the capability being architected and that the value of the capability has a positive effect on the value of the business.

Capability is Architected with a focus on performance and cost so that one can see the net-present value for launching the Capability. Key elements of the underlying Services[37] of each Capability are engineered[38] to minimize risk and to assure that delivery is within cost and schedule. Note, in the case where the services are acquired, the service provider should provide blueprints and for legal reasons the blueprints (architecture and engineering data) should be placed into escrow.

The U.S. Federal Government was instrumental in establishing an architectural approach to agency modernization. They did so through the Clinger Cohen Act of 1996 and also in documents such as the Federal CIO Council's "Practical Guide to Federal Enterprise Architecture"[39]. While the focus of the act was on IT modernization, people realized the need to be more formal and systematic in their approaches to documenting both the business and the supporting IT. This included working definitions like the one provided in The Practical Guide. The Practical Guide asserted that the Architecture of an Agency is:

---

35 While there is revenue in some government agencies, we also talk about appropriations.

36 The terms "Operating Unit" and "Non-operating Unit" as synonyms for Business Line and Business Area Respectively.

37 Services may be designed, developed, and offered internally or acquired from other service providers

38 The details of a Capability are categorized and defined as Doctrine, Organization, Training, Materiel, Leadership, Personnel, Facilities (DOTMLPF). This set of categories comes from The U.S. Department of Defense.

39 The *Practical Guide to Federal Enterprise Architecture* can be found at https://www.gao.gov/assets/590/588407.pdf

"A strategic information asset base, which defines the mission, the information and the technologies necessary to perform the mission, and the transitional processes for implementing new technologies in response to the changing mission needs".

The definition also asserts that the architecture *"includes baseline architecture, target architecture, and a sequencing plan"*[40]. Our definition builds on this one to emphasize the business and the idea that technologies are introduced in support of the capabilities and operating models. Our new working definition then, is:

Architecture and Engineering as applied to businesses, is a discipline resulting in a strategic information asset which defines a business including the mission and business models chosen to assure the delivery of value in the midst of changing market conditions and mission needs. The architecture includes Doctrine / Policy, Organizational information, Training, Materiel in the form of processes, roles, and information and technologies necessary to perform the mission, Leadership, Personnel / staffing, and Facilities that underpin the capabilities. These piece parts of the mission and architecture are referred to as the DOTMLPF.

Given the fact that the architecture addresses changing social and market conditions, and given that the architecture covers both current and target states, it must include a time element so that executives can see the current state of the business by fiscal or calendar year and see that improvement or degradation is taking place over time.

---

40 This definition comes from the "*Practical Guide to Federal Enterprise Architecture*" found at https://www.gao.gov/assets/590/588407.pdf

PART II – SUCCESS FACTORS

OVERVIEW

The components of a successful architecture and engineering endeavor are typically minimized or overlooked. As a result, architecture and engineering efforts fail and get a bad rap. We believe that each of the components presented here is, in itself, a critical success factor not to be excluded. The components of a successful architecture and engineering approach for managing day to day business operations and to managing business transformation are as follows:

- **Architecture Policy** with teeth and an executive team that is prepared to enforce the policy. Leadership then, goes hand in hand with policy and is a critical success factor

- **Architecture Organization** starting with an internally owned and staffed **Initiative** because a vendor should not own your architecture and intellectual property. The Initiative is then supported by an embedded **Program** to handle some of the mechanics and house commodity resources

- **Education and Training** because guaranteed, all levels of your organization are going to have to get knowledgeable about and accustom to this new way of doing business. Without really knowing it, almost everyone in the organization produces and consumes architecture information and they need to know how that information is structured and stored.

- **Architecture Approach** because people need to understand the outcome and how to get there. With so many people involved in the production of the architecture everyone should know the approach and related processes

- **Leadership in the form of a Chief Architect** and supporting organization positioned at the VP, or Deputy Commissioner level in a government setting. Good leaders of any mission establish vision, actionable goals, and concrete objectives. They know how to inspire people to achieve objectives

- **Management System / Governance** (more leadership) because you need to control the development and quality of the Architecture and one person shouldn't be making decisions regarding what it good / right for the business

- **Communications Approach and Plan** because Architecture is not a closet or siloed function.

- **Marketing Approach and Plan** because people are constantly asking "what is it?" and "why do I need that?". Marketing will build backing and help manage the nay-sayers
- **A concrete and intuitive set of building blocks** that appeal to both the business and IT folks
- **An Architecture Framework** that is proven, like the Zachman Framework® or the other specifications / frameworks discussed back in the *Introduction* to *Part I – Setting the Stage*. Make the framework a hybrid framework if you'd like
- **Tool Environment and Architecture Repository** because the business needs tools that guide the creation of high-quality data and identify when and where data is missing. And the business needs a place to put the data, a system that enables the generation of reports
- **Architecture Enabled Strategic Planning Process** because there is no "Architecture Process". The Architecture is both an input to and output from your Strategic Planning Process and the Program Management Process
- **Architecture Enabled Program Management** because you want to minimize risk associated with the delivery of transformation programs and supporting IT Systems / Applications. The business also needs a group of people to manage the organizational change that is documented in the architecture.
- **Zoning Maps or Reference Models** because you need to set the stage and provide a context for the supporting architecture work that will ensue
- **Blueprints for Key Capabilities** because large investments in new Capabilities or capital investments designed to refresh existing Capabilities need to be assured. Formal and complete documentation provides a better level of assurance
- **The right Staff** because Architecture and Engineering is no different than any other facet of your business, it requires the right people with the right skills

In addition to assuring that components are not excluded; the Chief Architect and leadership team should maintain an eye towards the target state. Many business transformation initiatives spend years making up for the fact that the organization operated without architecture. They spend years documenting the current state and they spend an inordinate amount of time educating people on why architecture and engineering are important. This is why Leadership and Education are such important ingredients.

BUILDING BLOCKS AND REPOSITORY

One cannot Zone a Business, Architect Capabilities, or Engineer DOTMLPF without understanding the Building Blocks of a business. The Architecture of a business, in its' noun form, is fundamentally data and information about the Building Blocks of the business, including information about how the blocks are interconnected.

> You may find it odd that we start with the Building Blocks and the repository, but there are two good reasons for this.
>
> First, most architects today focus on diagrams developed in an Office Suite where the symbols have no standard meaning and where there is no underlying data or repository to store decision making data. These are diagrams, presentations, and drawings, masquerading as architecture. They are drawings designed to get one individual or an organizational unit through their business day.
>
> Second, most organizations that do use architecture tools use multiple tools so a tool agnostic repository is required for warehousing the architecture / planning and engineering data.

The building blocks of a house are easy, one has cement blocks of a certain size that can withstand certain pressure, rebar of a particular size, cement that is also designed to withstand a specified pressure. A building has structural timbers and beams of varying sizes and types with the ability to support certain spans / loads. And buildings have boilers, pipe, wire, and breaker boxes that can support the electrical load in Amperes. Buildings also have simple things like windows and doors. As with traditional building architecture where the data is about the structure and building blocks of the building, we in the business world need building blocks of a business and information about how those business building blocks are composed and interconnect.

One basic difference between this and traditional building architecture is the need to maintain the data electronically and the daily use of the data[41].

---

41 In "Smart Cities", todays building architecture must be digital and online just like Business Architecture; society is beyond the point where paper blueprints can be considered acceptable. A perfect example is, the need for layered building blueprints so that first responders have immediate access to the blueprints for the building that

While building architects and engineers have AutoCAD®[42] and other tools, for legal reasons, blueprints were traditionally delivered in paper form[43] and used primarily for and during construction. In the business / government world, the customer has a vested interest in having the entire architecture in a machine-readable form and electronic copies of the blueprints for each Capability. To facilitate this electronic transfer, we store the building block data in industry standard formats. One can then receive and store both the drawings and the underlying data in a local (business / agency owned) repository. More importantly, one can interrogate a particular building block and all of its' constituent parts, or a set of building blocks regardless of scope. The scope of your inquiry might be a segment of your business (Business Area / Line) or a particular Application / System.

While your business might choose a different framework, or create a hybrid framework, the authors have aligned the Building Blocks with the rows of the Zachman Framework®. There are approximately 360 building blocks in total, there are 200 that are important to the business and IT folks. A summary is provided in *Figure 4: Summary of Building Blocks by Role/View*. This figure shows the number of building block and how they are distributed among the rows of the Zachman Framework®.

---

they are rushing off to. Those blueprints need to be layered so that they can also focus on certain information without being burdened by extraneous data.

42 AutoCAD is a registered trade mark of Autodesk, Inc. https://www.autodesk.com/company

43 This may certainly change over time although standards need to be formed so that cities and towns are not required to have multiple architecture tools/products and multiple versions of those tools. Cities in particular have a vested interest in having architects provide building architecture electronically because the information held in the architecture is required by first responders and the information needs to be provided to the first responders in real-time. People cannot be fumbling with paper blueprints. The need for making traditional building architecture data available on a day to day basis is becoming more apparent and is happening with the digital transformation that society is undergoing and with the concept of smart cities.

Count of Name	Column Labels			
Row Labels	Atom	Element	Particle	Grand Total
⊞ Planner Level		79		79
⊞ Owner Level		69		69
⊞ Engineering Level		52		52
⊞ Builder Level	23			23
⊞ Subcontractor Level			3	3
Grand Total	23	200	3	226

Figure 4: Summary of Building Blocks by Role/View

Note that the heavy lifting is done up front by the Planners and Owners. The business and IT folks directing and shaping strategy and plans need to focus on the top 3 rows depicted in *Figure 4: Summary of Building Blocks by Role/View*. Seventy-nine (79) Planner Level building blocks plus sixty-nine (69) Owner Level building blocks plus fifty-two (52) Engineering Level building blocks makes for two Hundred (200) building blocks.

As a prelude to our discussion on the applications of Architecture and Engineering in the business world, we introduced some of the Building Blocks (of a business) via some basic questions about your business / agency. For instance, in *Figure 3: Key Building Blocks of a Business*, we introduced the concept of Business Areas and Business Lines. It is natural then to ask, does your business have a repository containing a list of Business Lines (Operating Units) and Business Areas (Non-operating Units) that comprise it[44]? There are many related questions that can be posed based upon the framework and knowledge of how the building blocks relate to one another. For instance, one might ask:

- o For each Business Area / Line does the company have a list of underlying business capabilities?
- o Are the Capabilities comprised of Services[45] being rendered?
- o Have you documented who is consuming the Services?
- o Does each Service have a list of well-defined processes where the processes automate the delivery of those Services?

---

44 We are talking about an inventory of the Business Areas and Lines with a mapping to their respective Capabilities and an understanding of their respective missions and how they are performing. We are speaking of models with underlying data, and not just a pretty picture.

45 We are using the word Service with a capital S; these are business services being offered by organizations executing processes which are automated by IT. We are not talking about Software as a Service (SaaS).

- Does the repository have the goals for each Area / Line on a calendar or fiscal year basis? Are the Goals comprised of concrete and actionable Objectives?
- Does the organization know if any of these Objectives have been achieved?
- Do each of the Business Areas / Lines have a strategy for achieving each goal?
- Have organizational and process measures and metrics been established and are they being monitored?

This is, in part, the top of your architecture posed in the form of questions.

The next three figures depict the Building Blocks of a business. The first figure (*Figure 5: Planner Related Building Blocks of a Business*) presents the Planner related building blocks, the second figure depicts the Owner Building Blocks, and the third is the Engineering related building block. Given the number of building blocks, we've taken some liberties in placing multiple Building Blocks in a single square. In *Figure 6: Owner Related Building Blocks* we see more granular Building Blocks like Processes, Activities, and Business Scenarios that the owners, as stewards of a Business Area / Line, need to support. Note that there are (in Yellow text) a few touch points between the Planner and Owner views, so coordination is required. Finally, in *Figure 7: The Engineering Elements of a Business* we depict the Building Blocks that Engineers concern themselves with.

Before we move on, note that in *Figure 5: Planner Related Building Blocks of a Business,* we presented the "Business" as though it were a building block. In reality, it is not a building block, the Business is the thing that building blocks comprise. The Business, be it a company, an organizational unit within the business, or a government agency, is an Element in the repository and the anchor point for all the information comprising the reference models depicted in *Figure 8: The Business as an Element* and the Capabilities depicted in *Figure 9: Capability has a set of blueprints*. It is also the source of information required to publish the Annual Business Plan and the Annual IT Strategic Plan. These are reports that are generated from the Architecture Repository at the appropriate time in the budget cycle.

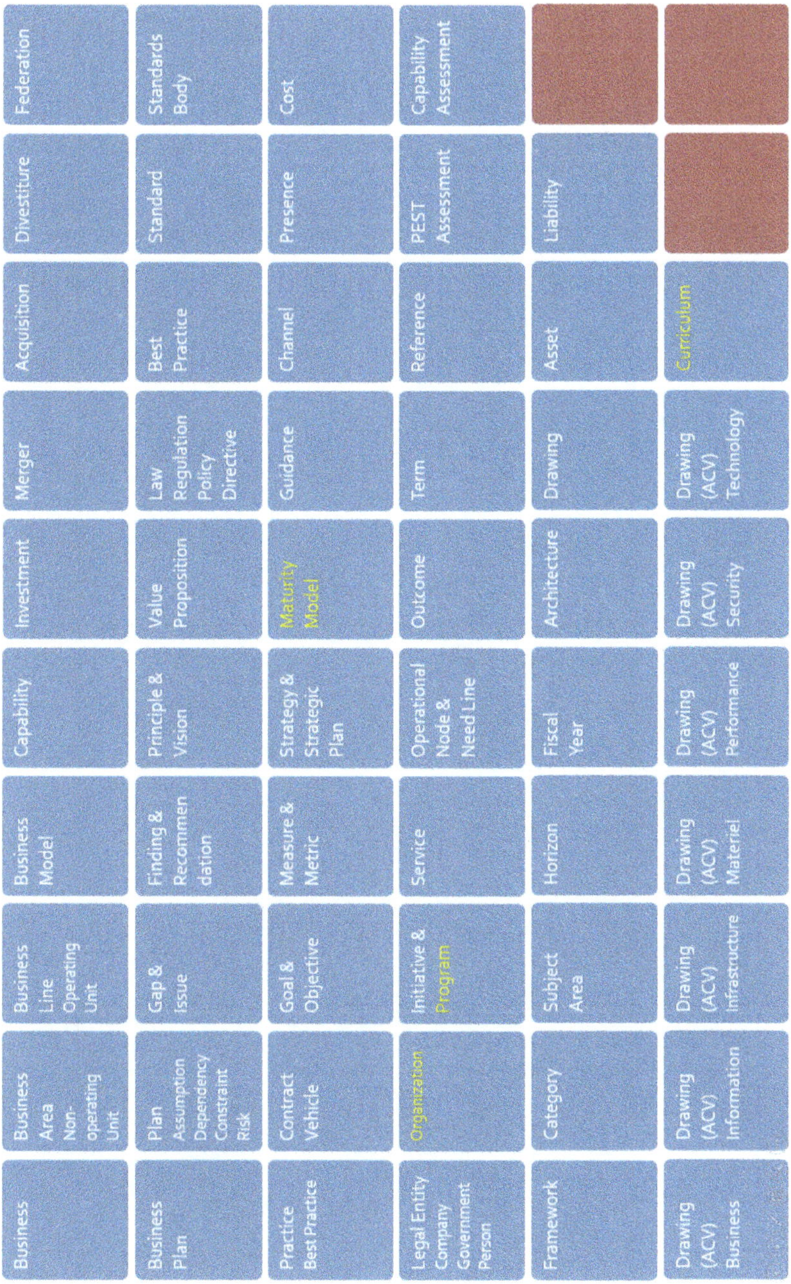

Federation	Standards Body	Cost	Capability Assessment		
Divestiture	Standard	Presence	PEST Assessment	Liability	
Acquisition	Best Practice	Channel	Reference	Asset	Curriculum
Merger	Law Regulation Policy Directive	Guidance	Term	Drawing	Drawing (ACV) Technology
Investment	Value Proposition	Maturity Model	Outcome	Architecture	Drawing (ACV) Security
Capability	Principle & Vision	Strategy & Strategic Plan	Operational Node & Need Line	Fiscal Year	Drawing (ACV) Performance
Business Model	Finding & Recommendation	Measure & Metric	Service	Horizon	Drawing (ACV) Materiel
Business Line Operating Unit	Gap & Issue	Goal & Objective	Initiative & Program	Subject Area	Drawing (ACV) Infrastructure
Business Area Non-operating Unit	Plan Assumption Dependency Constraint Risk	Contract Vehicle	Organization	Category	Drawing (ACV) Information
Business	Business Plan	Practice Best Practice	Legal Entity Company Government Person	Framework	Drawing (ACV) Business

Figure 5: Planner Related Building Blocks of a Business

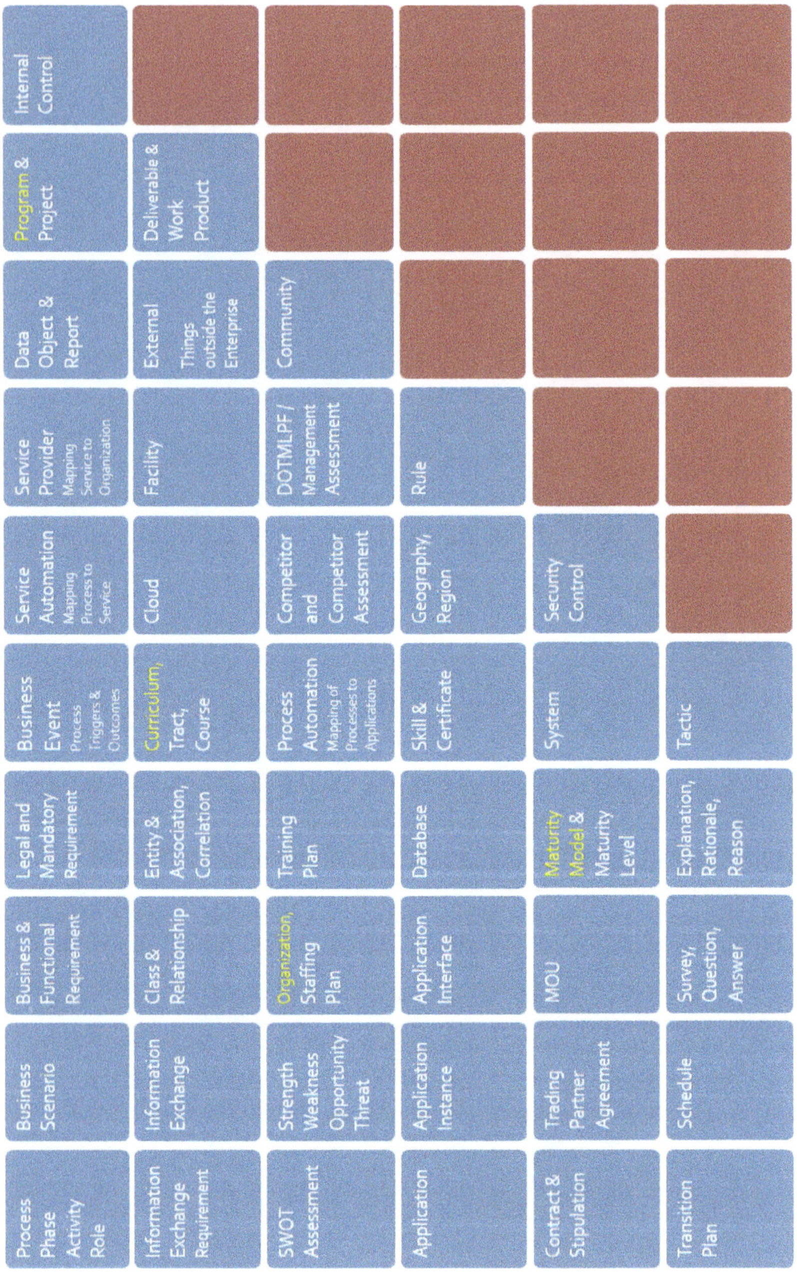

Internal Control					
Program & Project	Deliverable & Work Product				
Data Object & Report	External Things outside the Enterprise	Community			
Service Provider / Mapping Service to Organization	Facility	DOTMLPF / Management Assessment	Rule		
Service Automation / Mapping Process to Service	Cloud	Competitor and Competitor Assessment	Geography, Region	Security Control	
Business Event / Process Triggers & Outcomes	Curriculum, Tract, Course	Process Automation / Mapping of Processes to Applications	Skill & Certificate	System	Tactic
Legal and Mandatory Requirement	Entity & Association, Correlation	Training Plan	Database	Maturity Model & Maturity Level	Explanation, Rationale, Reason
Business & Functional Requirement	Class & Relationship	Organization, Staffing Plan	Application Interface	MOU	Survey, Question, Answer
Business Scenario	Information Exchange	Strength Weakness Opportunity Threat	Application Instance	Trading Partner Agreement	Schedule
Process Phase Activity Role	Information Exchange Requirement	SWOT Assessment	Application	Contract & Stipulation	Transition Plan

Figure 6: Owner Related Building Blocks

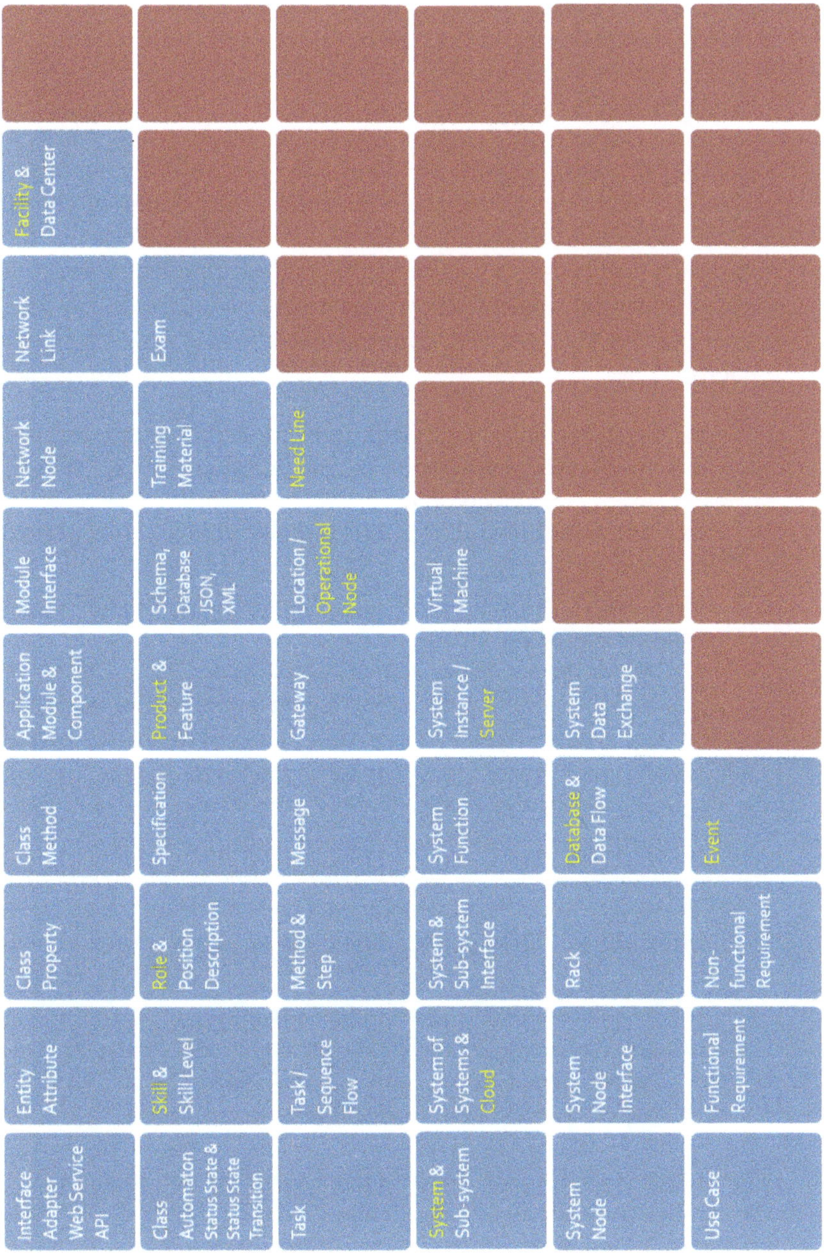

Facility & Data Center
Network Link — Exam
Network Node — Training Material — Need Line
Module Interface — Schema, Database JSON, XML — Location / Operational Node — Virtual Machine
Application Module & Component — Product & Feature — Gateway — System Instance / Server — System Data Exchange
Class Method — Specification — Message — System Function — Database & Data Flow — Event
Class Property — Role & Position Description — Method & Step — System & Sub-system Interface — Rack — Non-functional Requirement
Entity Attribute — Skill & Skill Level — Task / Sequence Flow — System of Systems & Cloud — System Node Interface — Functional Requirement
Interface Adapter Web Service API — Class Automaton Status State & Status State Transition — Task — System & Sub-system — System Node — Use Case

Figure 7: The Engineering Elements of a Business

Having introduced the Building Blocks of a business, this is a good time to talk about the levels of detail. There are times when one does not need detailed knowledge about the building blocks. Generally speaking, if any Building Block is outside of the business then you may not need to know anything about the internal structure and operations of that building block.

Let's consider two examples, one for the business folks and another the IT folks. For the business folks, a great example of this is a Business Line that is a wholly owned subsidiary with its' own Architecture. For the IT folks, the example is Software as a Service (SaaS). In the case of SaaS, your business needs just enough documentation required to be successful as a user, to assure that the business has a copy of all data, and to assure continuity of operations.

Whether one is documenting a single Building Block or the entire business, there are three levels of detail that one needs to be aware of. They are:

- **Black box detail** – in this case the internal structure and operations of the box is immaterial, so it is referred to as a black box. But one needs to know why the thing / box itself is important, dependencies, and (if appropriate) inputs / outputs.
- **Gray box detail** – in the case of gray boxes, one needs to know about some of the internals. A great example is a Process Owner needing a Gray Box view of his / her Processes in terms of the Activities that comprise each Process, but they need not have a view of the internal operations of each of those Activities. The Process Owner might know what Business Scenarios each Activity supports, but they don't have to know exactly what tasks get one from trigger to outcomes. Certainly, they need to know that the engineers have modeled the workflow and understand the workflow, but that Clear box view of each Activity is the realm of the engineer.
- **Clear box detail** – in this case, more than likely, you own the building block and you are going to build and manage that building block. In this case you need to know internals and need to be able to unambiguously present to a Builder or Sub-contractor

One final note about the concept of Black Boxes, if something is outside the business, this doesn't mean Architecture is not needed. For legal reasons, the business has a vested interest the Architecture. One should also assure that the Architecture has passed an Independent Verification & Validation (IV&V) and that the Architecture is placed in escrow.

Now that we've introduced some of the higher order Building Blocks of a Business and the concept of building block detail, we can tie this back to the metaphor and the idea that one Zones the Business and Architects Capabilities. Zoning the Business starts with two key Building Blocks generally referred to as Functional Areas. There are two types of Functional Areas, the first called Business Area (Area) and the second Business Line (Line).

- o *Business Areas* are organizations that conduct back office functions that keep the business running. They are also referred to as cost centers and *Non-Operating Units.* Business Areas are work horses that support the Business Lines so that the business lines can focus on their customer facing responsibilities.

- o *Business Lines* are customer facing organizations that have responsibility for profit and loss. *Business Lines* are also called *Operating Units.*

These Business Areas / Lines and the building blocks that comprise them are documented in the architecture repository and the resulting structure and outputs from a business point of view are depicted in *Figure 8: The Business as an Element*. This figure depicts some of the reference models and some key reports that are generated using the data in the repository. The reports include the "Annual Business Plan" and the "Annual Technology Plan".

Each of the Business Areas and Business Lines have Capabilities germane to the Area / Line. These Capabilities are architected and the resulting structure and output is as depicted in *Figure 9: Capability has a set of blueprints*. This figure shows the data about each Capability as a set of blueprints. The collection of blueprints, in turn, comprise the *Capability Architecture and Engineering Design Package*. The diagrams are created using Architecture and Engineering tools that feed the underlying data into the Architecture Repository.

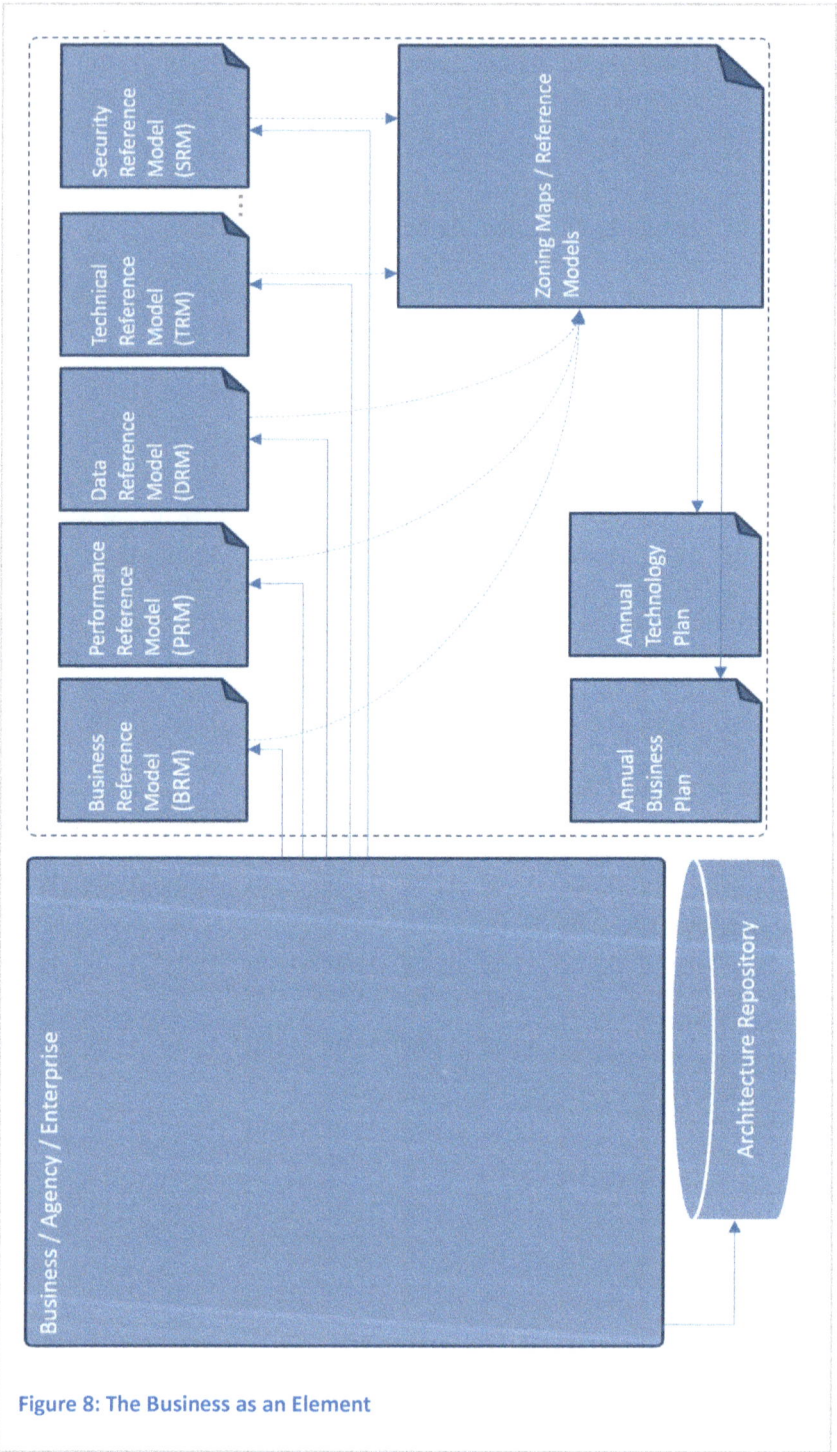

Figure 8: The Business as an Element

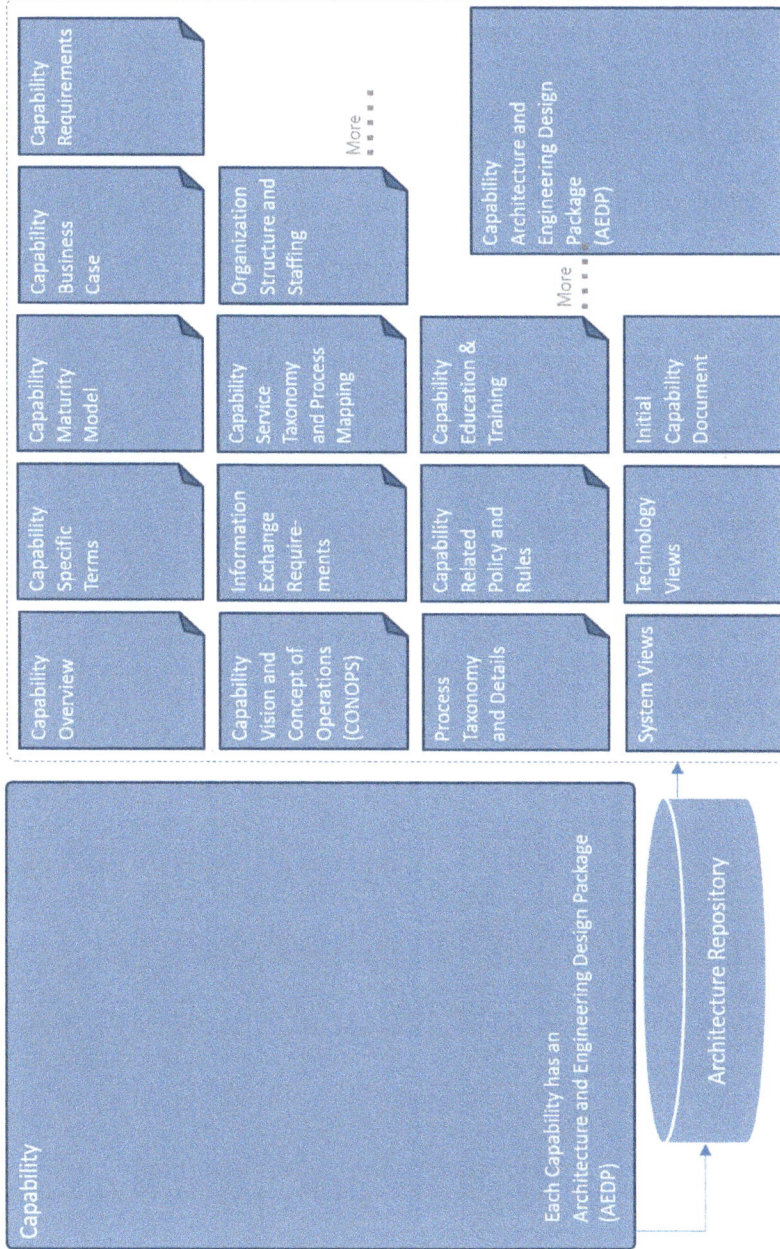

Figure 9: Capability has a set of blueprints

The inventory or portfolio of Capabilities is in that portion of the Architecture Repository that we refer to as the Business Reference Model (BRM). Details about each Capability are gathered in the Program and Project Management Process. That is, when a Capability needs to be introduced and when a capital investment needs to be made in an existing Capability, a Program is formed and the Program executes the Program and Project Management Process along with the embedded architecture activities. The resulting output is a set of blueprints for the Capability.

Business Area, Business Line, Capability, and the Services that comprise a Capability are the building blocks that an Agency Commissioner, a CEO, a Venture Capitalist, or a Chief Architect focus on in planning or Zoning the Business. Starting with the Business Areas and Lines, we form a view of an Business (see *Figure 10: Business Areas and Lines as Building Blocks of the Business*) where the organizational units comprising the Business Areas provide Services to the business at large and the Business Lines.

As an example, consider a conglomerate with multiple business lines catering to distinctly different product lines. Those Business Lines are served by a common Human Resources Business. Another example of a well-accepted Business Area is *Finance* and one of the best-known Services offered by *Finance*, is Payroll. This Service is part of a Capability called *General Accounting*.

In *Figure 10: Business Areas and Lines as Building Blocks of the Business*, you get a glimpse of how the buidling blocks of a business are used to Zone the Business. This depiction applies whether the business is a public company or a governmental body like an Agency or Authority. In the United States Federal Government, the Agency's can be viewed as Business Lines.

It is not obvious, but this structure is recursive insofar as, each Business Lines may be another business having the same structure depicted in *Figure 10: Business Areas and Lines as Building Blocks of the Business*. A real-life example of this is a Business Line which is a wholly-owned subsidiary. Another real example from the public sector (Governments) is a Federation where each Business Line in the Federation is itself, a business. Specifically, the US Federal Government is an example where each Agency is treated as a business having its own Architecture.

The Zoning of your Business also entails the identification of key suppliers, Communities or Markets being served, and Channels to be employed to get your offerings (product / information / programs / services) to those Markets.

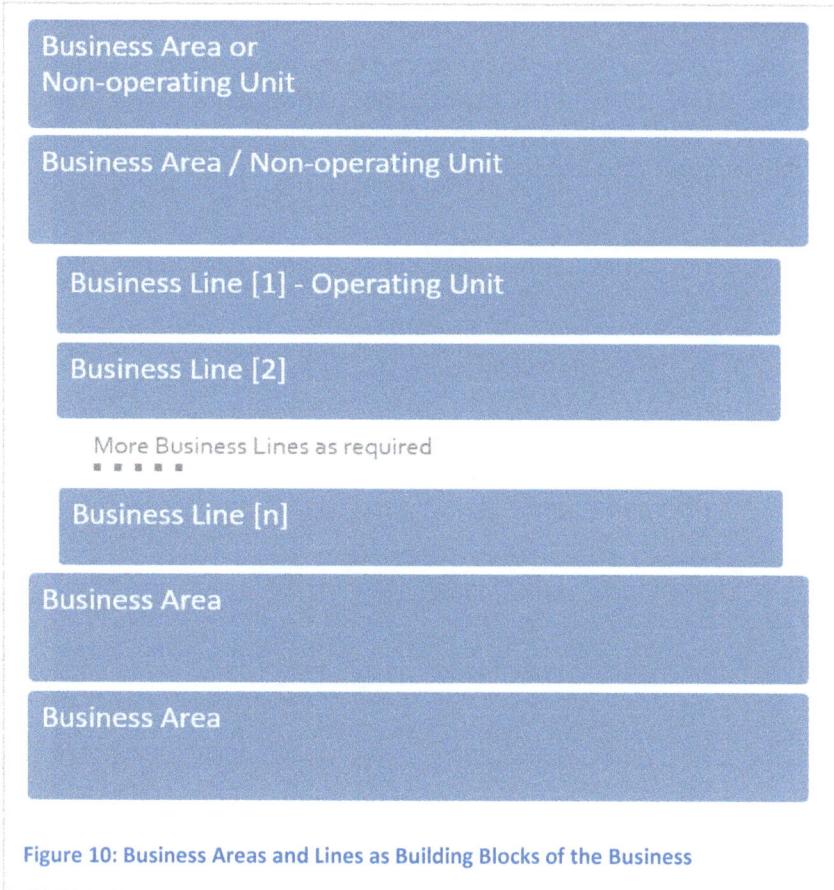

Business Area or
Non-operating Unit

Business Area / Non-operating Unit

Business Line [1] - Operating Unit

Business Line [2]

More Business Lines as required

Business Line [n]

Business Area

Business Area

Figure 10: Business Areas and Lines as Building Blocks of the Business

Going back now to the concept of Business Areas and Lines as Build Blocks of a business we provide a more complete example as depicted in depict in *Figure 11: Sample Business Areas and Lines and the Positioning of the Architecture*. In this example, the Business Area at the top is *Strategic Planning and Budgeting*. This is the business area where your Chief Architect and architecture initiative reside[46]. The Business Lines are sandwiched between *Strategic Planning and Budgeting* and *Financial Management and Accounting Services*. Some company's house budgeting

---

[46] Your architecture initiative, just like all other non-operating units and the Strategy organization itself, are overhead. But your business should not operate without an architecture initiative and without a heart and brain.

along with Finance. The separation of concerns depicted (architected) here is designed to prevent any conflict of interest.

At the bottom of *Figure 11: Sample Business Areas and Lines and the Positioning of the Architecture*, is a foundational Business Area we refer to as *"Corporate Facilities and Information Technology (IT)"*. With this particular model, and with the current state of technology (Cloud Computing), IT is more or less a business unto itself. Although, keep in mind that the business may be using Cloud Computing Services provided by multiple Cloud Service Providers.

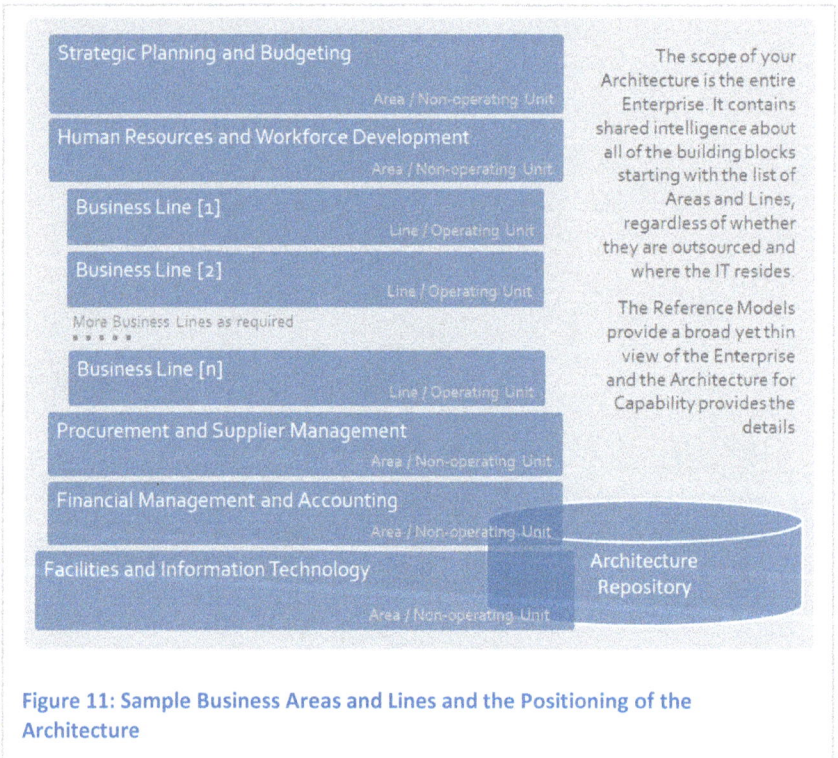

| Strategic Planning and Budgeting | The scope of your Architecture is the entire Enterprise. It contains shared intelligence about all of the building blocks starting with the list of Areas and Lines, regardless of whether they are outsourced and where the IT resides. |

Figure 11: Sample Business Areas and Lines and the Positioning of the Architecture

We also depict in *Figure 11: Sample Business Areas and Lines and the Positioning of the Architecture*, Procurement and Human Resources as company-wide Business Areas supporting the business at large. Last but not least, there is *The Heart and the Brain* of the business: The Architecture. The positioning of the Architecture is not meant to associate it more with IT, rather it is intended to show how foundational it is.

Aside from *Strategic Planning and Budgeting*, *Financial Management and Accounting*, and *Corporate Facilities and IT*, the Business Areas and Lines are said to be *"non-integral"*. This means that, for reasons of acquisition and divestiture, one can slide any one of these Areas / Lines in or out. The business knows all the integration points from a business (Process) and IT (Systems) perspective. For an Acquisition, when the company is brought in, it is wired in. For a divestiture, all interfaces are severed and the Area / Line is slid out.

Your business and a depiction of it can be based on the ones shown in *Figure 10: Business Areas and Lines as Building Blocks of the Business,* and in *Figure 11: Sample Business Areas and Lines and the Positioning of the Architecture* but more than likely your depiction would not show all Business Areas. The model / drawing would just be too large. To augment that model and depiction, we suggest a companion model that shows all Functional Areas and their respective Capabilities. A sample / fragment is depicted in *Figure 12: Model depicting Capabilities by Business Area / Line.*

A model of this sort is created to show the association and alignment of Capabilities to Business Areas and Lines. Our preference is to show these as vertical stacks where each stack is a stack of Capabilities topped off by the Business Area / Line that they are germane to. Underpining that model is yet another model with the *Services* that comprise each capability. These

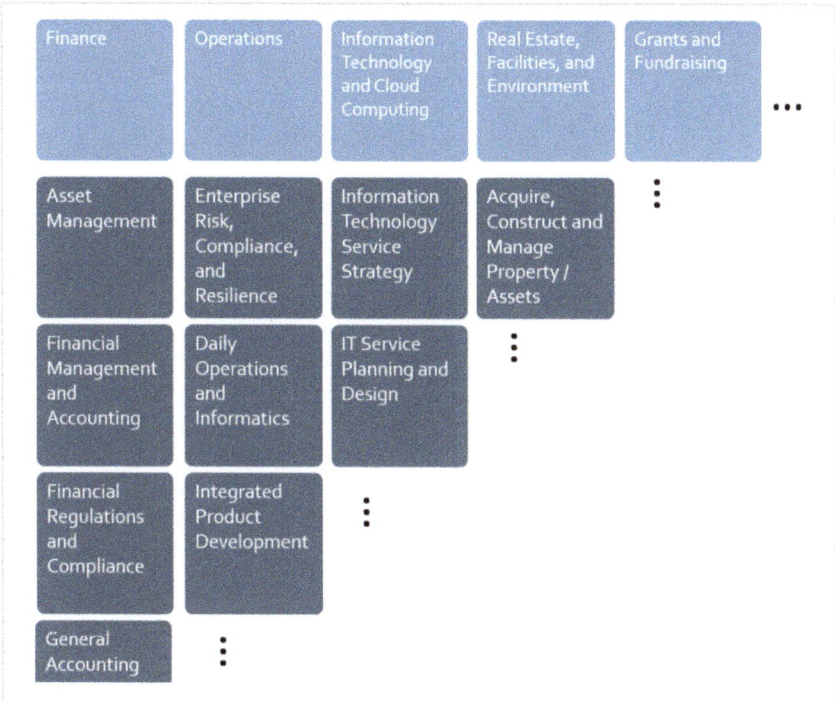

Figure 12: Model depicting Capabilities by Business Area / Line

models combined comprise a *Capability and Service Taxonomy* and complete view of the business in terms of where in the business the capabilities reside and what Services are being offered. This Capability and Service Taxonomy is a complete macro view of what the business does.

ARCHITECTURE FRAMEWORK

In following suit with the *CIO Council's Practical Guide to Federal Enterprise Architecture[47]*, we've asserted that architecture in its noun form is an "information asset base", so we need to understand how one gets the information that goes into the architecture. How does one document the building blocks of their business? This is done using a framework that helps stage the gathering of the information and then positions that information. The information is gathered by asking key questions designed to ferret out the necessary details. With this idea in mind, some have asserted that "architecture is a set of questions". It is a set of questions, but this is an oversimplification. Implicit in the Architecture is the set of questions posed by an organization about its' structure, performance, etc. But the architecture is also the set of answers that one hones in on as the questions and tradeoffs are explored. These questions include the mission and capability requirements / needs posed in the form of questions.

Architecture frameworks and supporting engineering methods are the tools for documenting these questions, the answers, and decisions made in getting from question to answer. In business terms, the framework is a tool and technique for creating "formal descriptions" of a business. It is a tool and technique which facilitates an understanding of value, cost, health, and where to invest.

Using the Zachman Framework® as an example, the questions can be organized and posed by people playing roles in the organization and, the questions are then categorized. It is in this organization that a two-dimensional framework can be formed. Looking at *Figure 13: The Zachman Framework®*, the roles are:

- o   Planner
- o   Owner
- o   Designer / Engineer
- o   Builder, and the
- o   Sub-contractor

---

[47] The "*Practical Guide to Federal Enterprise Architecture*" can be found at https://www.gao.gov/assets/590/588407.pdf

Those roles are represented by the rows in the Zachman Framework®. The Zachman Framework® then categorizes things by overlaying the rows with a set of columns. The categories / columns are referred to as "the six interrogatives". The columns are:

- o Who
- o What
- o Where
- o When
- o How, and
- o Why questions

While the Zachman Framework does not prescribe an order for information gathering, there is an implied logical ordering by role. That is, one might want to establish a Planner's View of the Business and each Capability to set the stage for and before establishing the more detailed Owner views.

	What	How	Where	Who	When	Why
Planner						
Owner						
Designer						
Builder						
Sub-contractor						
Functioning Enterprise						

Figure 13: The Zachman Framework®

With the metaphor and a framework in mind one can think of architecture and the application of the framework at two basic levels: (A) at a company / agency-wide level to Zone the Business, and then (B) at the Business Area / Line or Capability level to Architect each Capability. This means that we apply the same framework to position and stage the gathering of information about the business, and then again to position and stage the gathering of information about the Capabilities of the business. We say then, that the framework is applied recursively[48].

At the company or agency level, architecture is viewed as a set of zoning maps or a master plan primarily containing the information (lists of things) required to make investment decisions. As depicted in *Figure 14: The*

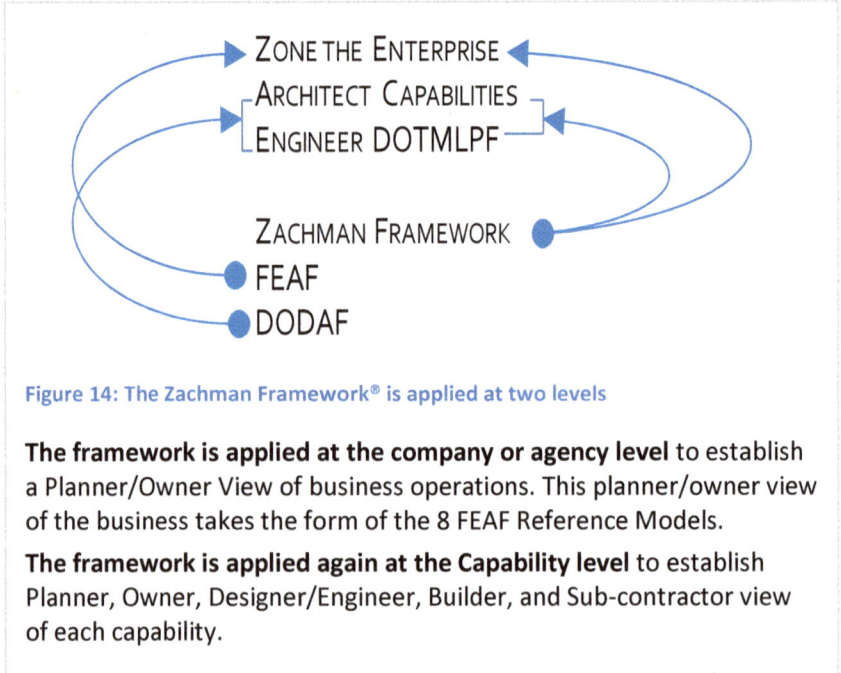

ZONE THE ENTERPRISE
ARCHITECT CAPABILITIES
ENGINEER DOTMLPF

ZACHMAN FRAMEWORK
FEAF
DODAF

Figure 14: The Zachman Framework® is applied at two levels

The framework is applied at the company or agency level to establish a Planner/Owner View of business operations. This planner/owner view of the business takes the form of the 8 FEAF Reference Models.

The framework is applied again at the Capability level to establish Planner, Owner, Designer/Engineer, Builder, and Sub-contractor view of each capability.

Zachman Framework® is applied at two levels, we use the FEAF as a specification for what comprises zoning maps as a planner / owner view of the business. Our thoughts on how the FEAF plays this role is described, for

---

48 Note that there are two forms of recursion or, recursive approaches that one can take. Given the use of the word mission in our working definition and the implication that if every organizational unit within the business has a well-defined mission then each org unit can be treated as a business and the Architecture for the business at large can be produced recursively by producing an Architecture for each organizational unit until one gets to the leaf nodes in the org structure. While recursion of this sort is valid, this approach would be impractical given the number of organizational units within a large business and given how difficult it can be to get people to cooperate. We take a slightly different approach; we still apply the framework recursively but we simplify by applying it at only two levels: once at the top level when we Zone the Business and then again at the Capability level when we Architect each Capability.

each reference model, in the section entitled *Zoning Maps or Reference Models* on page *81*.

At the capability level, one can think of architecture in terms of blueprints as a source of information required for the business case of an investment in any one capability, and as requirements and specifications used for both estimating cost and for construction. Here we use the DODAF as a specification for the structure and content of the blueprints.

While the framework is applied recursively, the questions posed by the architect at each level can vary. For instance, at the highest level of the business one asks how many organizations are delivering the Services that comprise a Capability. At the Capability level, the architect asks how many process variations exist for the delivery of a particular Service and how many different systems automate those processes. It is at both the Business and Capability levels that we ask ourselves about the number of technologies and products being used and ask ourselves if there are technological gaps and if there is a glut of products.

These two aspects of architecture are different yet complimentary. The company or agency level is broad yet thin. It is a Planner's View of the business where most of the information is recorded in the form of lists and where one emphasizes meaning and cost. There can be diagrams at the top level of your architecture, but the lists are important because at this level the primary purpose of the architecture is analysis. With the right set of lists and attributes one can create charts to facilitate one's analysis. Additionally, with the right data in place one can create advanced visualizations like mathematical graphs. One such list is the complete list of Capabilities that comprise the Business.

If the reference models are a broad yet thin view of the business, then the blueprints that document each Capability are narrower in scope than the entire business and are deep. Being focused on one capability and having to provide detail necessary for construction, is what gives the blueprints depth. At both levels, it is important to focus on the data because decisions are based on the data and a diagram with no underlying data / information does not enable decision making. The importance of data is exemplified by blueprints for a house. One can look at a pretty picture drawn by the architect and say; "that is what I want". But that pretty picture does not enable the owner to make a decision about the affordability. Those decisions are typically made by looking at the costs of the building blocks, cost of construction, and the aggregate cost. This cost data is in the architecture, but not in the pretty picture.

Before moving off of this topic, we provide a graphic depiction of Capabilities, Services, Processes, Activities, etc. to emphasize the relationships between them and the difference in granularity. Capabilities are large grained activities[49] (see *Figure 15: Capabilities and Services*) performed by the business or agency in support of its mission. Detail about a Capability starts with the architect documenting the smaller grained activities that we refer to as Services. These Services[50] are said to comprise the Capability, and the delivery of those Services is performed by organizational units executing business processes. The business processes are comprised of Activities and the activities are further broken down into Tasks. Tasks are, at times, performed using methods getting one down to

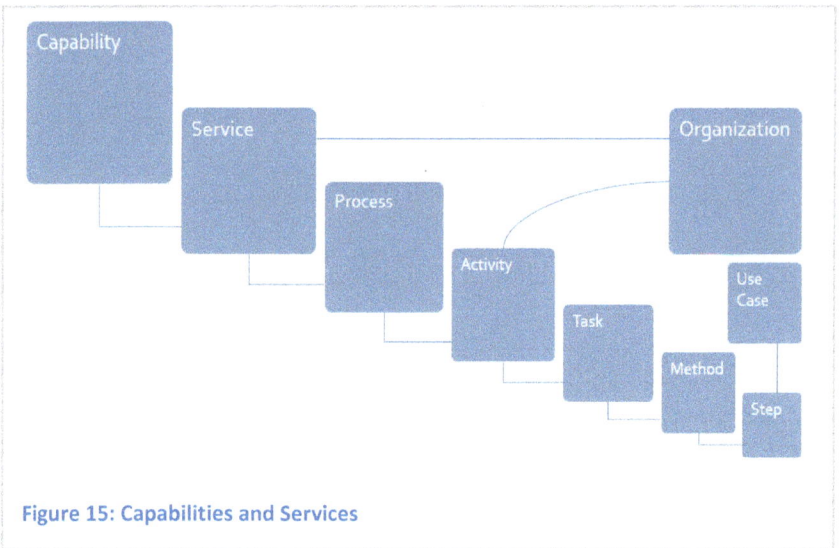

Figure 15: Capabilities and Services

the step level. This gives one a feel for the growing level of detail and depth that is in the architecture as one traverse from the Planner View to the Sub-Contractor View in the Zachman Framework®.

Having just introduced the concept of process as it relates to capability and having talked about the need for an architecture ability, we'd like to comment on the notion that there is an "architecture capability" and

---

49 As depicted in *Figure 15: Capabilities and Services,* the authors differentiate Capabilities from Services, Services from Processes, and Processes from Activities. They are each first order objects. In our building block approach, we talk about Capabilities getting broken down into Services, the Services being delivered through the execution of well-defined Processes, the processes getting broken into Activities, Activities into Tasks and Tasks being prescribed by a Method that comprises Steps.

50 These are Business Services rendered by organizations to internal and external clients. They are not to be confused with software provided as a service or web services. We have those forms of services much lower in the architecture stack.

"architecture process". The authors position architecture and engineering work below the Capability, Service, and Process levels. It is positioned at the activity level and we assert that these activities are performed in the context of other business processes[51]. For instance, businesses develop investment plans in a cyclic process, referred to mostly as the Strategic Planning Process. The Federal Government calls this process the Capital Planning and Investment Control (CPIC) process. From a process point of view, Architecting is a practice with one set of activities supporting the planning process and another set of activities that support the program management process where investment and structural detail is gathered for a particular Capability.

Strategic planning processes are typically broken down into phases where, in the initial phase, a draft plan is developed and then, in a later phase, the strategic plan is finalized. It is in between these two parts of the planning cycle where transformation programs gather, refine, and scrutinize information about proposed capabilities / investments. This information is used to determine if each investment has a positive net-present value. It is through the architectural analysis conducted in the program management process that a business builds more confidence in planned investments and reduces risk.

What the authors have introduced here is a hybrid framework that combines the Zachman, FEAF, and DOD Architecture Frameworks. It is a unified framework and while there are discussions about a Unified Architecture Framework®[52] and efforts under way by the Open Group® (OMG®) to develop a specification, the framework and building blocks presented here represent a unified set of building blocks that have been applied at client engagements conducted by the authors.

Now that we understand what Architecture is, what the Building Blocks of a Business are, and now that we have a framework for documenting the Building Blocks, we have to visit the topic of leadership and having an executive in charge.

CHIEF ARCHITECT

To be successful with the Architecture and Engineering of a business requires an executive level Chief Architect who is well versed and knowledgeable about all aspects of architecture development,

---

51 In particular, the strategic Planning and Program Management Processes
52 The development of this Unified Architecture Framework is under way by the Object Management Group® (OMG®) https://www.omg.org/

maintenance, and use. Ideally, they are well versed in the business and industry that the business is part of. The Chief Architect is also a person who can coordinate the efforts of the Chief Information Officer (CIO), Chief Data Officer (CDO), Chief Information Security Officer (CISO), and Chief Technology Officer (CTO), and who can serve as the interface between the business and IT communities. Accordingly, a business should have a Chief Architect who owns the Architecture and Engineering Initiative and also directs the embedded Architecture and Engineering Program Manager handling some of the mechanics. This person has overall responsibility for the ongoing development, delivery, and use of the architecture.

The Chief Architect is an executive that, depending on the size of the business, is a Director or Vice President. Their background and qualifications span both the business and technology sides of the organization. Because the Chief Architect also directs the Architecture and Engineering Program Manager, this person should be knowledgeable about program management. Because the Chief Architect is facilitating the development of formal strategic plans, they are versed in Capital Planning and Investment Control.

The Chief Architect, working in collaboration with other executives and the company leadership, is instrumental in obtaining organizational buy-in for the Architecture. This include support from the Business Areas / Lines, building the architecture and engineering team, and securing resources to support architecture management functions such as risk management, configuration management, and quality assurance. As such, the Chief Architect acts as the organizational spokesperson and advocate for the adoption and use of architecture.

When hiring a Chief Architect, develop a job description targeted at hiring a candidate with the following set of skills, abilities, and experience:

- Leadership ability, including strong team building skills, and the ability to make decisions. The Chief Architect must be perceived as a leader by the stakeholders he or she serves, the IT organization, and management
- Personal and professional skills, including communication and relationship-building skills, problem solving, and negotiation.
- Experience with how businesses are structured and Business / Operating Models that various businesses employ.
- Industry experience to understand the business processes of the organization and understand how the organization relates to peers in the industry.

- Ability to draw connections between marketplace trends and specific organizational strategies and correct flawed processes within the organization.
- Extensive technical breadth along with technical depth in one or more areas. This breadth should cover:
  - Application development and deployment
  - Creation and maintenance of technology infrastructure
    - Cloud Computing
  - Multiple platforms, including web and phone-based platforms and inter-operability and integration of platforms
- Proficiency with multiple Architecture and Engineering frameworks and design methodologies
- Experience with all phases of Strategic Planning
- Experience with program / project management, including the management of scope

This is a clear departure from trends starting years ago with Chief Technology Officer (CTO), Chief Data Office (CDO), and Chief Information Security Officer (CISO) either as peers to or direct reports of the Chief Information Officer (CIO). The advent of the Chief Architect role provides a logical anchor point and reporting structure with the CIO, CTO, CDO, CISO reporting to the Chief Architect. In this respect, some organizational change management will be in order as one attempts to integrate and unify the efforts of these roles under your newly appointed Chief Architect.

ARCHITECTURE POLICY

While we started with the Building Blocks of a Business, hiring your Chief Architect should come first, and on the heels of that, the development of an Architecture Policy. The policy should focus on the roles and responsibilities of the various organizations involved and how they contribute to the development and use the architecture. Given the systemic nature of architecture, almost everyone in the business is in some way a contributor to and / or user of the Architecture, so they need to know about it and their responsibilities.

If your company has a framework in mind, then it is best to state those roles and responsibilities vis-à-vis the framework. In particular, state which organizations are responsible for certain data and views of the business. The role and responsibility descriptions should include the owner of the architecture and a responsibility matrix like a RACI chart including all parties involved. A RACI charts describes who is "Responsible",

"Accountable", "Consulted", and "Informed". Ask yourself the following questions and assure that the policy provides answers:

- o Who is responsible for the executive or planner's view of the business? Who is responsible for Zoning the Business?
- o Who is responsible for the architecture detail (owner views) about each Business Area / Line?
- o If you are using the FEAF or a hybrid framework that includes the FEAF, who is responsible for the FEAF-based Reference Model details?
- o Who is responsible for Architecting Capabilities of your business?
- o Who is responsible for Engineering the DOTMLPF of a Capability?

If the management system and frameworks to be used are yet to be determined, then provide some introductory material on these topics and be sure to add the detail in the form of addendums.

In terms of ownership and touching on the management system a bit, architecture is not a command and control function, nor is it dictatorial. Architecture and Engineering is democratic in nature, so the organization that has been tagged as the owner is also the chairperson of the Architecture Board. In Integrated Product Development (IPD) terms, the Architecture Board can be viewed as an "Integrated Portfolio Management Team (IPMT)" that answers to an "Investment Review Board (IRB)". Each of the stakeholder organizations has a seat at the architecture table and is involved in decision making. The policy should cover these governance topics as well, although to keep the policy succinct, the policy can be augmented by a charter for the governance bodies.

The policy needs to call out the Chief Architect as the owner of the Architecture and Engineering Policy, with the Chief Financial Officer as a possible co-owner. These roles both have a vested interest in assuring the policy has teeth and that it is enforced. Teeth may come in the form of positive and negative covenants or business rules. For example, what happens if a particular stakeholder is remiss and their portion of the architecture does not pass the audit of an independent verification and validation group? Does a particular business Area / Line get funded if their architecture is incomplete? Is the executive in charge replaced? Is any business Area / Line permitted to make capital investments in Capabilities without architecture / blueprints?

Make sure that the policy defines the scope of the business. If the scope is the entire company / agency, are there exclusions? For example, if your company has wholly-owned subsidiaries, then for legal reasons the scope does not include those subsidiaries. But through policy those subsidiaries should be required to have an Architecture. In this case you are dealing with a federation and the policy may have to deal with how the architectures are aligned, reviewed, and if necessary approved.

Typically, the scope is the entire company and the development of the Architecture is treated as a company-wide effort requiring people from throughout the company. Business Area / Line executives need to hold a seat at the architecture round table and bring the appropriate resources to document the Area / Line business operations in accordance with the chosen framework. These executives must also assure that the Area / Line operations are aligned with the company's vision of the future, and that investments being made at the Area / Line level are aligned with company goals and objectives.

Implicit in what we just mentioned is that Architecture and Engineering is systemic, so coordination, cooperation, and buy-in are all tantamount to the success of the effort and a smooth transition to a Target Operating Model. Policy establishes that buy-in by having stakeholder sign the policy. As stated in the Practical Guide to Federal Enterprise Architecture:

> "An EA program calls for sustained leadership and strong commitment. This degree of sponsorship and commitment needs the buy-in of the Agency Head, leadership by the CIO, and early designation of a Chief Architect"[53]

In the United States Federal Government, policy at the highest level took the form of legislation: The Federal Information Technology Reform Act[54] and the Clinger Cohen Act[55], [56]. As a result of the Clinger Cohen Act, each

---

53 Don't capitulate; go by the numbers on your dashboard. If the business is faltering, do some root cause analysis to get to the heart of the problem and fix the problem. The problem might be process related, in which case the business may take one of two approaches. If the problem can be addressed by tweaking existing processes then the business may embark on a Business Process Improvement (BPI) initiative. Alternatively, existing processes might need to be re-engineered. In this case, one wipes the slate clean to develop new processes.

54 The Federal Information Technology Reform Act can be found at: https://www.congress.gov/bill/113th-congress/house-bill/1232

55 The Clinger-Cohen Act of 1996 was originally enacted as the Information Technology Management Reform Act of 1996 (Divisions D and E of P.L. 104-106). The law was renamed the Clinger-Cohen Act by Pub. L. 104-208,110 Stat. 3009-393 (1996)

56 Having cited the Information Technology Reform Act and the Clinger Cohen Act, we'd like to point out that these acts were designed to have the agencies invest in and modernize IT. This was the primary purpose then of the Architecture that the agencies were to produce. We make this point given our emphasis on business operations and IT as an enabler. One uses Architecture to document and modernize a

Agency was viewed as a business. This is an example of a federated approach because the business at large is the U.S. Federal Government as a collection of agencies, each being treated as a Business with its' own Architecture. A federated approach can have weaknesses and complexities that are worth avoiding[57]. For example, in the federated approach the company / government may never have a holistic view of the target operating environment.

While policy in the form of legislation has teeth, there are some potential drawbacks. In the public sector, as an example, governmental bodies (Agencies and Authorities) take the position that they need additional funding to do the architecture work, above and beyond the current level of funding. You need to determine if additional funding is required within your business and if the architecture produced has value and is being put to use.

You may also consider an example on the other end of the spectrum, where a company has consolidated IT and has defined the scope of the Architecture to be just the IT organization. This is typical given the IT myopia that exists today and also given that most people view architecture and engineering as an IT discipline. Ask yourself, what is the benefit to the company at large if only the IT organization has an Architecture?

If your company is a Cloud Service Provider (CSP), then the company is in the business of offering infrastructure, platform, and software used as a service. The scope then, is the CSP as a company and it should consider the whole of the business including financial management, budgeting, procurement, human resources management, etc. The architecture is not limited to just Cloud infrastructure and IT.

In addition to the scope, roles and responsibilities, and the business rules, the policy document should cover the following:

- o Purpose for the Architecture. Make it real, intuitive, and compelling.
- o Value proposition. Here again, be intuitive and compelling because people will waste your time asking you, repeatedly, what is the value and why are we doing this?
- o High level scope of the architecture in terms of data to be captured

---

business, the IT of which is a very small part. Budgetarily speaking, IT is typically such a small percentage of a company's budget that they don't bother trying to make it more efficient.

57 One of the authors has delved into the subject of federating architecture, to the tune of an eighty (80) page white paper. Readers should feel free to reach out to the authors for more information and guidance on this subject.

- o   Timing in terms of when certain architecture / data is due
- o   Reviews
- o   Independent verification and validation
- o   Variances / exceptions

It is worth mentioning in the policy the breadth and depth of the Architecture and how both are defined. In the model presented here and given our discussion about frameworks, the content of the Architecture is defined by the application of the FEAF, DODAF, and the Unified Modeling Language (UML)®[58]. Implicit in the definition of these specifications is an understanding of the data to be gathered. The breadth is defined in terms of the FEAF Reference Models which are defined in the glossary. The depth is defined in terms of the information required in a set of DODAF-based blueprints. Depth is extended when one is dealing with custom software, which takes one down to the UML level.

It is also worth mentioning the depth of the architecture vis-à-vis the perceived overlap between Architecture and Engineering and ITIL / Service Management[59]. Architecture and Engineering and Service Management are completely different disciplines although the Architecture and Engineering does push some information into your Service Management system and Configuration Management Database or CMDB[60].

Another key thing to have in the policy is a glossary. The policy comes before the Architecture, so be sure that the policy spells things out for all parties in lay terms. Be sure that those terms are in the architecture repository once that is established.

Finally, sign out the policy and publish it on your company / agency intranet for all employees to see. It is through the signing of the policy by executives and stakeholders that you obtain and then maintain buy-in and support. It is official and non-discretionary. If not signed out and not enforced, just walk away. Walk away now before you invest too much time, effort, and attempt to operate without funding and executive backing.

---

[58] Unified Modeling Language (UML) - http://www.uml.org/what-is-uml.htm
[59] Information Technology Infrastructure Library (ITIL) -
    https://en.wikipedia.org/wiki/ITIL
[60] Configuration Management Database (CMDB) -
    https://en.wikipedia.org/wiki/Configuration_management_database

MANAGEMENT SYSTEM / GOVERNANCE

The management system documents how the architecture evolves in a controlled manner and the publishing of the architecture. This includes how and when new content is added and how existing content is changed. In effect, it is about release management and change control. In particular, it covers the decision making that goes into approving new content and changes to existing content. The management system is synonymous with the term "Governance". A candidate management structure and set of bodies is depicted in *Figure 16: Governance Structure* which may include:

- o An Investment Review Board (IRB)
- o An Architecture Board (AB) as an active body of people that drives the business transformation[61]
- o A Functional Capabilities board (FCB)[62], and a
- o A Technical Review Committee (TRC) that deals with technical and security issues primarily from an IT point of view.

The Architecture Board, being an active body, is not a review body waiting for people to submit their architecture for review. That function is handled by your internal QA team or by your external IV&V team. The AB is an executive steering committee and Integrated Portfolio Management Team (IPMT)[63] that is managing the architecture supporting the portfolio of business capabilities. Based on industry analysis, the AB makes decisions along with the FCB on how the portfolio should change and where investments are required. The AB reports to the IRB and makes funding proposals in accordance with the strategic planning process.

The Functional Capabilities Board is a group of executives that preside over the portfolio of capabilities. Depending on the size of your organization there may be multiple Functional Capability Boards. The FCB works in conjunction with the AB in performing three forms of analysis:

---

61 The Architecture Board is not a passive review body waiting for others to specify changes, change is driven by the body from the top based on business goals and objectives. For this reason, we don't refer to the board as an "Architecture Review Board (ARB)". Architecture reviews are conducted by the quality Assurance team or the Independent Verification and Validation (IV&V) team.

62 The concept of a Functional Capabilities Board (FCB) comes from the Department of Defense https://www.dau.mil/acquipedia/Pages/ArticleDetails.aspx?aid=ad729538-8b5b-41fe-a0ef-c24ca8309888

63 This concept comes from Integrated Product Development (IPD). More information on IPD can be found at https://www.acq.osd.mil/se/docs/DoD-IPPD-Handbook-Aug98.pdf

- SWOT Analysis – an analysis of Strengths, Weaknesses, Opportunities, and Threats (SWOT)
- PEST Analysis – an analysis of Political, Economic, Social, and Technology (PEST) factors affecting the business
- Competitor Analysis

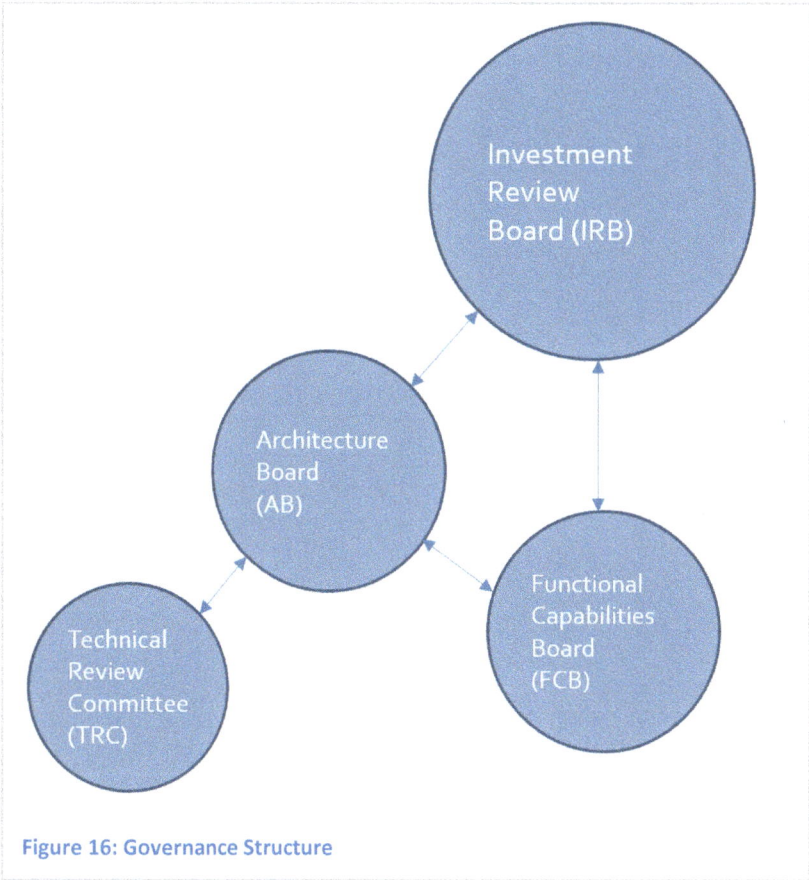

Figure 16: Governance Structure

These forms of analysis, augmented by Scenario Planning[64], are used to determine where investments need to be made. To make investment decisions, the Functional Capabilities Boards leverage the Capability Models in the architecture. An example of a Capability Model was provided in *Figure 12: Model depicting Capabilities by Business Area / Line*. While not depicted in that figure, there are three colored overlays that one can create on the Capability Model to facilitate decision making. These colored overlays are sometimes referred to as heat maps and they stem from the

---

64 For a brief description of Scenario Planning you may refer to https://www.economist.com/news/2008/09/01/scenario-planning

above-mentioned analyses. The overlays graphically highlight the results of those analyses to show where revenue / appropriation opportunities lay, where cost optimization opportunities lay, and where the business needs to invest in order to address legal and mandatory requirements.

Your company's / agency's management system documents how these boards operate and who is on them. The policy may also contain business rules that guide these boards on how to deal with day to day operational issues. For instance, the policy may specify if and when delegation is permitted for attendance at board meetings. Generally, delegation should not be permitted because decision making / voting should always be done by the board member, not his / her delegate.

It is important to note two things here. First, that these bodies are organization agnostic insofar as they stand alongside and independent of the org chart. Second, they persist while participating organizational units of the business may come and go. In light of this, each of these bodies must have a clear and concise charter and these bodies must be operating under the auspices of a high-level body.

Supporting the idea that these boards are active bodies that launch work, the organization that houses and funds the Architecture and Engineering should have a resource pool providing skilled resources to projects launched by the abovementioned boards. Those people provide the following services which can be made available through the company's service catalog:

- o A Requirements Management service
- o Architecture service including business analysis / diagnosis
- o Engineering service
- o Architecture and Engineering Tools (Software as a Service)
- o Education and training service

The tools and services are also provided to the Business Areas / Lines as they launch efforts to look at facets of their business and report back with the necessary and agreed to architecture detail, to include "Findings" and "Recommendations".

This is what makes the AB an active decision-making body rather than a passive review body. In addition to supporting the Business Areas / Lines in their analyses, they charter project teams that conduct analyses of cross-cutting facets of the business. The teams are managed on behalf of the AB by the Architecture and Engineering PMO so each project is managed against plans and properly staffed. On a weekly and monthly basis, the project teams report back to the PMO which facilitates the comeback to the AB for decision making. If the AB decides favorably then the architecture needs to get promoted and published. This is where the Independent Verification and Validation (IV&V) team comes in: the architecture must pass IV&V before it can be published.

The Architecture Board is not strictly technical. In support of the management system then, there has to be a group of people that review architecture from a functional / business point of view and subordinate to that group, a Technical Review Committee (TRC) that handles the technical part of any architecture. The basic flow of the architecture work includes the Project Team passing architecture off to the QA. From QA the material can go on to the TRC which renders a decision to pass work on to the AB. The AB then passes approved work on to IV&V.

Having an independent verification and validation (IV&V) team is a key component of the management system and an enabler for informed decision making. It is the IV&V team that returns their decision back to the AB on whether a particular release is ready to be published. Publishing includes the promotion of content to a production level repository, updating static web pages, checking operation of dynamic web pages and visualizations. And more importantly, the Investment Review Board should only approve investments that have supporting architecture which passed IV&V. This includes a verification of the proposed net-present value.

This entire section might lead the reader to believe that "Agile" software design and development is being overlooked and precluded. On the contrary, we are merely highlighting some of the things that need to be in place prior to one's attempts at applying Agile frameworks and approaches for software development. Without getting into the details of Agile frameworks, we assert that the discipline presented here improves agility. For example, having a process taxonomy in place facilitates the development of Agile Themes, Epics, and User Stories that appeal to the business community. The very same process taxonomy and Themes, Epics, and Stories can be used to evaluate Commercial-off-the-shelf (COTS) systems. Today the trend is toward the use of Commercial-off-the-shelf (COTS) systems. For an example of a highly iterative and spiral approach to IT that transcends software development, we recommend the Evolutionary Process for the Integration of COTS-based System (EPIC)[65]. The EPIC was published back in 2002 by the Carnegie Mellon Software

---

65 The Evolutionary Process for the Integration of COTS (EPIC) can be found on the Internet at:
https://resources.sei.cmu.edu/asset_files/TechnicalReport/2002_005_001_14021.pdf

Engineering Institute work in conjunction with MITRE® and the United States Airforce (USAF). The authors of the EPIC assert: *"this alternative approach is a risk-based, disciplined, spiral-engineering approach which leverages the Rational Unified Process®[66] (RUP®)"*.

ARCHITECTURE APPROACH

The architecture approach outlines how you intend to produce the architecture and realize the purpose of the Architecture as stated in your policy document. To an architect, this is also known as your Concept of Operations or CONOPS. It describes in lay terms, how you intend on producing the FEAF-based Reference Models and DODAF-based Capability Blueprints. Our approach to producing a purposeful Architecture is twofold: **(A)** working in collaboration with the business Areas / Lines, publish FEAF-based reference models yearly to establish a broad yet thin (Planner's View) of the business that is used to inform the budget, and **(B)** create Capability Architecture and Engineering Design Packages that document proposed investments. The investments may be in existing and / or new capabilities. This level of architecture is to assure that the efficacy and net-present value of each investment is clear.

> It is commonplace to find references to an "Architecture Process", but stay clear of a unique or standalone "Architecture Process" that **(A)** people execute outside of the architecture and engineering team, and **(B)** the results of which no one uses.

Our approach is to embed architecture and engineering activities in two key processes that most companies have and then to generate reports that are used by governance bodies to assure that their decisions are informed. The two processes are the Strategic Planning Process / Capital Investment and Control Process, and the Program Management Process. In order for this approach to work, these processes should be in place and documented. Additionally, **(A)** the Reference Models discussed are both an input to and output of the Strategic Planning Process, and **(B)** Capability Blueprints are an input to and output of the Program Management Process.

Implicit in this, is the approach for developing investment plans. For each proposed investment, staff continue to conduct architecture and engineering activities designed to establish an Owner View of each capability. These activities and the architecture and engineering outputs

---

66 The Rational Unified Process and RUP are trademarks of the IBM Corporation

show if the proposed investments and business cases are sound or not. The approach is to launch a transformation program to do a deep dive on each of the proposed investments. In architectural terms, we say that they Architect the Capability and it is through the architecture effort that we gain a complete understanding of how much it will cost to build out / adjust each capability and what the capital investment will be (Full life cycle cost). The information produced in this deep dive is then incorporated into the reference models to qualify the plan. The result is an investment plan where investments are qualified and sound.

Note that in any one particular year your planners and architects are working on the plan and architecture for the next fiscal year and while you are doing this, there are other work streams building out what you said you were going to do in the current year. Please also note that the above-mentioned detail is atypical of some reference models. We recommend this level of detail though, given that the reference models are used to generate the strategic business and IT plans for your business.

ARCHITECTURE ORGANIZATION

The organization / initiative is the home and funding mechanism for the Architecture and Engineering leadership team, and for the embedded Architecture and Engineering Program. It is responsible for funding all aspects of both the Initiative and the Program. While the program owns and manages the tool environment, the Initiative owns the data / content and the quality of the data. The Initiative owns the relationships with stakeholders and assures that the needs of the stakeholders are being met.

> The Architecture and Engineering effort is conducted by an organization, not a single person with the title of Architect. It is a VP / Director level organization and initiative with an embedded architecture program.

The embedded Architecture and Engineering Program owns the mechanics of continuous operations and rendering of Architecture and Engineering Services. The Architecture Program, provisions the Architecture and Engineering Services to the Business Areas / Lines, houses a Program Management Office (PMO) that manages transformation projects chartered by the Architecture Board, and configures and maintains the tools and the tool agnostic repository.

Whether you are a public company, a privately-owned company, or a governmental body, it is important to position the Architecture and Engineering Organization at the right level. If you are a public or privately-owned company, we recommend that you position the organization at the Vice President level within the Strategy group. This is the option depicted in *Figure 17: Recommended Organizational Positioning*. If you are a U.S. Federal Agency, we recommend positioning an architecture group within the agency at the Deputy Commissioner level and above the CIO, CTO, CDO, and CISO. For State or local Government, we recommend that you treat the that State / City / Local Government as the Business (no Federation) where the architecture and engineering organization is positioned at the Deputy Commissioner level within the Office of Management and Budget / Department of Budget.

The size of the business determines if your architecture and engineering organization is at the Vice President or Director level. If at the Director

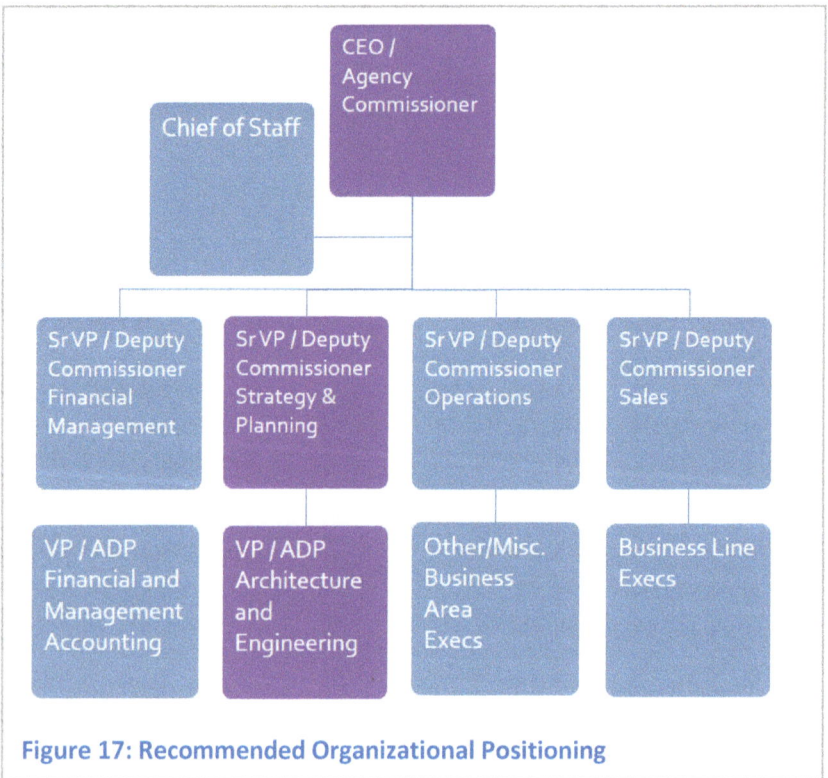

Figure 17: Recommended Organizational Positioning

level the organization should assure that the Chief Architect is treated as an executive in his / her own right and that they have the authority to enforce the framework and methods and mandate work to improve quality of the data and the performance of the organization doing the architecture and engineering.

The *Practical Guide to Federal Enterprise Architecture* provides some great guidance on the positioning of the Architecture effort and on the stature of the person filling the Chief Architect role. For example, the guide states that the Chief Architect should be a "*Friend and liaison to the business units*", and a "*Good communicator who can bridge the cultural differences that often exist between the business and systems organizations, and facilitate interaction and cooperation between these two cultures*".

In *Figure 18: Recommended Organizational Structure and Positioning of the Reference Models* we continue with the public / private company example where the CIO, CDO, CTO, and CISO are direct reports to the Chief Architect as the head of your Architecture and Engineering Organization. Also depicted is the ownership of the Reference Models.

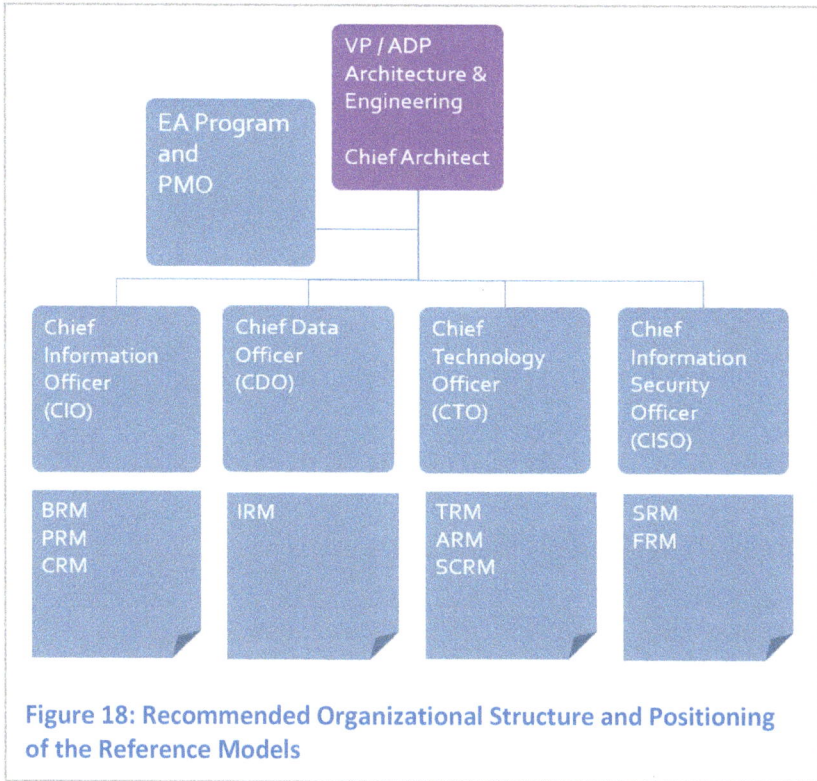

Figure 18: Recommended Organizational Structure and Positioning of the Reference Models

The reference models depicted are:

1. Business (BRM)
2. Performance (PRM)
3. Information (IRM)
4. Technical (TRM)
5. Application / System (ARM)

6. Service Components (SCRM)
7. Security (SRM)
8. Facility (FRM), and a
9. Common (CRM) containing data common to one or more reference models

This top-level portion of the Architecture and Engineering Organization is the Architecture and Engineering Initiative as described earlier. Note that the Architecture and Engineering Program (also depicted in *Figure 18: Recommended Organizational Structure and Positioning of the Reference Models)*, is above the CIO, CDO, CTO, and CISO. Having said this, the Program does serve those roles and facilitates their respective reference model responsibilities.

The Architecture and Engineering Program (further detailed in *Figure 19: Program Structure and positioning of Key Functions*) operates like a consulting company with a resource pool. It provides people resources to internal clients as they approach the organization for assistance in planning, budgeting, architecting, engineering, and with transformative projects. The Architecture and Engineering Program provisions of all Services, including:

1. Architecture & Engineering Services (People)
2. Strategic Planning Services (People)
3. Program Management Services (People)
4. Education and Training:
   For professional services
   For Frameworks and Methods
   For tools
5. Architecture and Engineering Tools (Software as a Service – SaaS)

Don't take it to heart if no one wants your architecture and engineering professional services. In this case, let the business Areas / Lines go to the outside, with the caveat that contracts are written to require:

o Architecture and engineering detail / data in the needed formats,
o That the architecture drawings and data pass your internal standards,
o The architecture passes Independent Verification & Validation (IV&V), and
o After successful IV&V, the architecture repository is loaded.

The Architecture and Engineering Program and the basic program structure is depicted in *Figure 19: Program Structure and positioning of Key*

Functions. The PMO manages transformation projects and engagements. Staffing should be handled based on the scope of the effort and what Business Areas / Lines have a stake.

The PMO also manages teams formed using a matrix management approach[67] to update the reference models each year. The Business Areas and Lines obviously need to divvy up people for the reference model updates, but that is a staffing issue rather than a structural consideration.

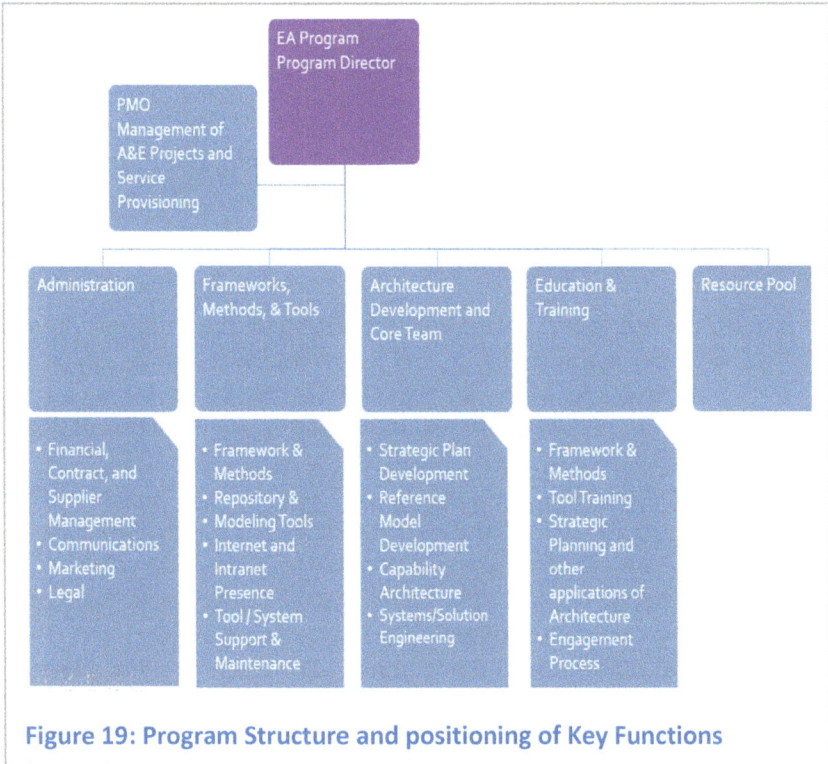

Figure 19: Program Structure and positioning of Key Functions

The Architecture and Engineering Program also has a lead architect responsible for the framework and methods and a chief engineer that is responsible for the Architecture and Engineering tool environment where the tool environment includes the architecture repository, the architecture

---

67 A matrix organizational structure is a company structure in which the reporting relationships are set up as a grid, or matrix, rather than in the traditional hierarchy. In other words, employees have dual reporting relationships - generally to both a functional manager and a product manager

and engineering tools like UNICOM® System Architect®, and web accessibility to all content.

A quality assurance team which can also serve as the AB's Technical Review Committee (TRC) should be in place to review architecture work products and deliverables before they are submitted for presentation to your Architecture Board. This QA team / TRC would also conduct ongoing reviews of the reference model content. This group defines and delivers QA reports to the Chief Architect to drive improvements to the architecture and engineering realm. Remember that there are positive and negative covenants in the policy and those organizations whose architecture quality is lacking are accountable and negative covenants may be imposed.

Architecturally, one should have an IDEF0® Activity Model that describes what the Architecture and Engineering organization does and Roles required to handle each Activity. Given our experience in this space we recommend the following roles:

- **Chief Architect** – this role is responsible for the entire Architecture and Engineering Initiative and the embedded program. It is responsible for all the Services provided by the organization and the Activities performed for day to day operation of the organization. In general, the role is responsible for the health, well-being, and value realization of the Architecture and Engineering organization. They are responsible for the underlying DOTMLPF, sales, employee happiness, and the customer satisfaction. The person filling this role is also responsible for the health of the architecture through the application of and adherence to the chosen framework and methods. Being responsible for the health of the architecture, the quality assurance function also reports into the Office of the Chief Architect.

- **Chief Technology Officer (CTO)** – this role reports to the Chief Architect and is responsible for the Technical Reference Model (TRM), the IT software and hardware product inventory, and the IT technology forecast. It is important that this role also provide guidance on the difference between a Technology and a Product that implements a particular Technology. In doing so, the role is then responsible for the Technology Inventory, the Forecast, and qualifying Products. The person filling this role should be adept at identifying places where technologies can be applied within the business to improve the customer experience and the profitability of the business, if profit applies.

With the popularity of Cloud Computing and with the proliferation of Clouds, this role is also responsible for the Service Component Reference Model and the inventory all Clouds and Software being used as a Service.

o **Chief Data Officer (CDO)** – reports to the Chief Architect and is responsible for the Data / Information Reference Model which includes an understanding of all semantics, all meta-data, the inventory of all databases / repositories, and publishing certain data and meta-data to the Internet. They are also responsible for working with the Chief Information Security Officer (CISO) to document where sensitive data resides, both in-flight and at-rest. Working along with the CISO, they know exactly where all Personally Identifiable Information (PII), Payment Card Information (PCI), Personal Health Information (PHI) resides, and they assure that the appropriate protections are in place for these types of data.

This role assures that there are either IDEF1X® data models or UML Class Models in place for all relational and object repositories. If the organization is also using NOSQL and Graph Databases, this role needs to assure that the appropriate metadata is in place for those repositories as well.

o **Chief Information Security Officer (CISO)** – reports to the Chief Architect and is responsible for the Security Reference Model (SRM) and information technology security reports including application and data security and security assessments. This role is responsible for documenting audit activities and corresponding workflows as well as Security Controls by facility type. So, the CISO is responsible for documenting what Security Controls must be met for Public, Private, and Hybrid Clouds and then executing the audit activities to assure that the Applications / Systems are meeting the controls. The CISO organization then, is the organization that issues certificates of Authority to Operate (ATO) and generates ATO reports that the Chief Architect needs to act upon.

o **Lead Architect and Head of Reference Model Development** – this person and role is responsible for all reference model content and coordinating efforts to ensure that the necessary content is there for all business units (Areas / Lines) as well as the CTO, CDO, CIO, and CISO. In architecture terms, this person is responsible for assuring that the reference models comprise a planner's view of each business unit and the business at large and that the Annual Business Plan and IT Strategic Plans are published in a timely manner. They are also responsible for working with the internal quality assurance team and perhaps the Independent Verification & Validation (IV&V) team. The purpose of working with these teams it to assure that the reference models are ready at each phase in the Strategic Planning cycle and that they are ready for the associated executive / board meetings. This role reports to the Architecture and Engineering Program Director / Manager.

o **Business Subject Matter Expert** - a business subject-matter expert (SME) or domain expert is a person who is an authority in a particular area or facet of the business. In this particular case, the organization needs subject matter experts in the different facets of the business that are undergoing transformation. Keep in mind that industries will have industry specific business capabilities and therefore industry specific subject matter experts. For example, you typically only find mining experts in the mining industry but all industries have financial management experts[68].

o **Engineer / Engineering Specialist** – Engineers are people who design and can oversee the implementation of the DOTMLPF of a Capability and the DOTMLPF of the Services that comprise each Capability. They do this while considering the limitations imposed by practicality, regulation, safety, and cost. [69] [70] There is one sentence in the WIKI page for "Engineer" that we like so we thought I would add it here. The citation actually comes from the Bureau of Labor Statistics: *"The work of engineers forms the link between scientific discoveries and their subsequent applications to human and business needs and quality of life"*.[71]

68 The American Productivity Quality Center (APQC®) https://www.apqc.org/ is a great source for understanding what is unique to an industry and what is common across industries
69 Bureau of Labor Statistics, U.S. Department of Labor
   (2006). "Engineers". Occupational Outlook Handbook, 2006-07 Edition. Retrieved 2006-09-21.
70 National Society of Professional Engineers (2006). "Frequently Asked Questions About Engineering". Archived from the original on 2006-05-22. Retrieved 2006-09-21. "Science is knowledge based on observed facts and tested truths arranged in an orderly system that can be validated and communicated to other people. Engineering is the creative application of scientific principles used to plan, build, direct, guide, manage, or work on systems to maintain and improve our daily lives."
71 Bureau of Labor Statistics, U.S. Department of Labor
   (2006). "Engineers". Occupational Outlook Handbook, 2006-07 Edition. Retrieved 2006-09-21

We differentiate the architecture and engineering disciplines and place greater weight and importance on the engineering side. For this reason, we need engineering specialists that understand the detailed and subtle nature of their particular field and DOTMLPF for their respective field. The fields include network engineering, data engineering, application / software engineering, process engineering, and systems (computing systems) and hardware engineering.

- **Application Engineer / Specialist** – is an engineering specialist that has depth of knowledge in one or more classes of applications (web based, mobile, Enterprise Resource Planning (ERP), etc.) or perhaps a single application or a company's family of applications. This role may also entail application ownership in which case the person specializes in the application that they own. If the application is COTS based, they may additionally have knowledge of the underlying commercial-off-the-shelf (COTS) product.

- **Information / Data Engineer and Data Scientist** – is an engineering specialist that understands all forms of data modeling including object / class modeling via the Unified Modeling Language (UML) and relational data modeling via IDEF1X®. The information / data specialist also understands, and is intimate with, all approaches to storing and reporting on data including operational data stores, data warehouses, and data lakes. They also understand and know where to apply the relational and NOSQL database management systems and underlying schemas like XML and JSON.

- **Network Engineer / Specialist** – a network specialist understands all types of modern networks, networking protocols, and both the internet and intranets. They understand how to model networks and the interconnection of internal networks with the internet. Network Engineers understand the network as reusable infrastructure and Infrastructure offered as a service (IaaS). They understand, apply, and adhere to the Open Systems Interconnection (OSI) model.

- **Systems Engineer / Specialist** – a systems specialist understands all modern physical and virtual computing systems and, on the physical side, related sub-systems like racks, blade computers, networking hardware, storage devices and storage area networks, printing and power management (uninterruptible power suppliers) sub-systems. In short, they understand the physics of a traditional data center and Cloud infrastructure. They also understand how a data center participates in the Internet and how a data center interoperates with the Clouds that they are using.

o **Cloud Computing Engineer / Specialist** – a cloud computing specialist is an engineering specialist understands the various computing layers in cloud computing, including but not limited to the, Infrastructure layer (infrastructure as a service), operating system and middleware layers (platform as a service), and application structures when engineered for the cloud and the multi-user implications (application as a service). Given the breadth and depth of the various Clouds available today, this role may further specialize in a particular Cloud. Examples include the Microsoft Azure, Amazon, and ORACLE Clouds.

o **Operating Systems Engineer / Specialist** – an operating system is the software that supports a computer's basic functions, such as scheduling tasks, executing applications (processes / threads), and controlling peripherals. An operating system specialist understands this software and how it supports those basic computer functions. They understand the internals and operations of both desktop and server operating systems and in particular how they provide for multi-tasking.

o **Middleware Engineer / Specialist** – middleware is the software that acts as a bridge between an operating system and the software which enables the development of business applications or systems. A database engine is a perfect example of one form of middleware and a web application server is another example. The two of these provide for the bulk of the ability for a programmer to develop business applications or systems. Middleware falls into many categories so the organization may need as many middleware specialists as they have categories. Example of some typical middleware categories include:
Relational Database Engines
Web Application Servers
Rules Engines
Etc.

o **IT Security Engineer / Specialist** - computer security, also known as cyber security or IT security, is the protection of computer systems from the theft or damage to their hardware, software or information. Also included is the protection from disruptions or misdirection of the services they provide.[72] An IT Security Specialist is a person that understands how to protect and monitor computers, Applications / Systems, and information from attack. They may specialize in physical devices / mechanisms, virtual, or cover both physical and virtual. An IT Security Specialist also understands the audit activities that are required to assess and remediate security risks.

o **Technical Writer** - a technical writer is a professional writer who produces technical documentation that helps people understand and use a product or service. This documentation includes online help, manuals (system manual, end-user manuals, training manuals, etc.), white papers, design specifications, project plans, test plans, business correspondence, etc.[73] The products may be a computer hardware or software products. A technical writer is not restricted to any one particular medium although they do typically publish via word processing software and then with the assistance of a web content management specialist or a web page designer publish via the inter and / or intra net. A technical write may also drive and or support the development of non-technical documentation.

o **Chief Engineer** - the chief engineer has deep knowledge of architecture, methods, and engineering tools. They understand how those tools are being used, configured, and how they are integrated to support the architecture and engineering work being conducted within your business. The Chief Engineer typically has a group of supporting engineers that are responsible for the architecture and engineering tool environment. In support of the chief architect he / she assures that the environment meets the needs of the business and that it performs satisfactorily given day to day usage by both internal and external users. They are responsible for all modeling tools, web-based browsing and management of architecture content, the repository, a warehouse, search, reporting, and mass import / export of content.

o **Project Manager** – a project manager is a professional in the matter of managing a group of people working together to achieve a concrete and actionable objective which may be the development of a well-defined product. Project managers have the responsibility of developing project plans based on well-defined activities and tasks, assigning resources, procurement, and execution of the plan. Project

---

72 https://en.wikipedia.org/wiki/Computer_security
73 https://en.wikipedia.org/wiki/Technical_writer

managers are the first point of contact for any issues or discrepancies that arise. They help to resolve issues before the problem escalates to higher authorities. In this architecture and engineering context the project manager is responsible for properly documenting each transformation project including risks, issues, and dependencies. Given that transformation programs are typically established to launch or upgrade a business capability and since Capabilities are comprised of Services, the program manager responsible for the transformation program may decide to treat each Service as a project each with a dedicated project manager. It is then the responsibility of the program manager is to assure that dependencies between the projects (if any exist) are addressed.

o **Program Manager** – a program manager has oversight of a related set of projects in a program and can use this oversight to ensure that the program goals and objectives are met. They provide for a decision-making capacity that cannot be achieved at project level and provide project managers with a program perspective when required. This person also acts as a sounding board for ideas and approaches to solving project issues that have program impacts.[74] A Program that is large enough to contain other Programs is typically managed by a Program Director. In this case a Program Director has oversight of the embedded Programs and each Program is managed by a Program Manager.

o **Business Analyst** - a business analyst (BA) is someone who analyzes an organization or some facet of a business and the business operations (existing or planned) in that area of the business. They document the business or processes and supporting systems, assessing the business model and its automation with technology.[75] The International Institute of Business Analysis (IIBA) describes the role as "a liaison among stakeholders in order to understand the structure, policies, and operations of an organization, and to recommend solutions that enable the organization to achieve its goals"[76]. Having a business analyst on every transformation program is a key and critical success factor for all such programs that are dealing with business capabilities, services, processes, roles, policies,

74 https://en.wikipedia.org/wiki/Program_management#Overview_and_definition
75 https://en.wikipedia.org/wiki/Business_analyst
76 International Institute of Business Analysis (IIBA). A Guide to the Business Analysis Body of Knowledge®, 2.0 (BABOK® Guide 2). Cited in: Jerry Lee Jr. Ford (2010), UML for the IT Business Analyst. p. 2

business rules, etc.

Note that, at this time, business analysts and business Architects are viewed as different roles. It behooves industry at large and companies to broaden their view of these roles and observe the similarities between them. They are actually more than similar; they are the same.

o **Head of Education & Training** - is the equivalent of a program manager that is responsible for all education and corresponding training material. They are responsible for education and training experts that are employed by the Architecture and Engineering organization and the curriculum of courses that is required to make the business successful in developing and using architecture. This person and role are responsible for making architecture and engineering training material available electronically via the worldwide-web and / or in a traditional class room setting. The training material must cover processes and tools for the various skill levels like Expert, Advanced, Novice, etc.

o **Head of Marketing and Communications** – is the equivalent of a program manager that is responsible for marketing the architecture and engineering services. This organization promotes the architecture and the associated services offered by the architecture organization. They may also take the lead on managing both internal and external communications. This role and the supporting team are responsible for helping all parties understand the value and business case for Architecture and Engineering. Through a positive marketing campaign, they keep the nay-sayers in place and prevent nay-sayers from becoming obstacles to success. Depending on the size of your business, this role and the Head of Education and Training role may be combined.

o **Head of QA & Risk Management** – this role is the equivalent of a program manager and is responsible for the quality assessments of all architecture and engineering work products and deliverables. This includes the FEAF-like reference models, DODAF and UML models, and the underlying data for all models. This role is also responsible for establishing a risk assessment process / activities and publishing risk assessments not just on the risk of the architecture but also the business.

- Head of Independent Verification &Validation (IV&V) – the head of IV&V is the equivalent of a program manager that is responsible for all independent verification and validation of architecture. The validation is focused on assuring that the architecture meets the specifications imposed by the chosen framework and specifications like the FEAF and DODAF. Verification is focused on assuring that the objectives and needs of the business have been met. This role, in effect, duplicates what the QA team does although it is an independent team. To minimize cost associated with IV&V it is recommended that the organization contract this service and only invoke it when there is a dispute that the internal QA team is unable to adjudicate.

- Capital Investment Council (CIC) / Investment Review Board (IRB) – this council / board is responsible for the cyclic investment plans and decisions to make investments in capabilities. While the content of those plans comes from various legs of the organization including the Architecture Board, the CIC / IRB is responsible for reviewing and then approving those plans. The plans stem from an architectural analysis performed by architects and supporting teams that are operating under the auspices of the CIC / IRB.

  The CIC / IRB is responsible for the evaluation and ongoing management of risk associated with each investment so they need a common risk assessment method in place that all the teams operating under them can leverage.

- Architecture Board (AB) – the AB is group of executives managing a portfolio of transformation projects and, in particular, the architecture and engineering for each of the projects. The AB presides over transformation projects that span functional areas (business Areas / Lines) of the business.

  The AB also governs the content of the architecture. The AB is both plan and issue driven. In either case the board charters transformation programs to look at and architect Capabilities that address needs identified in plans and issues.

- Functional Capabilities Board (FCB) – is a group of executives that presides over a set the capabilities germane to a business Area / Line. Depending on the maturity and lifecycle of the capabilities the FCB may meet more or less. For instance, a mature Business Area / Line with a mature set of capabilities does not require much attention or investment. In this case the FCB may only meet twice a year to facilitate the spring and fall planning cycle. On the flip side of this coin, a capability that is nearing end of life requires market research and attention so that FCB might meet quarterly or even monthly to review the results of all architecture and engineering activities and the activities of the transformation projects established to either launch a new capability or refresh and existing one.

- **Technical Review Committee (TRC)** – the Technical Review Committee (TRC) is a matrix managed team. They operate under the auspices of the Architecture Board. As a committee, it is chaired by the head of Quality Assurance with representation from the technical community including IT Service Management / Operations. The Technical Review Committee is the technical arm of the Architecture Board and performs technical reviews upon request from the AB. The AB is not able to sign-off on any architecture / proposal without the review and approval of the TRC.

Each of the boards mentioned above (three of them), plus the Technical Review Committee, require charters that cover, among other things, mission, authority, membership, voting, decision making and records, business rules, and attendance.

EDUCATION AND TRAINING

The education and training organization provides both architecture and engineering training services at the discipline, method, and tool levels. This means that they educate parties involved on the services offered, processes being applied, they cover both frameworks and methods, and they teach people how to use the tools. The organization may customize training for audiences that are internal to the Architecture and Engineering organization and external. Internally, the architecture and engineering staff in the resource pools need to be trained. In covering the activities that are performed, the training must also address the accompanying deliverables, and work products that go into building the deliverables.

The tool training must go above and beyond vanilla tool training to cover specifically how the tools are to be used within your organization. The more tools you have the more custom training is required. Generally, only two tools are required, **(A)** a web accessible architecture repository to house architecture and engineering data and for reporting, and **(B)** an architecture tool for architecting a business capability top to bottom and left to right (hint, Unicom System Architect®). The latter (B) includes the engineering of DOTMLPF.

Depending on the level of maturity of your organization and its' familiarity with Architecture and Engineering, the training organization may have to provide general Architecture and Engineering training so that everyone knows what it is and how it is to be used within the organization. As the organization at large matures, the training may wane or the delivery may become purely electronic via your company's intranet.

The education and training group collaborates with the marketing group and the communications group so that the curriculum and the training are marketed and communicated. To this end the Architecture and Engineering website should have a section on the curriculum and classes offered. The website also provides a user friendly and intuitive shopping experience so that people can sign up for courses by placing them in a shopping cart and then completing the purchase or registration. If managerial approval is required for such a purchase, make that part of the workflow that is automated by the website.

Your company / agency may want to establish internal certification program. This provides some level of surety that when one requests an architect with a particular skill level that they are getting what they asked for.

We recommend that the curriculum cover the following areas:

- o **The processes in which the Architecture and Engineering activities are embedded:** The Architecture enabled Strategic Planning Process (Zoning the Business) and the Architecture enabled Program and Project Management Process (Architecting and Engineering a Capability)

- o **The chosen Architecture Frameworks and how they are being used, examples:**
  FEAF
  DODAF
  ZACHMAN®
  TOGAF®
  etc.

- o **Architecture / engineering methods, examples:**
  IDEF0®
  IDEF1X®

BPMN®
DODAF methods
UML®
Other methods given your choice of frameworks

- o **Tools**
  Architecture Repository
  UNICOM® System Architect®

  Sparx Systems Enterprise Architect®
  Other Architecture and Engineering tools that meet needs and fit the budget[77]
  etc.

If your organization is using some other tool for requirements management, another tool for Entity Relationship (data) modeling, another tool for UML modeling then the organization needs training for those tools as well. Regardless of how many tools are being used, the curriculum should include a course on the tool agnostic and web accessible repository and the use of business intelligence tools for creating reports from that repository.

The architecture core team can help develop the curriculum and teach courses. Courses can also be farmed out to suppliers. Either way, your organization should have training and the organization should re-train as required.

COMMUNICATIONS APPROACH AND PLAN

Communications and marketing are areas that most organizations neglect when it comes to Architecture and Engineering. A lack of marketing and communications and the fact that Architecture and Engineering is treated as something done off in the corner are two key reasons for failure. Architecture and Engineering deals with almost every facet of your business and all parties should be aware of the Architecture. Develop a communication plan that deals with all the basics like (A) who the Architecture and Engineering folks need to speak with (what internal and external groups are you speaking with), (B) what the architecture and engineering team needs to say, (C) how often you need to communicate,

---

[77] Remember that only the architects and engineers need direct access to the modeling tools. This is why a web accessible repository is an important part of the tool environment. Much of the architecture and engineering data can be accessed, recorded, and later edited directly in the repository and through the browser.

(D) the mechanism or vehicle; is it a face to face meeting or an electronic update / presentation. External groups are important because they should know that your business values its' architectural approach and what an integral part it is in your business.

The communications team can also help with the periodic reports that need to go out. Although, to a large extent that can be automated by the architecture repository. If the architecture repository has stored procedures, the stored procedures can be scheduled to create and distribute reports. Those stored procedures can EMAIL the reports to an individual or all people assigned to a particular role, like a role called "Architecture Board Member". The architecture can also enable people to subscribe to reports and publications. Perhaps the communications team should be publishing a business transformation journal as well.

This is your opportunity to really shine because the communications team can help sell people on the value of the architecture.

MARKETING APPROACH AND PLAN

According to an online source "*Marketing is based on thinking about the business in terms of customer needs and their satisfaction*"[78]. This same source states that marketing organizations take a holistic view of the market, the product, and the customer. Marketing is viewed as a "*tightly integrated effort to discover, create, arouse and satisfy customer needs*". This is exactly what is needed for an Architecture and Engineering Initiative from both internal and outward facing perspectives. Your company's clients should know that your company has an architecture in place. After all, would you engage a company to establish your architecture if they themselves do not have an architecture?

Internal to the business, the marketing group is responsible for developing a demand for both the Architecture and the Architecture and Engineering Services being offered. The group is also responsible for assuring that the Architecture and Engineering Organization is filling the needs of the internal clients. In this respect, they can help you better understand your customers and their needs. Your customers being, the leadership team / Investment Review Board (IRB) and the business Areas / Lines that need to develop strategic / investment plans. Marketing can also help in the area of performance measurement. Your customers may be individually launching their own efforts to establish performance measures and performance

---

78 Marketing - http://www.businessdictionary.com/definition/marketing.html

dashboards. This is something that the architecture and engineering team does and they can do it for all organizations that comprise the company. The legs of the business need to know that the Architecture and Engineering Organization provides those services, and your marketing team will facilitate awareness.

To streamline architecture and engineering operations, the marketing and communications groups can be a single organizational unit.

TOOL ENVIRONMENT

Just as companies typically prefer one accounting system to ten different ones, you would expect a company to want a single architecture and engineering tool environment. And preferably, the company would want as few general-purpose modeling tools as possible. Interestingly, most businesses or agencies that we've worked with, while generally reluctant to invest in modeling tools, have more than one modeling tool. Over time, individual organizational units within the company / agency go out and make tactical investments in modeling tools. This results in a plethora of tools because there is no coordinating body in those companies / agencies.

Complicating the problem, many companies don't properly document the architecture and engineering tool environment. As an example, one of our clients was responsible for housing the agency's' architecture. The organization owned the tool environment but had no architecture documenting how the organization operated and no system views documenting the supporting tool environment.

If your company is already down the path of "10 of these tools and 5 of those tools" and no repository, then take an inventory of all the architecture and engineering products that the company has and start a set of system views of the current and target operating environments.

The system views of your Architecture and Engineering tool environment get created in an architecture tool like UNICOM® System Architect®. Once agreed to, the list of Architecture and Engineering Tools and the underlying Products are registered in the Application Reference Model (ARM) and Technical Reference Model (TRM) of your architecture repository. If you haven't purchased a repository and haven't set up your reference models, then by all means make sure a repository is part of the architecture tool environment that you architect.

Develop all the technical views of the architecture tool environment in accordance with your chosen architecture framework. Assure that technical building blocks, like the systems / applications that automate the strategic planning and program management processes, are properly related to the operational aspects of your Architecture and Engineering ability. Yes, you need IDEF0®[79] based activity models and BPMN®[80] based process models of those processes with a mapping of the Applications / Systems to the Activities they automate[81]. This enables you to identify gaps in terms of the parts of those processes that are not automated. At this point and by this time, you also need the IDEF0® based activity models for all the architecture and engineering activities that are to be embedded into the aforementioned processes. Those are the activities that require your attention as they need to be automated by the tool environment. Generally, the tool environment should contain components that enable:

- Reference Model Development and Monitoring
- Capability Modeling
- Service Modeling
- Organization Modeling
- Policy Modeling
- Modeling of Education and Training Material
- Concept of Operations Modeling
- Information Exchange Modeling
- Process Decomposition and Information Flow (IDEF0®)
- Workflow Modeling (BPMN®)
- Requirements Management
- Data Modeling
- Object Modeling (UML®)
- Application Design
- Network Modeling
- Systems Modeling
- Technology and Product Modeling
- Reporting
- Search
- Web browsing / navigation of the architecture

We mention these forms of modeling in particular because given the current level of Architecture maturity in the industry these are generally thought to be disciplines performed by different people and falling outside of Architecture and Engineering space. For instance, today the requirements management is thought to be done by "Business Analysts"

---

79 Integrated Definition Methods® (IDEF®) – http://www.idef.com
80 Business Process Modeling Notation (BPMN) – http://www.bpmn.org
81 We have models in the UNICOM System Architect which may eventually be made available.

and most business analysts don't know that requirements management is part of Architecture and Engineering and something that all Architects and Engineers do. As a result, industry has developed dedicated and standalone requirements management tools and for similar historical reasons has develop separate data modeling tools.

In the end, you really only need two tools and people trained in Architecture and Engineering. Today, those tools are: a tool agnostic repository to store you're Architecture and Engineering data, and a holistic modeling tool like UNICOM® System Architect® to Architect Capabilities and to Engineer the underlying DOTMLPF. Your repository, by its' very design, should enable the business to make all content web accessible.

A candidate tool environment is depicted in *Figure 20: Depiction of the basic tool environment.* Note the various disks in lower right-hand corner and in particular the ITIL-based Configuration Management Database (CMDB).

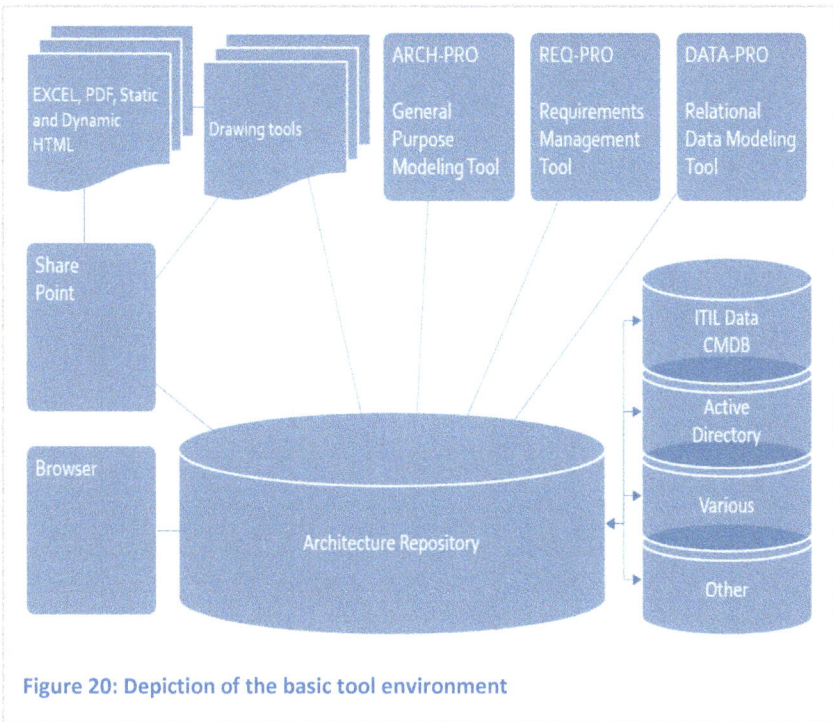

Figure 20: Depiction of the basic tool environment

Certain architecture and engineering data come from other systems and, upon approval, certain IT data must be pushed from the Architecture to the CMDB. This includes, but is not limited to, Application / System data at the instance level where each environment (with potentially multiple production environments) is an instance of the Application / System. Each instance needs to be managed by the IT organization or the Cloud Service Provider (CSP).

The other system worthy of noting and depicted in *Figure 20: Depiction of the basic tool environment* is the corporate directory containing person and organization data. This is typically the MS Active Directory® underpinning your EMAIL system. It is important to acknowledge the Architecture as the authoritative source of the Org chart and to acknowledge the need to synchronize person and organization data between the architecture and that Application / System. Person data must be kept in the architecture and kept in sync with the Active Directory so that, as an example, when someone is assigned as the owner of an Application / System the Architecture has the name and other key information about the person. In this scenario, if the person leaves the company, then the Architecture needs to be updated as the Active Directory is.

You may add other tools as you see fit but treat each of the tools as an Application / System so that you list them as such in your Application Reference Model (ARM). As an example, if you were to purchase UNICOM® System Architect® it gets recorded as a product in your product inventory (Technical Reference Model) with all the associated costs including the initial purchase price and then annual maintenance. You then associate the Product with the Application / System that it automates. Let's call the Application / System "ARCHPRO". And when someone asks you what Application / System you are using you say ARCHPRO. The point here is that the Application / System is not the Product and vice versa; they are two separate and distinct things.

ARCHITECTURE ENABLED STRATEGIC PLANNING

The ability to Plan and Budget goes by different names but is generally referred to as Strategic Planning and Budgeting or simply, Strategic Planning. While they are not equivalent to one another, the U.S. Department of Defense (DOD) refers to this as "*Programming, Planning, Budgeting, and Budget Execution (PPBE)*" and the U.S. Federal Government refers to the Strategic Planning Process as the "*Capital Planning and Investment Control (CPIC)*"[82] Process. There is guidance indicating that the CPIC Process is supposed to be architecture enabled, although most treat

---

82 Information about the Capital Planning and Investment Control (CPIC) Process can be found at https://www.ocio.usda.gov/about-ocio/information-resource-management/capital-planning-and-investment-control

architecture as a separate and distinct process from the CPIC process and it is up to the individual agencies to assure that these two processes are integrated.

Your company may have a strategic planning process, but it may not be informed by architecture and engineering methods and the information that stems from the application of those methods. In this case, document (architect) the relevant Zoning / Architecture / Engineering activities and show where they are imbedded in the planning process[83]. Document why these activities are relevant to your planning process. The relevance will become apparent in documenting the inputs and outputs of each activity and observing that some of the data flows right into your company's strategic plan. You may also find that the strategic planning policy and business rules guide and / or constrains these activities.

A high-level depiction of an architecture enabled budget process is depicted in *Figure 21: Architecture and Engineering Activities in the context of a Budget Lifecycle.* Here we show the budget cycle with five embedded architecture activities. We show where those activities are positioned relative to the fiscal year and the phases of the budget cycle. The activities depicted are ones from the Andersen Consulting® *Business Integration Methodology (BIM)®.* Other activities and analyses that comprise the Strategic Planning Process are also depicted in *Figure 28: A Top-down Strategic Planning Process.*

The depiction provided in *Figure 21: Architecture and Engineering Activities in the context of a Budget Lifecycle* was developed for a client that wanted an architecture program to facilitate the merger of some fifty organizations that each had their own CIO and IT department . The depiction re-enforces the business focus and the budget cycle as the context of that client's IT Strategic Planning efforts.

A key takeaway here is that the strategic planning process updates and maintains your company's Reference Models which house data required for the Annual Business Plan and Information Technology Strategic Plan.

---

83 To document where these activities are performed one creates IDEF0® based Activity Models down to the task level, and subsequently creates BPMN based workflow models using the tasks created in the IDEF0® Activity Models.

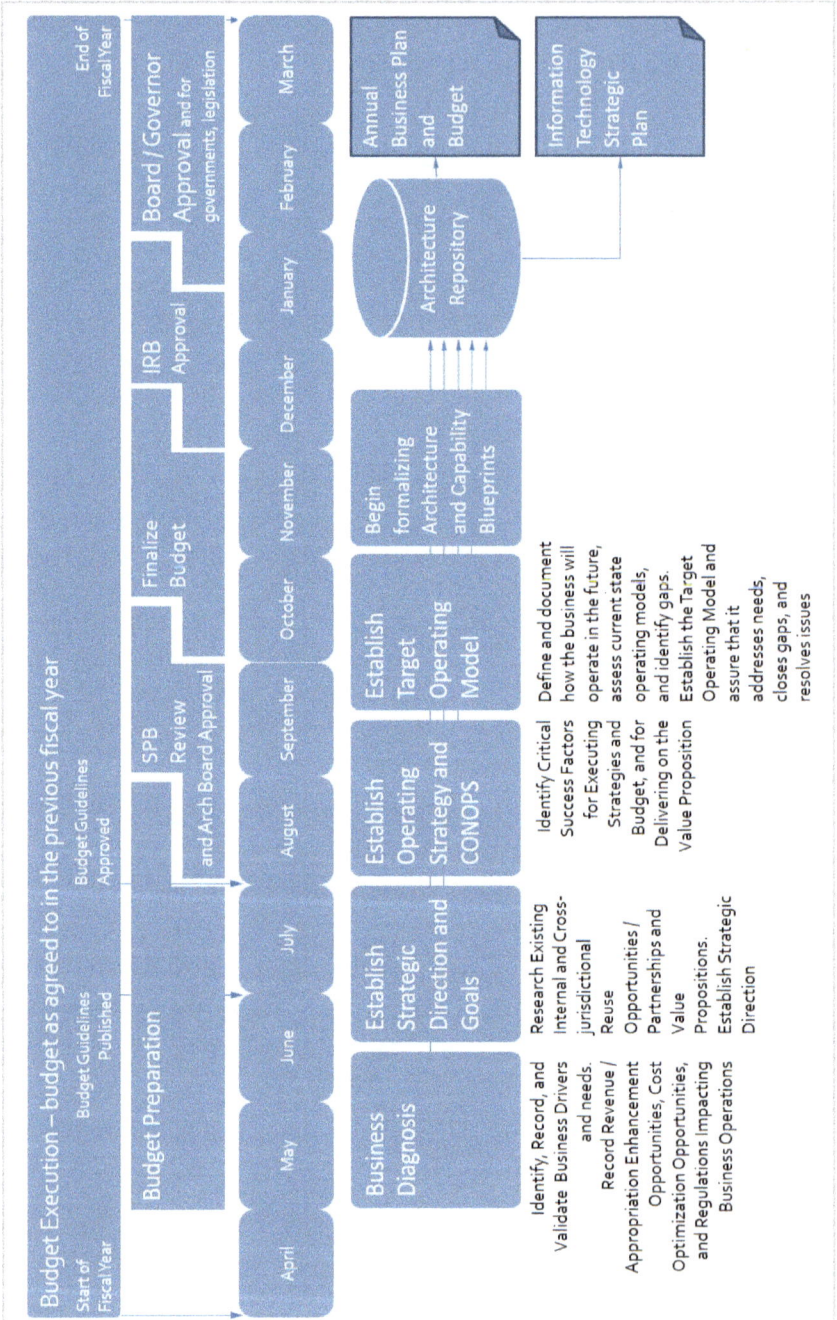

Figure 21: Architecture and Engineering Activities in the context of a Budget Lifecycle

ARCHITECTURE ENABLED PROGRAM MANAGEMENT

Initiatives, Programs, and Projects are bodies of people that are brought together to realize a mission, launch a product, etc. They are established within companies and governmental bodies in the course of doing business. We are speaking here of Transformation Programs designed to either introduce new Capabilities or to make capital investments in existing Capabilities. These Transformation Programs are typically chartered and launched by the Business Areas / Lines or the Architecture Board acting as a body that looks across the Areas and Lines.

A Transformation Program is responsible for an agreed to investment and a decision that was made during the early stages of the Strategic Planning and Budgeting Process to pursue the investment. While a certain amount of Architecture was developed during those early stages[84], the transformation program now needs to expound upon that architecture to form a complete set of blueprints for the Capability being introduced or refreshed. Note that the idea of producing a complete set of blueprints does not preclude agility: the IT detail is produced by applying agile techniques within the context of the transformation programs. Additionally, some of the data being produced in the architecture and engineering activities (like the process taxonomy) make agility feasible, and other more detailed IT data is fed to the Service Management / Operations team or directly fed into the Service Management System and Configuration Management Database (CMDB).

A few notes about these Transformation Programs:

o They are business focused, meaning that they are typically looking at a new Business Model or analyzing aspects of existing business models and operations.

o Their scope is typically the full DOTMLPF spectrum and rarely deal solely with IT. It is a common mistake to think that these programs are IT only. For instance, many businesses launch programs to establish company-wide Systems / Applications like a Financial Management System / Application. Setting aside the fact that they are creating a silo, they tend to gloss over the Policy and

---

84 A Planner's View of the Capability is produced during the Strategic Planning and Budgeting Process and that Architecture and Engineering information should be in your Architecture Repository.

Organizational impacts and changes, they overlook education and training, and they ignore skills and staffing plans, etc.

- o If programs are company-wide or span more than one Business Area / Line, then they should be driven by the Architecture Board with stakeholder representation from Business Areas / Lines, as required. If they do not span more than one Business Area / Line then the Business Area / Line may drive the transformation project

- o The programs are governed by the established management system. This is to avoid indiscriminate decisions and single person decision making

- o They begin in one fiscal year as part of the Strategic Planning and Budgeting Process and then continue on after the proposed investment and the budget has been approved.

Transformation programs are responsible for the Architecture the Capability and the Engineering of the underlying DOTMLPF.

There are several Commercial and Government Off-the-Shelf (COTS / GOTS) Program Management Processes with varying degrees of embedded architecture and engineering. As an example, there is one published by NYS Government called the *NYS Guidebook*. The *NYS Guidebook*[85] has an embedded Software Delivery Lifecycle (SDLC). Another business focused process is the Anderson Consulting® *Business Integration Methodology (BIM)®*. The BIM does an excellent job at integrating Strategic Planning at the corporate or executive level with the creation and delivery of Capabilities. The key here is to choose a process that is holistic and begins with an analysis of business operations as opposed to one which is focused on the delivery of an Information Technology System / Application alone.

There is another process that is definitely worthy of mention here given the trend to buy Commercial off the shelf systems. *The Evolutionary Process for the Integration of COTS-based Systems (EPIC)*[86] is a great approach to follow and leverage for the architecture and engineering activities that need to occur in the context of your broader Transformation Program Management Process. This process is noteworthy because it iterates acquisitions and contract development as one converges on a solution.

---

85 https://its.ny.gov/nys-project-management-guidebook-release-2
86 https://resources.sei.cmu.edu/library/asset-view.cfm?assetid=6093

Staff / Staffing and Skills

Building on a concrete set of roles likes the ones in the "*Architecture Organization*" section, assures that the business has well-defined position descriptions and corresponding skills and skill levels for members of the architecture and engineering team to successfully perform their jobs.

In some cases, existing employees may perform new duties as part of their involvement in the Architecture and Engineering Initiative or Program. Be sure to refresh their job descriptions accordingly and train. An effective Architecture and Engineering Program will manage the necessary human capital changes proactively through planning and clear communication. This step requires a creation of an Architecture and Engineering human capital plan that:

- o Assesses skills on hand and documents required training
- o Documents staffing gaps to identify the positions to be filled
- o Assesses the need for contract staff
- o Addresses staff retention, development, recognition, and reward

A skills assessment typically provides a set of job families and related job functions as an output. It will be important for the Architecture and Engineering positions and functions to be represented in the skills assessment. The assessment also accounts for experience levels like "novice", "sophomore", "advanced", and "expert". The skills assessment will be a critical component in defining the Architecture and Engineering skills gap. However, at a high level, the following skills are required to successfully initiate and manage an Architecture and Engineering Program:

- o **Generic Skills** - Leadership; ability to work effectively on and drive teams; interpersonal skills; oral and written communication skills; and ability to think logically and structure problems.

- o **Business Skills and Methods** - Ability to prepare a business case, define a business process, conduct strategic planning.

- o **Business Architecture and Engineering Skills** - Ability understand Business Models, to model business processes, and design architectural building blocks.

- o **Program and Project Management Skills** - Ability to manage individual projects and an overall portfolio of projects using standard program and project management tools and techniques. Ability to manage budgets, contracts, business change, risks, issues.

- o **IT General Knowledge Skills** - Knowledge of Application / System design patterns and Cloud Computing. Experience with programming languages, brokering applications, storage systems, infrastructure, migration planning. Experience creating and managing custom and off-the-shelf software products. Ability to construct service level agreement and perform asset management.

- o **Technical IT Skills** - Knowledge and experience with software engineering, Systems / Software Development Lifecycle (SDLC), security, data interchange, user interface, data management, and networks.

- o **Legal Environment** - Knowledge of data protection laws, contract law, procurement law, and fraud prevention practices

Remember, "Skill" is a Building Block so just as one documents the skills required for Financial Management and Strategic Planning and Budgeting, one needs to document the Architect and Engineering skills for each role. For each Architecture and Engineering Activity being embedded in the Strategic Planning and Program Management Processes, one needs to know the Roles and Skills involved.

Staffing includes the development of a resource pool and a supply chain to handle unanticipated load. The primary purpose of the resource pool is for the Architecture and Engineering Program to provide the people to render the architecture and engineering services. When a service request is submitted for an architect or an engineer, resources need to be available to satisfy the request. To avoid having an idle bench, the Architecture and Engineering Program should be slightly understaffed and have contracts in place with Systems Integrators that can provide the architecture and engineering staff when needed. This is your Architecture and Engineering supply chain.

The resource pool can be built up based on capacity planning, but as you do bring people into the resource pool be sure that they are trained. Let the resource pool be a Center of Excellence that helps bolster and evolve the framework, the methods, and the value of the architecture. When people in the resource pool are not on assignment, leverage them to do research and to provide education and training.

People in the resource pool that are not on assignment can also help with market research, looking into new Business Models and technologies that the business can leverage. The results, the findings and recommendations, can be reported to the Architecture Board for action.

ZONING MAPS OR REFERENCE MODELS

Zoning or segmenting the Business entails breaking the business down into manageable and well-defined piece-parts. These piece-parts and other related building blocks are recorded in the FEAF-based reference models, where the Zoning is done primarily in the Business Reference Model (BRM). We recommend that you start with the Business Reference Model (BRM) to establish a clear understanding of the Business Lines (Operating Units) and Business Areas (Non-operating Units) that comprise the business. Then focus on the large-grained Capabilities of the Business Areas and Lines. Once you have the inventory of Capabilities, you may begin your architecture and later, the engineering of the DOTMLPF.

An example of Reference Models and their content is highlighted in one of our case studies presented in *Part IV – Case Studies* and the *State Government* case study (see *Figure 30: FEAF Like Reference Models* on page 135). That particular implementation was taylored for one of our clients that was focused more on Business Processes and Applications, moreso than Capability.

As depicted in *Figure 30: FEAF Like Reference Models,* the Reference Models do include inventories of some very basic Building Blocks that document how the business is structured and where investments are being made. The figure depicts some key relationships between building blocks, although in reality those relationships are not always direct relationships as depicted. There are, at times, other smaller grained intervening building blocks that comprise the relationship. Note that while Investments are part of the Performance Reference Model (PRM), "Investment" it is centrally located in this figure. This was done to emphsize the primary purpose of the Reference Models; to manage proposed Investments and to formulate the Budget.

In the outline below we take a look at what it means to Zone the Business, one reference model at a time. There are nine (9) reference models and in each case, to keep things simple, we've applied the "rule of three"[87]. This means that at most we explain the use and applicability of three elements.

❖ **Business Reference Model (BRM)** – Zoning entails breaking the business down into its' constituent parts: Business Areas and Lines. Once the Business Areas and Lines have been identified, document the Capabilities of each where a Capability is a large grained activity. For

---

87 An explanation of the Rule of Three can be found at:
https://en.wikipedia.org/wiki/Rule_of_three_(writing)

example, "Finance" and "Operations" are two well-known Business Areas. "Financial Management" and "Human Resources Management" are typical Capabilities. Looking back at **Figure 12: Model depicting Capabilities by Business Area / Line** you see a partial view of the Capabilities comprising those Business Areas. In summary, and applying the rule of three, the three building blocks of primary concern are:

Business Area

Business Line

Capability

As your Business Reference Model matures, it will look something like this:

> **Business Areas / Lines** are typically Sr VP level organizations that have germane
>> **Capabilities** which are comprised of
>>> **Services** which are delivered through well-defined
>>>> **Processes** which are comprised of well-defined
>>>>> **Activities** which are comprised of well-defined
>>>>>> **Tasks** which are guided by
>>>>>>> **Methods** that get you down to the
>>>>>>>> **Steps** Level[88]
>> **Organizational units**[89] within a Business Area / Line are assigned to deliver the Services that comprise the Capabilities within the respective Area / Line. This is done with the

---

88 Note, we are not suggesting that you get down to the step level in the first pass but as your architecture matures that Step level of detail should be there. We challenge you to get to first get the service level in place. Then leverage the APQC® models for the process and activity detail. Then move on to performance measures. You don't need task detail until you start modeling workflows (what most people refer to as process models).

89 Keep in mind that the organization and person information are both in a model we refer to as the "Common Reference Model (CRM)" This data really comes from your HR system so and interface to that system is required. With an interface in place, the org and person data copied into the architecture will be kept up to date. If the HR system uses a Lightweight Directory Access Protocol (LDAP) store for this information then the EA should have an event driven interface with the LDAP repository so that as changes occur in the LDAP repository the EA is automatically updated. Keep in mind that some changes in the EA should occur in advance of changes in your HR/LDAP. For example, if a person is a System/Application owner and that person is leaving the company then one needs to change owner just as one does in an org chart with "acting managers".

appropriate level of redundancy to accommodate Continuity of Operations[90].

❖ **Information / Data Reference Model (IRM)** – your data zones / segments are also known as data domains. They are a mirror of the business insofar as each data domain corresponds to the Business Areas. While not recommended, you may have your data experts take a stab at identifying the "Data Domains" and then later reconcile the data domains with the Business Areas. There may be justifiable variations between the business and data segments. Variations or not, consider creating a RACI chart of Business Areas to data domains so that you know which Business Area is Responsible, Accountable, Consulted, and Informed by that data domain. Your business may want to consult the NIEM[91] for their list of communities which may coincide with your data domains. The NIEM is also a good source for information exchange formats. Your reference model should get down to that level: the IRM and the Architecture and Engineering Program should be prescribing and enforcing formats for data at rest and in flight.
Applying the rule of three, start with
Data Domains
Subject Areas with each data domain
Information Assets / Classes of Data that fall within the subject areas
Ultimately your IRM should reflect this structure and contain:

➢ Data Domains / Categories
  ▪ Subject Areas
    • Classes of Data that fall within the subject area
      ♦ Entities
        ➢ Attribute / Property / Field
          ▪ Data Elements
  ▪ Databases / Warehouses
    • Tables
      ♦ Columns (meta-data about the atomic pieces of data that comprise an entity
  ▪ Master Data Repositories
  ▪ Data Lake

---

90 A definition for Continuity of Operations is provided in the Technopedia at:
    https://www.techopedia.com/definition/29823/continuity-of-operations-plan-coop
91 https://www.niem.gov and
    https://en.wikipedia.org/wiki/National_Information_Exchange_Model

Note that the table and column meta-data can be captured using the reverse engineering features of some architecture tools but the inventory of databases / schemas / warehouses is a prerequisite.

We advise close collaboration between the owners of the Information and Security Reference Models. For security reasons, take the time to mark Columns, Tables, and Databases that need to be encrypted at rest and call out the encryption methods. Don't wait until it is too late and data calls are required. Also take the time to get down below the Entity Attribute level. There is a key feature of UNICOM® System Architect® that enables you to do this: Data Elements. Define basic data elements like Social Security Number, Company Name, First Name, Last Name, Birth Date and then define your attributes as the assignment of these reusable Data Elements to an Entity. You will then know, ahead of time, everywhere in the entire array of databases that you have a Social Security Number.

Working together, the security and data teams also document the Confidentiality, Integrity, and Availability (CIA)[92] of your data. This is preferably done at the Data Element/Entity Attribute level so that the CIA of an Entity or Class of Data can be derived. As an example, a Database containing a Table with Person data will have a mix of data with High, Medium, and Low Confidentiality. The records in the Table will have the maximum Confidentiality of all Columns in the Table.

❖ **Performance Reference Model (PRM)** – the performance reference model is, in a manner of speaking, a mini-ledger. It contains proposed and subsequently agreed to investments that are itemized in accordance with your chart of accounts[93]. This includes the IT portion of any capital investment. Investments are tied to proposed or existing Capabilities in your BRM. The investment is made in the Doctrine, Organization, Training, Materiel, Leadership, Personnel, and Facilities (DOTMLPF) that is required for the Capability in question.

The performance reference model doesn't really contribute to the Zoning of the Business although you may think of it as the component of the architecture that tells you who and what is doing well. Given that Organizations are assigned to deliver Services and execute agreed

---

92 A write up on data Confidentiality, Integrity, and Availability can be found at https://whatis.techtarget.com/definition/Confidentiality-integrity-and-availability-CIA

93 Note that you will need an interface from your architecture and engineering tools to the General Ledger so that the chart of accounts can be pulled into the architecture and so that proposed investments can be itemized.

to Service Delivery Processes, the PRM documents which of these organization may need some help, what processes need attention, and who and what is shining. You can do this with a simple numeric measurement approach like Capability Maturity Model (CMM®)[94] which describes the maturity of a process as executed by a particular organization.

The FEAF enables the segmentation of Key Performance Indicators (KPIs) using the structure outlined below. We tend to avoid the complexity of this structure and opt for a simple KPI type where types might be "cycle time", "maturity", "monetary", etc.

- ➢ Measurement Area
  - ○ Measurement Category
    - ▪ Measurement Group
      - • Key Performance Indicator

You may use the measurement areas, categories, and groups as published in the U.S. Federal specification or, you may align (A) Measurement Areas with your Business Areas, (B) Measurement Categories with Capabilities within a Business Area, and (if categories correspond to capabilities then) (C) Measurement Groups would correspond to the Services that comprise a Capability. Again, you see the importance of the BRM and the basic Business Area, Business Line, Capability, Service, Process, Activity taxonomy.

The starting point for creating your Performance Reference Model is really the BRM because you need the inventory of Capabilities, Services, and Business Processes. Once you have these inventories, and once you know which organizations are executing those processes, you may rate the process-organization pair using the CMM® 1 thru 5 ratings.

CMM® level 1 indicates that the process is not defined and success is contingent on the heroics of one or two individuals within the organization. On the other end of the spectrum CMM® Level 5 is characterized by a process that is well-defined, communicated, and whose execution is being monitored on an ongoing basis.

If an organization executing a particular process gets to CMM® Level 5 for a particular process, or close to that, you might want to think about

---

94 Carnegie Mellon University® CMM® – see https://en.wikipedia.org/wiki/Capability_Maturity_Model_Integration and https://cmmiinstitute.com/

other key performance indicators aside from CMM® rating. Better yet, apply the "rule of 3" to master 3 KPI's, then fan out.

Knowing that Processes are executed to deliver Services, one can average ratings at the process level to provide a rating for a Service. One can then average ratings of the Services to establish a rating for a Capability. Note that the Service and Capability ratings, as averages, are not be organization specific. That is, if a Service is being rendered by 3 organizations executing 5 processes, then as an average the overall Service rating is organization independent.

To get a head start on both the process inventory and inventory of key performance indicators we suggest that you work with the American Productivity and Quality Center (APQC®)[95] as they have fairly complete inventories of process categories, processes, activities, and key performance indicators. Membership with the APQC® is required, but that may be less expensive than starting from scratch.

❖ **Application / System Reference Model (ARM)** – the ARM is the home of your Application / System inventory. This is where your company may gain the most up-front traction with the architecture effort because many companies don't have a company-wide inventory of the Applications / Systems. In terms of relationships to the other Reference Models, and in terms of portfolio management, you may focus on three things: (1) Capabilities / Services, automated by (2) Applications / Systems, that are built using (3) Products.

Bear in mind, that while Applications / Systems are built and supported by other software products, they are not the product. Your Product inventory, with part number detail, is in your Technical Reference Model (TRM) and the relationship between an Application and the Products that support it is across those models. The basic Application taxonomy is:

> ➢ Business Solution / Application Category as logical groups of:
>   ○ Applications comprised of
>   ▪ Modules comprise of
>   • Components

95 More information about The American Productivity Quality Center (APQC®) can be found at https://www.apqc.org/

If your company / agency uses the word "System" instead of "Application" then the taxonomy might look like this:

- ➤ System of Systems comprised of
  - ○ Systems broken down into
    - ▪ Subsystems which have
      - • Components

Applications / Systems also have, among other things, Tiers / Layers and multiple Environments which in the Cloud Computing world are comprised of virtual servers and, the Environments, are created as needed.

Here again you can reuse the Business Areas for categorizing your Applications / Systems. For example, if you have a company-wide Business Area called Procurement, then you can use "Procurement" as an Application / System category. Having said that, you can get that categorization through the extended relationship from Application to Business Area:

- ➤ **Applications** automates
  - ○ **Activities** comprises
    - ▪ **Processes** automates
      - • **Services** comprises a
        - ○ **Capability** is germane to a
          - ▪ **Business Area / Line**

The categorized list of Applications then, is nothing more than a query, and unique "Application Categories" are not required. Bear in mind though, Applications may be supporting multiple Business Areas so, an Application may fit more than one category.

You will need this extended relationship either way because you need to establish a matrix of Applications to Business Capabilities that they automate. Presenting this relationship in a matrix format, enables you to see if there is unnecessary or excessive duplication. How many procurement applications does your company have? How many Financial Management Systems does the company / agency have?

Zoning the business and then establishing a complimentary Applications / Systems design is an interesting and related subject. Companies have gone to one extreme or the other in emphasizing either (A) Applications / Systems that support a Business Line end-to-end (*Horizontally*), or (B) Applications / Systems that are functional in nature and support all the Business Lines (*Vertically positioned*). Rarely do we see a company in the middle that actually understands the need for both and that the two types of Applications / Systems are two parts of the whole. The balance comes from understanding which functions can be delegated to a master (vertical) system and which must remain "in-line" or horizontal. Remember that Business Lines (horizontally positioned) are like companies in and of themselves, and they have to have their own budget and ledger and end-to-end Resource Planning[96] systems. The Business Areas, with their specialty Applications / Systems, act as master systems that the end-to-end systems interoperate with.

Think about the implications of a design where the Business Lines are non-integral. Being non-integral means that the Business Line can be removed or slid out. From a Business Process perspective, you know how the Business Line inter-operates with the Business Areas and business at large, and the System perspective mirrors the business perspective. Think about a design like this from a merger & acquisitions point of view. If you are selling off one of those business lines, no problem; snip the interfaces and it is gone. The buyer gets the Business Line, the supporting ERP, and the blueprints.

In summary, understand what applications / systems you have and what they automate. If the company / agency has too many establish an Application / System Rationalization effort to systematically identify those Applications / Systems that can be sunset.

❖ **Technical Reference Model (TRM)** – zoning from a technical point of view is somewhat different from that of the other reference models; it is more standalone. The zoning or segmenting starts with the creation of standalone Product Categories. You may set up some product categories of your own or you can leverage categories that Service Management and network scanning tools have normalized on. In short, you need to partition / bucket your products and then see if, within each bucket, you have too much. Create a technology forecast for existing buckets and for new buckets that you anticipate creating. Look at the content of these buckets (software and hardware products) over time. Are the buckets continually growing and getting more expensive to maintain?

Take a simple and well-known example at this point in the evolution of business automation and Application / System development. One of

---

96 Enterprise Resource Planning (ERP) and ERP Systems are explained nicely here: https://softwareconnect.com/erp/what-is-erp/

the categories should be Databases and / or Database Management. Do you have some Business Areas / Lines that use different Relational Database Management Systems (RDBMS)? Are there other legs of the business using graph and NOSQL database management systems? Has any thought been put into what it takes to maintain all the disparate database management systems?

As your company / agency buys more Commercial-off-the-shelf (COTS) Applications and uses more Software as a Service (SaaS), there may be less of a need for the product inventory. This is because COTS products are black boxes to you and as a black box you know nothing about the internal structure and operations of the Application / System. That includes what database the COTS / SaaS uses. Having said this, we do caution our readers to ask what database management system is inside and ask what your choices are. More important, if you are dealing with SaaS, make sure that you own the data and that you maintain that data in house. At a minimum the company / agency should have a copy of the data.

Once the buckets are created and populated create side-by-side comparison of what the company looks like today compared to out years in a four-year planning cycle. This could be a rolling four-year cycle and report so that as each fiscal year changes, the report automatically changes / rolls.

❖ **Security Reference Model (SRM)** – there is plenty to zone / segment from a security point of view. We suggest that you start by defining security enclaves into which you place things that need to be protected in accordance with the definition of the enclave. These enclaves may be nested. For example, if you have an enclave called the DMZ then that enclave may be broken down into two sub-enclaves. Each Cloud Service Provider used may be an enclave for your company and the company needs to articulate what is permissible and not permissible in that cloud.

There is much more to the Security Reference Model though and we will not define it exhaustively here. Let's provide one more example which is related to the concept of a security enclave. Data needs to protected and secured and all information / data assets or "classes of data" require different levels of protection. To this end the security reference model should define those data security classifications and enable architects to classify the data that they are placing within a database and making accessible via some application. Tagging the data and then having the appropriate knowledge about what Applications / Systems are touching that data enables the business to identify security risks.

This security information can be used to create heat maps of the Database and Application / System portfolios. The heat maps provide a red, yellow, and green pictorial showing where there may be security vulnerabilities. It is important to note here, and in general, that to the greatest extent possible you need to focus on the data / metadata and let the tools do the drawing. Architects may do some drawing, but the hand drawing should be limited.

- ❖ **Service Component Reference Model (SCRM)** – the service component reference model documents the reusable IT services that have been established to support automation throughout the business. That is, it documents all Software being offered as a Service (SaaS) and the associated offering information. The offering information provides a list of features that one has access to given a particular level (Gold, Platinum, Free etc.).

- ❖ **Facilities Reference Model (FRM)** – the facilities reference model contains some important logistics information that can be used for Zoning purposes. For instance, if your company has regions then the regions need to be defined in the FRM. The FRM also contains the inventory of office and data centers locations / facilities.

- ❖ **Common Reference Model (CRM)** – the common reference model was introduced by the authors to house some important information that is used across the reference models and which is typically ignored in architecture efforts. This includes Organization (org chart) data, person data, and the assignment of people to organizations. Organizational modeling is the most common form of Zoning that people in business do every day without realizing that they are Zoning and dealing with data that is important to Architecture and Engineering efforts.

Remember, establishing your Reference Models is a one-time effort and after they are established one simply has to maintain them on a yearly basis. If you are starting from scratch, you can create the reference models simultaneously but with keen awareness of all dependencies between them. For example, the Application / System inventory is in the Application Reference Model, the Hardware / Software / Asset Inventory is in the Technical Reference Model, and software products in the TRM need to be mapped to the Applications / Systems in the ARM that are using them.

While your Application / System experts are creating the inventory of Applications / Systems, your service management people can be scanning your Network and Systems to determine what software is out there. From the scanned inventory and working with the suppliers you can get part number detail and both purchase and maintenance cost information.

Note that, under normal circumstances, much of the data in the Reference Models comes from your modeling tool. That is, it is created when you are Architecting and Engineering a Capability, or refreshing the Architecture, in your Architecture and Engineering tool. Only a portion of that data needs to be brought up into the Reference Models: the data comprising a Planner's View of the Capability, and perhaps some Owner View detail.

BLUEPRINTS FOR KEY CAPABILITIES

The architecture for your business has both breadth and depth. The breadth is covered by the Reference Models as a broad yet thin view of the business. The depth is established by creating a set of blueprints for each capability. We suggest a hybrid DODAF and UML specification that includes some diagrams and artifacts from both DODAF 1.5 and 2.0. In addition, we suggest some of our own diagrams and additions to the DODAF that are introduced to address gaps. A list of diagrams for Capabilities includes:

1. Capability Overview & Summary
2. Dictionary of Terms
3. Maturity Model including Operational Measures and Metrics
4. Business Case
5. Requirements
6. Common Canvas (do / draw what you want)
7. Capability and Service Taxonomy
8. Service to Process Mapping
9. Organization to Service Mapping (Who delivers the Services)
10. Operational Concept and Vision
11. Operational Node / User Group Connectivity and Information Exchange Requirements
12. Organizational Structure
13. Organizational Staffing Plans
14. Process Taxonomy
15. Process Context and Details (
    Triggers with attached Data Objects (inputs),
    Outcomes with attached Data Objects (outputs),
    Policies that constrain or guide each Process,

Roles,
Training, etc.)
16. Process Information Flow
17. Business Rules
18. Workflow Model
19. Education and Training (Curriculum and Courses)
20. Data Concepts / Objects
21. Data Classes (UML®), Data Elements, and Properties
22. Data Status State (UML®)
23. Data XML/JSON
24. Data Meta-model
25. Data Entities, Data Elements, and Attributes
26. Data Physical Schema
27. Application / System Interfaces
28. Systems Communications / Networks
29. Application / System Functionality and Data Flow
30. Application / System Portfolio Performance
31. Operational Activity to Application / Systems Function Matrix
32. Application / Systems Data Exchange Matrix
33. Application / Systems Performance Parameters Matrix
34. Applications / Systems Evolution Description
35. Applications / Systems Technology Forecast
36. Applications / Systems Rules Model
37. Applications / Systems Dialogs (UML Sequence Diagrams)
38. Technical Standards Profile and Product Inventory
39. Technical Standards Forecast
40. Supplier Schedule

The diagrams that are required for any one engagement depends on the Capability being architected. For now, we refer you to *Figure 37: DODAF Guidance for the applicability of Diagrams* (on page 158) for some scenarios that you might encounter. This DODAF v1.5 chart guides you on the applicability of the diagrams for each scenario considered.

PART III – ARCHITECTURE IN BUSINESS OPERATIONS

PUTTING THE ARCHITECTURE TO USE

The benefits of the metaphor and the uses of architecture are apparent from a builder and sub-contractor point of view. After all, what would a General Contractor (an Advisory Firm or a Systems Integrator[97] in the business world) do without blueprints and what would a builder do without building blocks? What would the sub-contractor do without the engineering detail required for them to put the building blocks together in the desired manner? But there are many other uses and benefits that are more important to the Chief Executive Officer (planner) and the executives running the Business Areas / Lines (owners). For instance, a formal architecture is used to facilitate:

- **Strategic Planning / Investment and Portfolio Management –** this includes a simplified and standardized approach for recording and analyzing alternatives, identifying reuse opportunities, eliminating redundancy, developing business cases, managing costs, and preventing duplicate effort. Without DOTMLPF and without understanding the Building Blocks of a Business, one cannot possibly compare apples to apples.

   The simplification stems from the centralized inventory of Capabilities and the Services and a clear understanding of the associated costs. Alternatives considered include outsourcing a Capability as opposed to keeping it in house and then on the IT side, the use of Software as a Service versus something hosted in house.

   The architecture answers questions that the planners and owners pose. Using the Service Management Capability as an example, questions like, how much did the business spend to launch its' Service Management Capability and what has the business spent annually to maintain the Service Management Capability?[98] Is it less expensive in the short and long term to use a Cloud provider? Do the Cloud providers provide a complete Service Management Capability and are the providers considered ITIL compliant?

- **Mergers / Acquisitions and Divestitures** by providing blueprints of what is being merged and how the merge of assets can be

---

97 For a description of a Systems Integrator see:
   https://en.wikipedia.org/wiki/Systems_integrator
98 Is that information in your company's ledger? If not and if your chart of accounts doesn't support that, no worries because that information needs to be in the architecture and is required to compute the net-present value of the investment.

handled and by providing the framework and strategy for handling the merger or the divestiture. What comes in? What needs to be eliminated / replaced because it is duplicative? What needs to be relinquished as part of the divestiture?

- o **Contract management** by clearly defining the program life cycle, acquisition lifecycle, software development life cycle, and architecture activities to be performed. Today more than ever it is important to specify the work products and deliverables associated with the activities, and the formats of those products. Moreover, one may want to contractually require the application of specific processes like the Evolution Process for the Integration of COTS (EPIC).

- o **Supplier Management** and a solicitation process are facilitated with well-defined activities, tasks, methods, work products, and deliverables; and by providing the solicitors with more accurate information about the current business and IT landscape. Many businesses delve into process improvement and re-engineering initiatives without creating simple process taxonomies or work breakdown structures that guide all parties on what needs to be done. In process terms, they delve into how they are going to do things (workflows) before they've even defined what they do (process taxonomies). Architecture also eliminates rediscovery costs that suppliers love to charge. It does this by recording information in standardized form to be held in perpetuity. With an Architecture Initiative in place re-discovery is really a matter of refamiliarizing oneself with the information in the architecture.

- o **Risk Management** is facilitated because architecture reduces risk for Program Managers by formalizing and standardizing the program management process. Risk is also reduced by making information available in a timely manner. Cost and schedule are always at risk when one cannot make informed decisions based on data.

- o **Operations and the maturation / optimization of the business** is facilitated by incorporating measurement techniques into the fabric of the business. The Capability Maturity Management (CMMI)® rating is just one example. In general, companies need key performance indicators (measures and metrics) that provide instantaneous feedback regarding the health of the company and the various business units that comprise it. In particular, measurement data held over time so that the business can observe improvements over the long haul. So, architecture helps the business mature by standardizing processes, monitoring performance, and making adjustments based on performance reports published by the Architecture system.

- o **Governance and Informed Decision Making** is facilitated by making key investment information (A Planner's View of the Business) Visible, Accessible, and Understandable (VAU)[99]. As an example, without such a system businesses resort to the use of spreadsheets for strategic planning and time-consuming data calls to pull together data for a simple metric like the expense to revenue (e / r) ratio and to determine the reasons why the ratio may not be in the desired range.

- o **Reporting** is facilitated by an automated dashboard and business intelligence tool as an integral part of the Architecture. Many companies that do leverage Architecture don't even realize that it is a Business Intelligence (BI) discipline. As an example, a major client did realize the need for a centralized reporting dashboard and reproduced the data and function of the Architecture in a standalone tool. This was done even though the client had an Architecture initiative in place.

- o **Records management and archiving**[100] is facilitated by the Architecture with more efficient access to information. The architecture maintains awareness of all repositories containing data records and the relationships between the repositories. This facilitates the ability of government agencies to support the Freedom of Information Act (FOIA) and the need to respond to requests for information in a timely manner. How can a business purport an interest in "Big Data" and the concepts of analytics and business intelligence if their historical data is locked in spreadsheets on desktop systems scattered throughout the business?

- o **Minimization of oversight** is facilitated by making quality an integral part of all the related processes and by making the

---

99 More information about making data Visible, Accessible, and Understandable (VAU) can be found at http://acqnotes.com/acqnote/careerfields/net-centric-data-service-strategy

100 Note that records management and archiving is problematic because not everyone wants records of what they did and some people would like to forget what they did. Unfortunately, this human behavior is at odds with having an architecture of your business and some basic underlying axioms that all the information in the architecture should be Visible, Accessible, and Understandable (VAU) to people within the business that have a need to know.

information gathered clear and unambiguous. Independent Verification and Validation (IV&V) is an example of oversight that can and should be minimized.

The Federal Government embraced architecture in 1996 with the Clinger-Cohen Act to facilitate IT Modernization. Approximately 20 years later, the discussion around the importance of architecture and the use of it is just heating up. But the applications of architecture are lacking and simultaneously there is trepidation over the use and cost of architecture tools. Businesses need to overcome this trepidation document business operations but they need to do this with the clear understanding about the two parts of the Architecture and how they will put the architecture to use.

Many companies purport their ability to provide you with Architecture and Engineering services when in fact they don't have an architecture or an organization to maintain one. Many companies leverage Enterprise Resource Planning (ERP) systems that support strategic planning yet when one asks for information on how they automate their Strategic Planning Process they show you spreadsheets and documents produced manually using an office suite. What is missing is Architecture and Engineering.

Architecture provides executives with real-time 'situational awareness' about the business and its' operations. In situational awareness terms, the Architecture and the "Intelligent Agents" that are part of it *put the right information in the right hands at the right time*"[101]. In Department of Defense *"Net-centric Data Strategy"* terms, architecture makes decision data "Visible, Accessible, and Understandable (VAU)".

The fundamental driver and use then, from a situational awareness perspective, is being able to readily answer executive level questions related to keeping the business viable and vibrant.

STRATEGIC PLANNING / INVESTMENT AND PORTFOLIO MANAGEMENT

Investment plans, strategic business plans, annual technology plans, etc. are outputs of the strategic planning process where the data is held within the Architecture. Whether you are a commercial company or a governmental agency you document how much money is required to keep current business operations going and what additional investments are to

---

101 The NYC Situational Awareness Concept of Operations was developed by Anthony Insolia in his role as Chief Architect for NYC.

be made. These are typically done in accordance with a Chart of Accounts[102]. In spite of the formality of the chart of accounts, the content of these plans and the process for developing them are both typically informal. Architecture Frameworks and tools formalize the content of these plans and bring some formality to the process for developing them.

We view the information that goes into a strategic business plan as a by-product of what architects call a planners' view of the business. A planner's view of the business documents things like business models, best practices, goals, objectives, and the portfolio of capabilities. The Architecture documents the initial outlay made to launch current Capabilities and the annual cost of maintaining each Capability. It highlights missing Capabilities / Services (Gaps) and Issues with the current operational environment. It includes proposed investments (outlined in accordance with the chart of accounts) that fill Gaps and address Issues demonstrating a clear path to achieving new business models and goals, including revenue goals for profit driven companies. For each Capability / Investment, the business owner and architect work to develop a more detailed owner's view of the Capability. The owner's view refines the cost estimates for new or updated Capabilities.

These planner and owner views of the business are augmented by design detail that is developed between the initial and final phases of the Strategic Planning Process. This design detail is developed to provide executives with the cost information required for making informed decisions about the proposed investments. Making an informed decision means knowing how much it will cost to launch / redress the capability, knowing what the annual maintenance is or the delta to the maintenance if existing, what the life span is of the capability, and what the cost is to replace the capability when it reaches end of life. This is all basic knowledge about the total cost of ownership and the information required to establish the net-present value of the investment. In that period between the early and late stages of planning, the architects and engineers also develop the engineering and builder detail required for acquisition programs to acquire and or build out the Capability and to simultaneously test proposed Processes and Products.

What are the building blocks facilitating investment planning? The primary building block is 'Capability' and the Business or Agency itself, where the Business or Agency is viewed as a portfolio of Capabilities. The building

---

102 Chart of Accounts is described at
   https://en.m.wikipedia.org/wiki/Chart_of_accounts

blocks that underlay each Capability and are required for investment planning are:

1. **Services** and underlying **Processes**
2. **Organizations** required to deliver the Services and staffing requirements or **Personnel**
3. **Policy** and underlying business **rules**
4. Education / **Training** material
5. **Applications** with key functionality exposed as web services
6. **Systems**, **networks**, printing, and other physical infrastructure
7. Independent governance and audit processes
8. **Facility**
9. **Business Models**, **Material Weaknesses**, **Best Practices**, **Gaps**, and **Issues** are all building blocks of the business and part of the strategic / investment plan

These are the basic building blocks that facilitate an initial look at the cost for building out or acquiring a Capability and determining if a particular Capability makes it into the strategic plan. The above building blocks help one to understand cost, but one must also consider the revenue / appropriation side of the capability benefits equation.

With this approach then, your company's strategic business plan and IT strategic plan are reports out of the architecture.

MERGERS / ACQUISITIONS AND DIVESTITURES

Mergers, acquisitions, and divestitures are all facilitated by an Architecture in many ways. Not only does the architecture provide the details on how the business Area / Line is structured, the Architecture augments the financial performance data in the company's ledger so one knows, in the case of an acquisition, what it cost to build and maintain the business and then, how well the business is doing.

Also, (A) if the company and its' assets are to be integrated then the Architecture serves as a set of blueprints on what gets integrated and what goes away, and (B) if the company is to operate as a wholly owned (non-integral) subsidiary and business line then the Architecture serves as a foundation to adjust and build upon. In this latter case, the Architecture provides the necessary detail required to establish interfaces between the operational data stores of the acquired company and master data repositories that are required in the parent company even though the company is non-integral.

CONTRACT MANAGEMENT

Contracts are comprised of terms and conditions that call for a supplier to perform certain activities and provide certain deliverables[103]. Managing a contract entails the assurance that one is getting what the contract calls for and determining if stipulations and requirements are being met. Making these determinations is next to impossible if there is any ambiguity in the Activities and Deliverables / Requirements. Architecture is important to contract management because architecture provides defined and unambiguous Activities, Deliverables, and Requirements whose definitions are refined over time. The architecture makes these Activities, Deliverables, and Requirements concrete by breaking them down. For instance, an Activity may be broken down into more granular Tasks; Task may be associated with Methods / Methodologies which break down the Task into Steps. The architecture also makes the Deliverables and the Work Products that go into making them unambiguous so that one knows exactly what they are getting.

Through repetition, continuous refinement, and the recording of historical information about the Activities and Deliverables, decision making is simpler. As an example, if one stipulates in a contract that a set of blueprints is to be developed using the Department of Defense Architecture Framework (DODAF), then given the maturity and detail behind the DODAF, one has a concrete way of determining if the contract stipulations have been met.

What are the building blocks that support contract management? They include but are not limited to:

- ❖ Capability
  - ➤ Service
    - ▪ Process
      - • Activity
        - ◆ Task
          - ➤ Method
            - ▪ Step

---

[103] As a side note, it is important to understand that architecture, from a contract management perspective, is important even when one in out-sourcing or purchasing 'Cloud Computing' services. To address risk and liability issues, contracts should call for architecture and engineering products to be placed into escrow just as businesses stipulate for the source code.

There are others like Contract itself with embedded terms and conditions and Doctrine / Policy. Most importantly, the architecture provides well defined and unambiguous work break down structures, work products, and deliverables that can all go into contracts that your company is developing with its' partners.

SUPPLIER MANAGEMENT

Supplier management has similar dependencies to contract management. For instance, supplier performance is monitored based on the Activities[104], Work Products[105], Deliverables[106], and performance expectations[107] called out in the contracts that one has with the suppliers. Architecture is then dependent on the business to be actively involved in recording suppliers, contracts, and performance measures. If this recording is done in Enterprise Resource Planning and / or Procurement systems, then the architecture should be integrated with those systems so that the key supplier information is brought into the architecture.

Those who have engaged architects to design a house know that a good architect has his / her fingertips on what builders to work with and what products to buy. The architects know both from quality and performance point of views which builders to work with. Good architects in the business world should have the same skill and information on hand. They should document candidate suppliers and required products and tools in the blueprints. This is done in supplier and product schedules, respectively. Albeit, the candidate supplier list is typically withheld during the solicitation process.

What are the building blocks that facilitate supplier management? From an architecture point of view, they include:

- Standards Body
- Standard
- Business Policy
- Capability,
  - Service,
    - Process,
      - Activity
        - Task

---

104 Well-defined activities
105 Well-defined work products
106 Well-defined deliverables
107 Well-defined measurements and metrics

> ➤ Method
- o Technology
- o Assessment
- o Dependency, Assumption, Issue, Risk ...
- o Skill
- o Requirement
- o Certificate

These basic building blocks enable the business to establish and then maintain ongoing no-frills relationships with suppliers. It is important though to acknowledge the establishment of the relationship as an (architectural) analysis of alternatives. The architecture documents the suppliers / alternatives considered and the decisions made as one honed in on a choice of suppliers.

Businesses that <u>don't</u> have architecture are vulnerable to suppliers they engage. When suppliers are brought in to do things like business process improvement / re-engineering or to automate some aspect of the business, the supplier asks for the architecture. When the architecture is not present, lacks quality, or is outdated, the supplier typically says that they need to reproduce it. This is referred to as supplier rediscovery. This rediscovery can be costly and alone is justification for the business to maintain architecture. To facilitate supplier management and to avoid supplier rediscovery, the architecture must be up-to-date, formal, and centralized.

RISK MANAGEMENT

A risk is the possibility of investment loss, one caused by an event or confluence of events which; if they occur, threaten the successful development, delivery, or deployment of one or more capabilities and / or supporting services. The threat or risk, based on probability of the occurrence of the event, is measured in terms of the monetary loss associated with the event. To avoid risk is to avoid unnecessary and unplanned costs.

Architecture minimizes risk by documenting the business and its' capabilities in an unambiguous way. Given the level of specification in the architecture, one avoids cost of schedule overruns. In short, advisory firms and systems integrators can readily understand what is required and how to provision needs. This form of documentation also helps to minimize risk through clear and concise performance measures that the business can monitor and act upon quickly if the measures are hitting pre-defined and agreed to thresholds. In this way, the business knows early on if issues are coming up, ones that lead to the occurrence of a risk.

What are the building blocks germane to risk management? They include:

o Risk
o Issue
o Finding
o Recommendation
o Gap
o Dependency
o Investment (given that a risk ultimately documents a potential financial loss)
o Event (given that a risk is the probability of an event or confluence of events occurring)
o Key Performance Indicator

Risks are documented by planners in establishing the investments that are to be made in the planning cycle. These risks can be business or agency wide and are associated with investments. In particular, associated with chosen strategies for achieving the goals related to the investments.

MATURITY OF BUSINESS OPERATIONS

Maturity management is a key byproduct of architecting and engineering businesses. To understand this, one first needs to understand maturity measures and metrics in business. We will consider two in this book. First, a very common metric applied to for-profit companies, is the expense to revenue (e/r) ratio. This is actually a metric formed using two measures: total expense and total revenue. Second, is a very basic measure that all organizations can apply called Capability Maturity Management Model (CMM®)[108]. While the CMM® was defined to formalize and mature software development processes it defines 5 levels of maturity that can be applied to processes in general. The five CMM® levels of maturity are paraphrased here:

o **Level 1** - no process, chaotic, ad hoc, success depends on individual effort and heroics
o **Level 2** - processes lack sufficient documentation, and are at times repeatable
o **Level 3** - processes are defined, confirmed as a standard business process and are predictable

---

108 The Carnegie Mellon® Capability Maturity Model is currently administered by the https://cmmiinstitute.com. Also see https://en.wikipedia.org/wiki/Capability_Maturity_Model_Integration

- Level 4 - projects follow the defined process, even under scheduled pressures
- Level 5 - processes are continuously improving; improvements are recorded

As the authoritative source of process details, the architecture facilitates process maturity. This is done by establishing a rating mechanism between process and the organizations executing them. This is an important point because one is not rating the process alone, rather, one is rating an organization as it employs and executes a process. This facilitation starts with an inventory of processes and associating organizations with processes. For the organizations that do not have processes in place, they can be associated with a process called "*None*" and rated "*Level 1 – no process, chaotic, ad hoc, success depends on individual efforts and heroics*".

Establishing this inventory and ratings in itself doesn't mean that the business has achieved a high maturity level though. For the business to achieve a high level of maturity the processes need to be institutionalized and just like a report card, grades (in your case CMMI® ratings) get averaged to provide an overall assessment and CMMI® rating for the organization.

Groups like the American Productivity Quality Center (APQC®)[109] have documented Key Performance Parameters (KPP's). They did this by first establishing a process taxonomy and then positioning these KPP's at various levels within the taxonomy. The taxonomy is as follows:

- Process Categories are broken down into
  - Process Groups which house
    - Processes which are comprised of
      - Activities, comprised of
        - Tasks

Key performance Parameters (Measures / Metrics) then, apply broadly to a process category / group or may be process and activity specific. One great example is expense to revenue (e / r) ratio. This is a very broad metric associated with the process category called "Manage Financial Resources".

Note that the APQC® is a consortium of companies and being a member of that consortium entitles your company to use the models and data. Being an active member of consortiums like the APQC® is itself a sign of your

---

109 For more information on The American Productivity Quality Center (APQC®), see: http://www.apqc.org

company's maturity. Also, the APQC® focuses on process taxonomies by industry. These are partial Planner Views of the respective industries. As a side note, they are not concerned with workflows. Workflows, as descriptions of how Activities are to be performed, vary from company to company. If they didn't vary then there would be no competition.

ARCHITECTURE REPORTS

We've said that there is no "Architecture Process" and that Architecture Activities are embedded in the Strategic Planning and Program Management Processes. Document the Work Products and Deliverables (Reports) that are outputs of those activities. The Activities that we are referring to result in very concrete and actionable Deliverables / Reports / Data Objects, they are **(A)** a Business Plan, **(B)** the Information Technology Strategic Plan, and **(C)** the Budget. More than likely you are developing your strategic plan using an office suite. You may put the office suite away; the architecture facilitates the gathering of the data and these publishable documents discussed are reports generated by the architecture.

We just named three reports, but there are others. Consider the following Reports by Reference Model:

A. **Business Reference Model**
   - Capability Report
      - Revenue / Appropriation Enhancement Opportunities Report, bearing in mind that some government agencies and authorities have revenue
      - Cost Optimization Opportunities Report
      - Regulatory Impacts Report
      - Capability Maturity Report
   - Strategic Plan (This is both business & IT, not just IT.)
   - Service Provisioning Report tells is how well are the service providers doing and at what cost
   - Organizational Staffing Plan / Growth Report
B. **Service Component Reference Model**
   - Service Component Utilization and Profitability Report
C. **Performance Reference Model**
   - Capability Maturity Report
   - Goal / Investment Alignment and Achievement Report
   - Report of the Top 10 Performance Indicators (for the business at large and then by Business Area / Line)
   - Policy Enforcement and Effectiveness?
D. **Security Reference Model**

- Security / Threat Risk Report (Risk Reduction)
- Confidentiality Availability & Integrity (CAI) Report for Data
- Confidentiality Availability & Integrity (CAI) Report for Applications / Systems

E. **Systems / Application Reference Model**
- Applications / Systems Report by fiscal year (Reward) tells us how many Applications / Systems we have and what category they fall in. Are they Strategic and Mission Critical? How many are neither Strategic nor Mission Critical?

F. **Infrastructure Reference Model**
- Server Utilization and Cost Report?
- Disaster Recovery Report?

G. **Facilities Reference Model**
- Office Center & Mixed-Use Space Report
- Real Estate and Facility Utilization Report, by Business Area / Business Line / Capability. Architected VS actual.
- Cloud / Data Center Report

If you want to be successful with your Architecture and Engineering Initiative, be sure that you generate reports that the business community is interested in. Get the business excited about your reports and have the architecture generate and distribute them automatically. Make canned reports available through your service catalog and or Intranet, let people subscribe, and for obvious reasons let people unsubscribe.

PLACING THE ARCHITECTURE INTO MOTION

Placing the architecture in motion, quite simply, means showing the change in the architecture and business over time. There are two somewhat related aspects to placing the architecture into motion, time-based visualization and Artificial Intelligence.

The visualization aspect is achieved by incorporating time into the appropriate architecture data structures and the use of modern visualization tools like D3js[©110] and THINKMAP®[111] to visualize the changes over time. As you will see, Time-based Visualizations are especially relevant to the monitoring of performance measurements, and they don't need to be complex in nature. Good old-fashioned bar charts do fine. The Artificial Intelligence piece is achieved through the creation of "Intelligent

---

110 For more information about Data Driven Documents (D3), see: http://d3js.org
111 For more information about THINKMAP®, see: http://www.thinkmap.com

Agents"[112] or advisors that facilitate the sort of analyses that architects are responsible for. This includes SWOT[113] and PEST[114] Assessments and Competitive / Competitor Analysis. In addition to facilitating assessments, the Intelligent Agents, with the assistance of people, learn and apply knowledge of things going on in the world to maintain situational awareness.

Note that this is a complete departure from the typical creation of static views (drawings) of the current business operations and the target state. The authors are a bit late in getting this message out, in spite of the fact that they have been doing advanced visualizations for years. One example is a visualization that one author did for a Federally Funded Research and Development Corporation (FFRDC). In that example, the author used THINKMAP® to show a time-based progression of all Systems in a Federal agency and how the systems landscape and expenditures would change over time.

TIME-BASED VISUALIZATIONS

For those of you that know "Ted Talks"®[115], there is a favorite of ours called *"The Best Stats You've Ever Seen"* [116] where Hans Rosling presents some data about families, family size, and life expectancy. We bring this up because what Hans is presenting is a time-based visualization. In introducing the topic and data and in showing how the demographics were changing over time, Hans says *"Let's see, we stopped the world"*. As depicted in *Figure 22: Ted Talk by Hans Rosling "Best Stats You've Ever Seen"*, Hans may have "stopped the world" in 1962 but he was about restart the visualization placing the historical data into motion. He was doing exactly what we are suggesting Architects do in architecting and engineering businesses.

Hans was able to start and stop the visualization because it employed software able display time-based snapshots of his bubble chart data. With

---

112 For a brief overview of Intelligent Agents see,
   https://en.wikipedia.org/wiki/Intelligent_agent
113 For more information about SWOT, see:
   https://en.wikipedia.org/wiki/SWOT_analysis SWOT Analysis is the analysis of
   Strengths, Weaknesses, Opportunities, and Threats of a business.
114 For more information about PEST, see: https://en.wikipedia.org/wiki/PEST_analysis
   PEST Analysis is the analysis of Political, Economic, Social, and Technological factors
   affecting a solution or business decision.
115 For more information about Ted Talks, see: http://WWW.Ted.COM
116 For direct access the above-mentioned Hans Rosling Ted Talk, see
   https://www.ted.com/talks/hans_rosling_shows_the_best_stats_you_ve_ever_seen

the proper model and data structures in place, one can and should do the same thing with Architecture and Engineering data. Using our own phrase, one can *"Place the Architecture into Motion"*.

Figure 22: Ted Talk by Hans Rosling "Best Stats You've Ever Seen"

Architecture and Engineering data is nothing more than time-based views of where the business has been, where it is now, and where it is going. Architecture (the Zoning Maps of the business and Blueprints for each Capability) provides time-based views of the business. If the architecture is maintained on a yearly basis, then rather than showing the static view of current and target state, we show the business changing over time. As an example, tying measurements and metrics to the changing Business Models and Architecture, enables one to make a correlation between the Architecture and Client / Constituent behaviors and business profits and appropriations.

In order to remain relevant in the market, the business and the architecture may be undergoing continuous change[117]. If the business is built and changed based on architecture, then the architecture is being kept up to date and visualizations of the business can be set into motion. The architecture should not be allowed to lag behind or fall by the wayside. One should *"Architect and Engineer First"*, without compromising agility.

---

117 It is important to get the Architecture established as quickly as possible and then get into steady state operations where, the architecture is merely being tweaked.

A Maturity Management Example, The Architecture as a Performance Dashboard

One of the authors had the opportunity to create this sort of architecture for an Agency of a US State Government[118]. The focus was on time-based visualizations of the agency's performance measures and metrics. There was no artificial intelligence, but nonetheless, the results were impressive. The State implemented a Performance Reference Model (PRM) as part of the Architecture and, that reference model housed the Measures / Metrics and the history data necessary to show how the agencies were doing over time.

The initial focus of the architecture team and the PRM, was on the building block called *Key Performance Indicators (KPI)* where Measures and Metric are types of Performance Indicators. The agency recorded their Key Performance Indicators and measurement history data directly in the web-accessible Architecture. While the architecture knows which system is storing the data for each KPI, the initial implementation required the data to be entered manually through the Browser[119]. Prior to using the web-based architecture repository, this had been done in spreadsheets and reporting was hindered by data quality issues that are germane to working in spreadsheets. The Architecture eliminated the data quality issues and also made the performance data Visible, Accessible, and Understandable (VAU)[120]. The Visibility, Accessibility, and Understandability was initially limited to all employees of the State. Ultimately, the State could decide what to publish publicly.

Reports for each KPI were made common using measurement history data as depicted in the data model fragment shown in *Figure 23: KPI data model fragment.* As an example of the time element and comparative views for each KPI, the architecture tool environment reported on an average for the:

- o Previous fiscal year (12-month average)
- o Current fiscal year, year to date, and
- o Previous fiscal year, year to date

These three numbers enable quick and easy comparisons. For example, one can compare the 3-month (January, February, March) average for the

---

118 This State government is a State within the United States of America (USA)
119 Any web browser like Chrome or Microsoft Explorer
120 United States Department of Defense Net-centric Services Strategy
  https://dodcio.defense.gov/Portals/0/Documents/DIEA/Services_Strategy.pdf

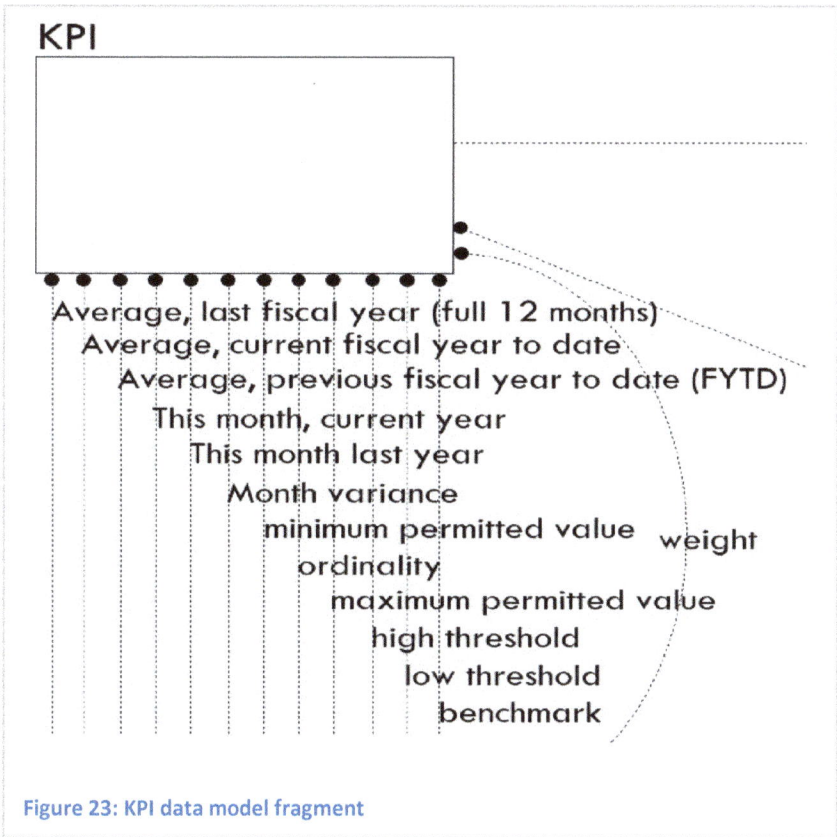

KPI

Average, last fiscal year (full 12 months)
Average, current fiscal year to date
Average, previous fiscal year to date (FYTD)
This month, current year
This month last year
Month variance
minimum permitted value   weight
ordinality
maximum permitted value
high threshold
low threshold
benchmark

Figure 23: KPI data model fragment

current year against the same 3-month average for the previous year. In this example, the State employees were able to observe how the agency was doing in March 2019 versus March 2018. One could also compare that 3-month average for the current year against the 12-month average for the previous year. The key point here is that the State was able to monitor performance indicators. Knowing which agency's owned which KPI's, the State was able to drill into the health of each Agency, and subsequently, into the health of each Capability.

The model had some features to facilitate dissemination of the performance data. For notification purposes, the model included high and low thresholds and a notification group. If the thresholds were hit, notifications were sent to everyone in the notification group. The model also provided a warning level in the event that numbers were getting close to a threshold. The architects didn't wait for numbers to get close or critical.

Some time back, the number may have grown, the APQC® had approximately 1500 performance measures and metrics documented across the various process categories that comprise the APQC® Process Classification Framework (PCF)[121]. We are not going to look at and discuss 1500 measures and metrics so, we will continue with a discussion on CMM® Rating and then a KPI relevant to the IT folks.

> We know some business and governments do this sort of monitoring, but they typically do it outside the context of the architecture which is where KPI's are born and maintained.
>
> In addition to centralizing performance reporting, the Architecture adds value by rolling numbers up and enabling drill down. The Architecture does weighted averages of select performance indicators and applies positive and negative covenants.

Before proceeding we'd like to comment on this idea of centralizing KPI monitoring in the Architecture. We are not asserting that the architecture become the data lake of all data in the enterprise. In reality, the data is decentralized and the architecture simply maintains awareness of where the relevant data is and what Application Programming Interface (API) is used to get the data. In this respect that Architecture has its' fingers on every pulse point of the business. This reinforces the role of the Architecture as the heart and brain of your business.

A PORTFOLIO MANAGEMENT EXAMPLE, FOR THE BUSINESS COMMUNITY AND EXECUTIVES

The set of Capabilities that comprise your business is a portfolio just like the portfolio of Applications / Systems that the IT folks care for and monitor. Here we focus on maturity as a Key Performance Indicator or KPI at the portfolio level and some related data that provides the business folks with insight into how their portfolios are doing.

As discussed, the Capability Maturity Model® (CMM®) rating is a measure of how efficient an organization is in executing a process. Knowing that processes are used to guide and automate the delivery of Services and knowing that Services comprise Capabilities, the business may average Service ratings to establish a Capability rating.

---

121 More information about The American Productivity Quality Center (APQC®) Process Classification Framework (PCF) can be found at: https://www.apqc.org/pcf

In this example, we present the health of the business in much the same way Doctors use Magnetic Resonance Imaging[122] (MRI) to provide a visualization of the body. In our Architecture and Engineering case we say we are creating an MRI-like view of the business. A view of this sort is also referred to as a "heat map" but more people understand what an MRI is than a heat map.

As you can see from *Figure 24: Business MRI looking at Capability Maturity* this sort of monitor is busy if you are looking at all Capabilities across the business. To get more focused, the monitor enables one to drill down into one particular area and, through filtering, focus only on those organizational units that are executing a particular Process or delivering a particular Service. If a company-wide view, like the one depicted in *Figure 24: Business MRI looking at Capability Maturity* is desired then, knowing the below structure, one can roll numbers up from the Capability to the top level of the business.

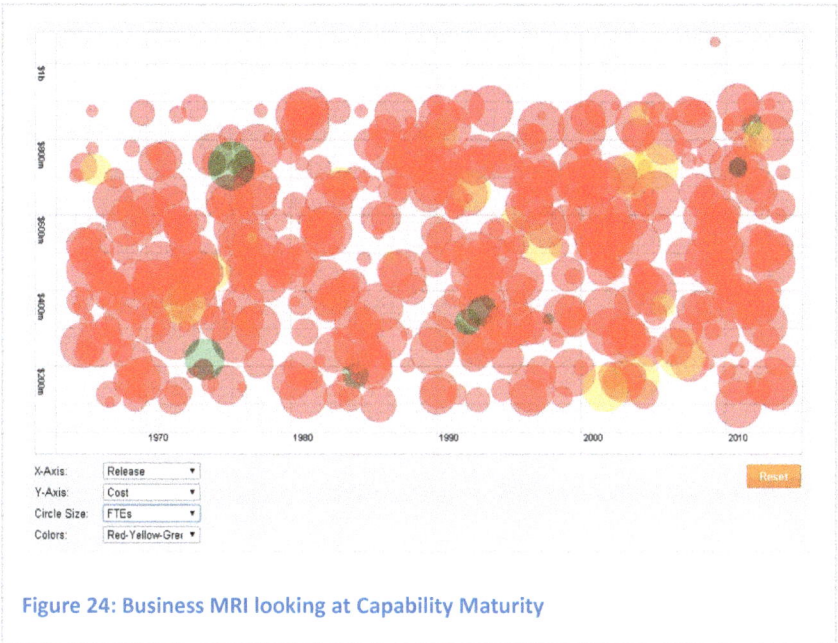

Figure 24: Business MRI looking at Capability Maturity

+ **Business or Agency** is comprised of
  o **Business Areas / Lines** that realize
    ▪ **Capability** that are comprised of
      • **Services** whose delivery is automated by

---

122 A description of Magnetic Resonance Imaging (MRI) can be found at
https://en.wikipedia.org/wiki/Magnetic_resonance_imaging

- o **Business Processes** executed by
  - ▪ **Organization**s to deliver **Services**

Starting at the Process level in this structure, one can derive the CMM® rating of a Service, the Capability that the Service comprises, the Business Area / Line that the Capability is Germane to, and then the Business / Agency.

Consider the trivial case where a Business Area has one Capability comprised of a single Service and one Process, and that only one Organization is involved in the delivery of the Service. If the Organization executing that process has a CMM® rating of 3 then the Service has a 3 rating, the Capability has a 3 rating, and the Business Area / Line has a CMM® rating of 3.

Having historical data, the executive is able to roll through time to see where the business is getting better or worse. Referring back to *Figure 24: Business MRI looking at Capability Maturity* and ahead to *Figure 25: Business MRI with a change in the x and y axis* you can see, in the bottom left of those figures, that the executive also has control over what the x and y axis represent and can also control what determines the circle size. These variables are based on attributes of the underlying CMM® Rating Records joined or augmented by some basic attributes of the Capability. This includes:

1. Number of people (Full Time Equivalents) associated with the Capability
2. Initial Standup Cost or cost to get to the Initial Operating Capability (IOC)[123]
3. Yearly maintenance cost
4. Demographics (is the Capability company-wide, segment-wide, or agency specific?)
5. Release Date
6. Rating
7. Rating Date

To make a monitor like this a bit more actionable one needs policy and rules for where to focus and invest, especially when there is so much red as in an example depicted in *Figure 24: Business MRI looking at Capability Maturity* and *Figure 25: Business MRI with a change in the x and y axis*.

---

123 For a description of Initial Operating Capability see:
https://en.wikipedia.org/wiki/Initial_operating_capability

Filtering a monitor like this helps the viewer focus, as does the ability to drill down into particular capabilities to see what is driving the problem. One also needs a way of prioritizing the issues and associated investments. As an example, one might want to act upon a red area in a highly profitable Business Line before certain Business Areas. Said another way, the business may want to enhance revenue before optimizing non-operating units.

In *Figure 25: Business MRI with a change in the x and y axis* we provide a snapshot of the same MRI depicted in *Figure 24: Business MRI looking at Capability Maturity* where the x-axis has been changed to "Cost" and the y-axis has been changed to "Demographic". Demographic telling us if the Capability is Company-wide, Agency-specific, or in-between.

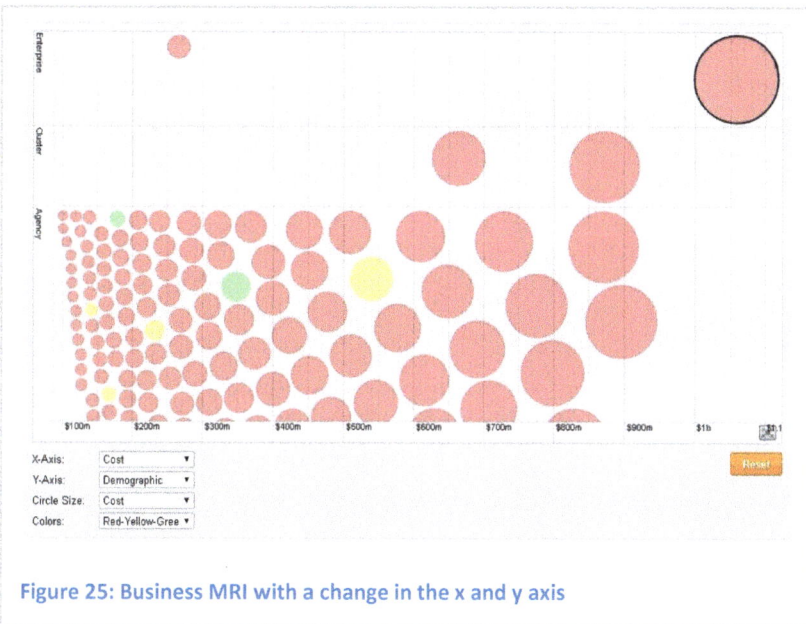

Figure 25: Business MRI with a change in the x and y axis

In summary, we are talking about Business Intelligence[124] formed using architecture data. Providing executives with a visualization of what the business does (large grained activities referred to as Capabilities), and insight into how efficient and effective the business is with each Capability.

This is done all the time in the financial world. Stock brokers look at visualizations (Heat Maps) of their portfolio on their cell phone, where the portfolios may be broken down by industry (their form of segmentation). A

---

124 A description of Business Intelligence can be found at:
https://en.wikipedia.org/wiki/Business_intelligence

portion of their portfolio may be showing some redness, and they drill in to take a more detailed look and to determine why.

An MRI like the one presented here can have motion as well. In the "CMM® Ratings" example presented, one can store the ratings by fiscal year and then set the bubble chart into motion to show change over time. Being one-year time intervals, there may not be much motion for a new company but there are other measures that are recorded daily, weekly, monthly, and quarterly.

Having performance measurements and not having accountability is useless. To this end, we add positive and negative covenants that the Business Areas and Lines agree to. Each KPI, being weighted, has certain pluses (+) for those that are making their numbers and minuses (-) for those that are not making their numbers. These numbers are tallied and checked on a periodic basis to form a simple scalar measure used to determine if Business Areas and Lines are doing well or not. The positive and negative covenants can be thought of as merits and demerits that incentivize the Business Areas and Lines to improve performance and adjust.

One cautionary note before we close on this topic and on the matter of performance measurement. There are very real and documented cases where people will go to great lengths to make numbers. This is an ethics issue that must be dealt with carefully. Don't get caught up in tactics of that sort, make sure that numbers are authentic and not contrived.

A Portfolio Management Example, for the IT Community

This example from the IT[125] world is based on a Best Practice from a well-known product and services company. The company used this technique internally. The services leg of the company also used the technique in client engagements. It is a monitor of the number of Applications / Systems by category[126]. The categorization of the Applications / Systems involves knowing if the Applications / Systems are (A) effective in terms of addressing business need with technologically sound and supported platforms, and (B) cost efficient. These two indicators (effectiveness and

---

125 Coincidentally, the measurement data for this IT related KPI come from the Architecture and in this case the Architecture repository needs to provide the API to call to get the measurement data.

126 While we differentiate Systems from Applications, some treat them synonymously and for those that do, this is a matter of "You say poe-ta-to and I say pa-ta-toe".

efficiency) are recorded for each Application / System in what we call "*Application / System Disposition Records*" which are stored by fiscal year.

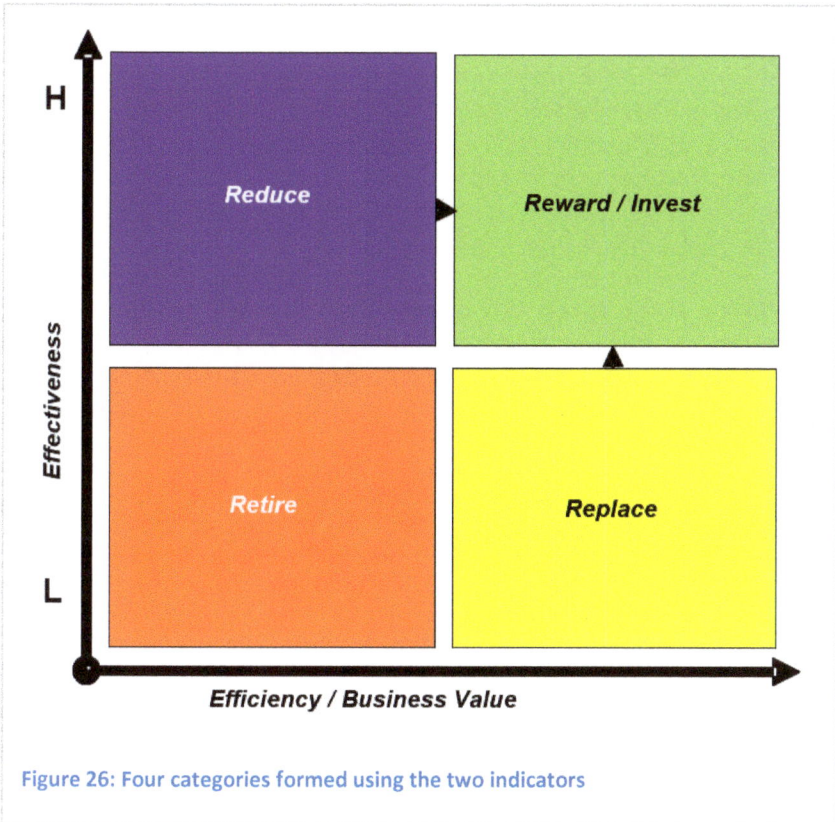

Reduce	**Reward / Invest**
Retire	**Replace**

Axes: vertical axis labeled *Effectiveness* (H at top, L at bottom); horizontal axis labeled **Efficiency / Business Value**

Figure 26: Four categories formed using the two indicators

The two indicators enable one to place the Applications / Systems in one of four categories as depicted in *Figure 26: Four categories formed using the two indicators*. While the axis in the figure shows High (H) and Low (L), the Disposition Records store a numeric value, for plotting and measurement purposes.

A variation on this is a pair of indicators called Operational Risk and Technical Risk. In both cases, the indicators can be set manually or they can be set based on a number of questions asked about each Application / System. Using the question and answer approach with numeric answers, the operational and technical risk indicators are formed quantitatively doing a weighted average of the answers to form the two risk indicators.

We call the records "*Disposition Records*" because they indicate how the Application / System will be dispositioned from an investment point of view. Applications / Systems that have low effectiveness and low efficiency

(Low, Low) fall into the "Retire" category and are dispositioned by shutting them down and eliminating maintenance costs. Applications / Systems in the "Reduce" category have critical business function that needs to be migrated to the appropriate Application / System in the "Reward" category. Once the mission critical functionality has been established in the correct Application / System, the Application / System that was marked for retirement can be shut down. The idea is to find opportunities to optimize the portfolio and to reduce expenses because the maintenance and licensing expenses associated with these Applications / Systems are affecting the expense to revenue (e / r) ratio.

Adding Fiscal year and some status information to the to the Disposition Records, and going through this exercise on a yearly basis, enables one to visualize the counts by fiscal year. One can visualize the portfolio in a bar chart like the one depicted in *Figure 32: Projecting Application Portfolio Size on page 146.*

We now have a visualization of the number of Applications / Systems in each category by fiscal year, and the visualization or report that is more actionable. Whereas before the portfolio manager, given a particular Application / System disposition, could act upon one Application / System; they can now observe and act upon the sets of Applications / Systems. Does this constitute Architecture in Motion? Not entirely, it is still a somewhat static presentation but at least there is a time element. We are making progress.

For one client, this bar chart was automated to roll by fiscal year. This added a sense of motion and time because the data and visualization would roll by 1 Fiscal Year. At one moment, the user was viewing 2007-2011 and with a click of the mouse, they were viewing 2008-20012, etc. The client also implemented a corresponding bubble chart depicting the Applications / Systems (represented by the bubbles) on a grid using the aforementioned operational and technical risk numbers as ordered pairs with an x-coordinate and a y-coordinate so that one can plot. The bubble chart could have easily been set into motion just like the Hans Rosling bubble charts. For yet another client, the authors enabled executives to carry the visualization through time using a slide bar.

Note that in addition to enabling motion, the use of a bubble chart adds yet another dimension to the report and decision making. The size of the bubble and the distance from the origin are both meaningful. The size of the bubble can represent something like maintenance cost of the Application / System and distance from the origin represents greater operational and technical risk.

THE APPLICATION OF ARTIFICIAL INTELLIGENCE

THE ARCHITECTURE AS THE HEART AND BRAIN OF A BUSINESS

In addition to maintaining performance data and history over time, the architecture includes Artificial Intelligence in the form of "Intelligent Agents"[127] (advisors) that interact with experts (people) to automate analyses of different facets of the business. These agents then systematically record the knowledge of experts[128] that they interact with. This knowledge is stored in the architecture and architects then use it to assess the direction that the business is headed in.

> More often than not, architects are consumed trying to establish the architecture that the company / agency has been operating without. They spend most of their time justifying the need for architecture and they focus entirely too much on IT. As a result, these forms of analyses are either ignored or performed by business analysts outside of the architecture organization.

In business terms, these Agents are nothing more than helpers. In computer and system terms they are asynchronous threads each corresponding to the uniqueness of the different types of analyses that are conducted in order to adjust the Architecture and Strategic Plans. The analyses that the Agents facilitate are analyses of:

1. Competitors[129] and Best Practices **(Competitive Analysis)**
2. Strengths, and Weaknesses, internal and externally driven Opportunities, and Threats **(SWOT Analysis)**
3. Political, Economic, Social, and Technological conditions **(PEST Analysis)**, and
4. DOTMLPF, associated with a Capability **(DOTMLPF or Management Assessments)**

---

127 Intelligent Agents Extend Knowledge-based Systems Feasibility, by G Elofson – IBM® Systems Journal Vol 34 NO 1 1995.

128 The business of recording the knowledge of knowledge experts is referred to as "Knowledge Caching" in the above-mentioned article by G Elofson.

129 Governments are not typically thought of as having competitors, ergo the introduction of "Best Practices" which other governmental bodies may espouse and automate. A perfect example which is becoming a nationwide standard is EZPASS. Another example is the use of camera technology to eliminate the need for toll booths.

These Intelligent Agents and the Knowledge Cache that each Agent maintains are represented in the lower right-hand corner of *Figure 27: The Architecture is a cache that houses Agent and Expert knowledge.* We depict the Agents exchanging information with their respective Business Areas / Lines. They also interact with Architects, Industry Experts, and Analysts to capture information from the outside world that is required for situational awareness.

The lead architect for a Business Area / Line determines if they want Agents facilitating their work. If chosen, the Business Areas / Lines have Agents performing Competitor, SWOT[130] and PEST[131] Analysis that are normally conducted by people alone where the knowledge resides with those people. Apprentices, operating under the auspices of the Agents, are responsible for maintaining a set of questions and for monitoring answers over time so that this knowledge is institutionalized and maintained in perpetuity. This structure of Agents with supporting Apprentices is depicted in *Figure 29: Agents and Apprentices.*

The Architecture, as envisioned, is started and stopped just as Hans Rosling started and then stopped the world. In this case, it is the Agents that are started and stopped along with the supporting Apprentices. Since Apprentices are defined dynamically by the architects and since they operate under the auspices of an Agent, if one stops an Agent then they stop all Apprentices under that Agent.

This class of problem is referred to by G. Elofson, in an IBM® Systems Journal Article, as the "Episodic Classification Problems (ECP)".[132] According to Elofson, *"Episodic Classification Problems are the transient responsibilities of the knowledge worker – growing and then receding in importance over time. Typically, episodic classification problems do not conform to traditional expert system solutions, and they require specialized architectures to offer decision support and increased span of control for those individuals whose task is expediting the problems."*

In our own words, certain problems and questions that architects and executives deal with are the realm of experts whose understanding of a particular industry or country is temporary. This includes, as an example,

---

130 SWOT Analysis is an analysis of Strengths, Weaknesses, Opportunities, and Threats that guide and inform the Strategic Plan of a business or agency
131 PEST Analysis is an analysis of Political, Economic, Social, and Technological factors that may benefit or inhibit the success of a business or agency given its' mission
132 Intelligent Agents Extend Knowledge-based Systems Feasibility, by G Elofson – IBM® Systems Journal Vol 34 NO 1 1995

things like the political conditions hindering market opportunity. In the proposed system, questions posed, answers provided, actions taken, and adjustments made to the Architecture are recorded by the system. The questions are typically posed in the context of the *Strategic Planning and Budgeting Process* with or without the Agents in place to maintain a record of:

1. The relevant questions asked,
2. Answers provided in the past,
3. What the answers mean, and
4. How the related issues or findings were dealt with.

Whether the agent / advisor is a person, machine, or combination of the two, the key functions performed are the harvesting and assimilation of knowledge that is relevant to the business. The architects are addressing the need to identify and monitor things like:

1. Revenue enhancement opportunities, applicable to the customer facing Business Lines in for-profit companies
2. Cost optimization opportunities, primarily in Business Areas
3. Regulatory Controls imposed by governmental bodies (Legal and Mandatory Requirements)

The knowledge of how revenue can be enhanced, how the business can optimize, and knowledge of regulatory controls that need to be addressed stems from architects and experts being engaged during the execution of the / a *Strategic Planning Process* in which one does the aforementioned forms of internal (introspective) and external (outward-looking) analyses. The added value of having the Architecture automate this is in the codification of expert knowledge. Knowledge that enables dynamic visualizations of the business and the abovementioned opportunities, over time.

These Intelligent Agents are depicted in Figure 27: The Architecture is a cache that houses Agent and Expert knowledge This figure provides a forest for the trees view of a business having Business Areas and Lines whose architecture staff is augmented by the Intelligent Agents. The coloring of the lines is not coincidental given the role of the architecture as Heart and Brain. This figure also depicts the Business Lines as somewhat autonomous in that they have their own operational data stores with which to conduct day to day operations. Not depicted, here are the lines showing that the operational data stores synchronize in real-time with the master data repositories across the bottom.

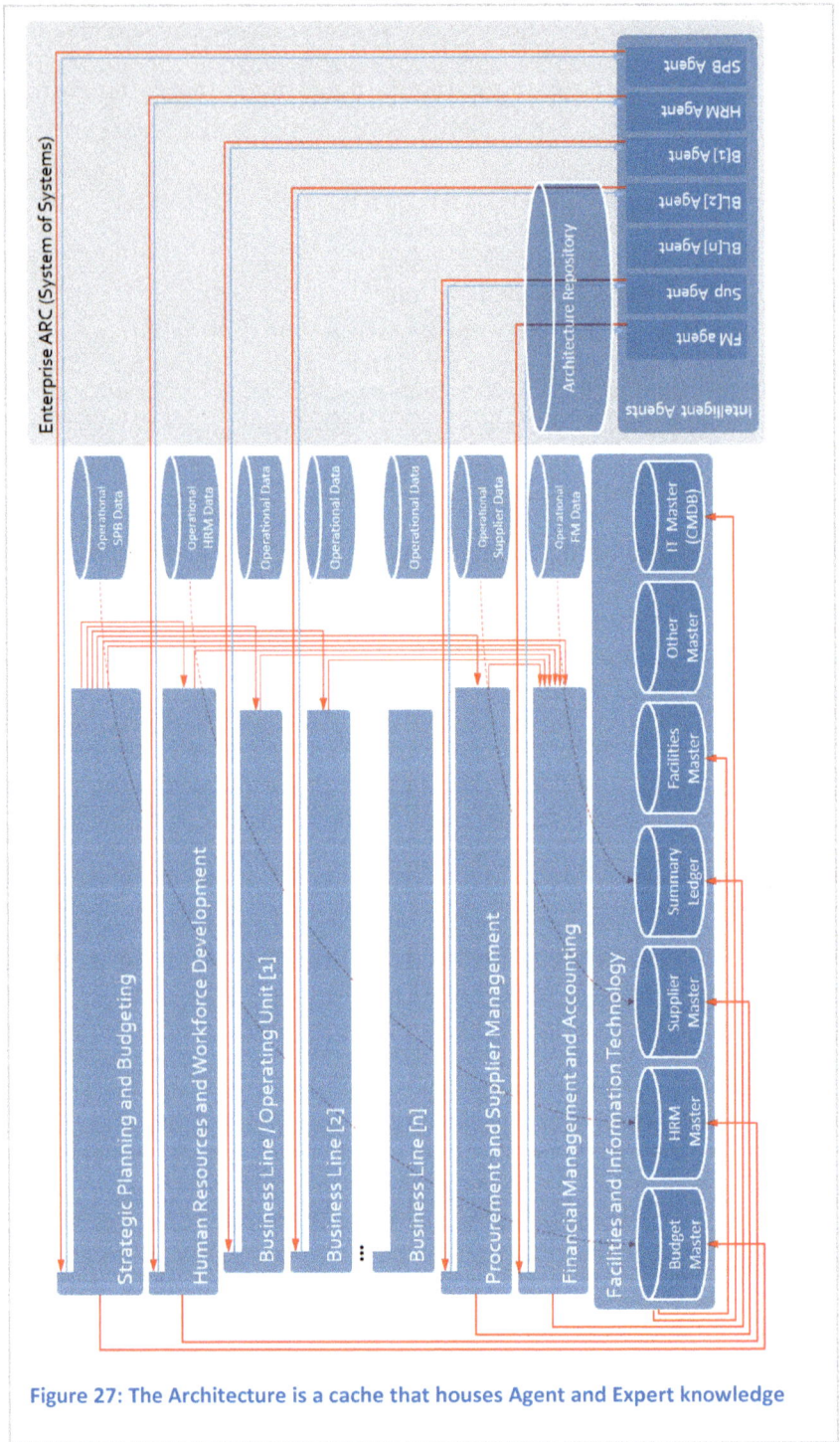

Figure 27: The Architecture is a cache that houses Agent and Expert knowledge

As described by Elofson, once certain questions and corresponding knowledge have been codified, the Agents can observe and record situations and provide advice just as an organizational unit within the business is assigned to do. The knowledge is institutionalized insofar as Agents are able to explain, to existing staff or new hires, how a particular issue was dealt with and why the issue was dealt with in the particular way.

Having automated agents supporting the codification and caching of knowledge is advantageous because most often, this sort of knowledge is held by people that come and go and the knowledge is lost when people move on.

Interestingly, with the recent literature equating this form of architecture with Strategy, Elofson cites as an example a *"Strategic Planning Function"* of a business where experts seek out information and provide recommendations back to executives, planners, and architects.

According to the *Internet Center for Management and Business Administration (ICMBA)*[133] a top-down or incremental approach to Strategic Planning starts with a clear and concise mission statement for each Business Area / Line. Based on those mission statements and knowledge of the current Architecture and *Key Performance Indicators*[134], goals and concrete and actionable objectives are established. A graphic depiction of a top-down Strategic Planning Process is depicted in *Figure 28: A Top-down Strategic Planning Process*.

Before the Strategic Plan can be finalized, the above-mentioned analyses are performed as they inform the Strategic Plan. This is an incremental approach insofar as; there is no major change in business models and one is establishing objectives that represent incremental improvements along existing trend lines.

The Architecture is designed to facilitate this process by enabling the architects and executives to assign Agents and then create Apprentices to handle related questions and provide advice. The architects and experts formulate the questions and the prospective answers. On a yearly basis,

---

133 The Internet Center for Management and Business Administration can be found at http://www.NetMBA.com

134 Citing an example from the American Productivity Quality Center (APQC®), there is a common process in the APQC® Process Classification Framework entitled" Perform Planning/Budgeting/Forecasting"134 and an associated KPI entitled "Total cost of the Perform Planning/Budgeting/Forecasting process as a percent of total revenue". For governmental bodies, this KPI can be a percent of total appropriations.

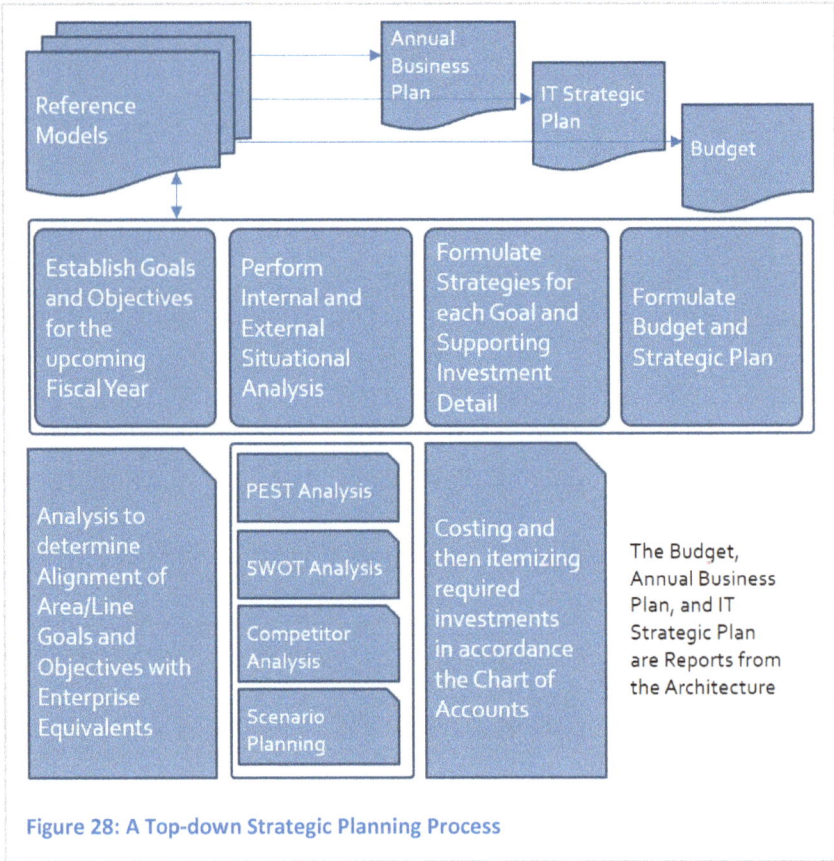

Figure 28: A Top-down Strategic Planning Process

the assigned Agents and supporting Apprentices pose agreed-to questions to Analysts for them to seek out and provide answers with the reason for each answer. Subsequently, Experts are re-engaged by the Agents to assess the answers and provide additional rationale for each answer.

The architecture system and tool environment required to support this is depicted in *Figure 29: Agents and Apprentices*. In that figure, we show the Business being comprised of Business Areas and Lines where each Area / Line has an Assigned Architect and optional Agents which can be started and stopped by the assigned architect or architect in charge.

This figure also shows the underlying Apprentices that may be created where each Apprentice is responsible for a set of Questions with prescribed (multiple choice) Answers. We also show that the Agents and Apprentices are assigned to work with an Industry Expert and an Analyst. Working together, the Agents, Apprentices, Architects, and Analysts record the Answers, Explanations, a Rationale provided by the Expert for each

Answer, and a set of Findings and Recommendations used to adjust the Architecture including new goals and objectives for the Strategic Plan.

In a manner of speaking, the act of assigning Agents and creating Apprentices resembles the staffing of people / positions. One is augmenting staff with automated Agents. The organizational chart for each Business Area / Line is staffed with an Architect, an Industry Expert, and supporting Analysts and, then one assigns Agents with supporting Apprentices to assist the Architect.

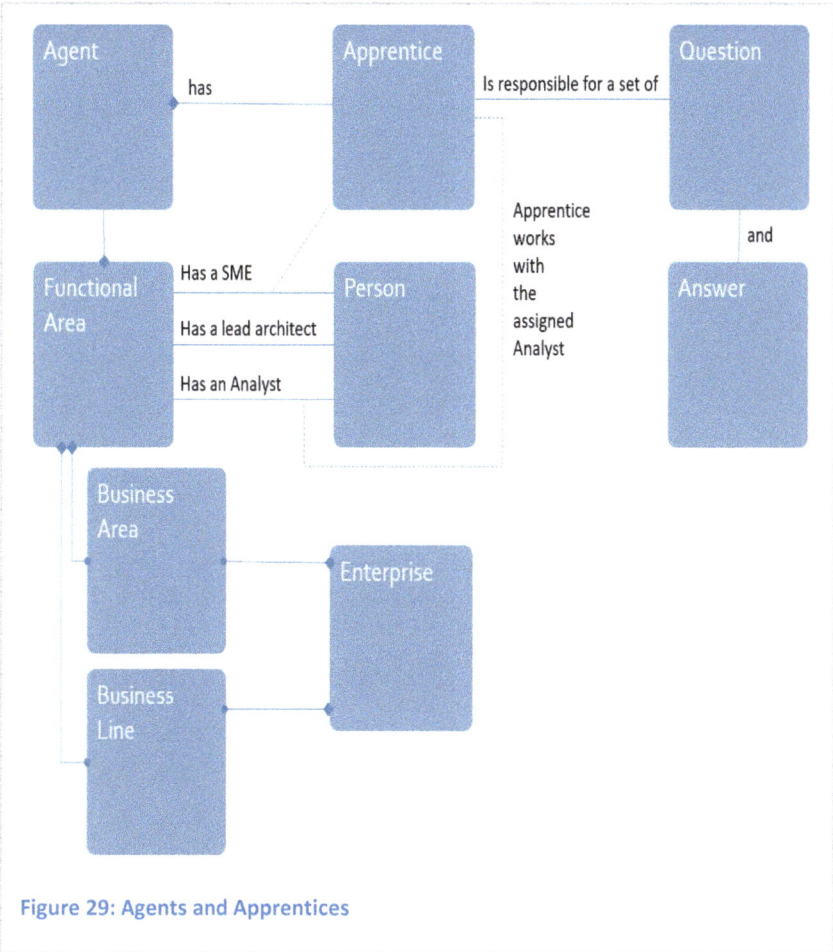

Figure 29: Agents and Apprentices

We will now consider each of these forms of analysis individually and in the context of each we discuss what Apprentices should be created.

ANALYSES CONDUCTED

SWOT ANALYSIS

A SWOT Analysis is an analysis of internal Strengths and Weaknesses, market Opportunities, and outside Threats. In doing internal analysis, the architects may look at the strengths and weaknesses of the Business at large, but more than likely they are focused on one particular Business Area / Line and perhaps even at one particular Capability. A company-wide view of SWOT is really an aggregated view of the SWOT for all Business Areas and Lines. If one is focused on revenue generating opportunities then one should be looking specifically at the Business Lines. Similarly, if one is focused primarily on opportunities to optimize cost then one should be looking at the Business Areas. This is not a hard and fast rule though because as you know, a Business Line may have grown to excess and may be in need of some cost optimization.

While the Apprentices can be more refined, the obvious candidates for Apprentices under a SWOT Agent are:

1. Market Strengths Apprentices
2. Apprentices to handle Market Weaknesses
3. Market Opportunity Apprentices
4. Market Threat Apprentices

The need for a more refined list is based on the potential need to break down the question sets so that they are more focused. Bear in mind though, that the Architect can create Apprentices and the corresponding set of Questions and Answers at will. Candidate questions for these Apprentices are listed below. Note, the obvious overarching question for the architect is "Will the Architecture / business need to be changed, and if so, at what cost?".

1. Can the business increase revenue in any of its' existing business lines? Architecturally, does anything have to change to realize suggested increases?
2. Can the business be more profitable in any of its' existing business lines? Should the business be leveraging other business models and associated channels? Architecturally, what needs to change?
3. Can the business increase its' market share? Can the business grow existing customer segments? Can the business break into new market segments?

4. Can the business be more efficient in any of the existing business areas? Is the business efficient in its' delivery of services and are delivery processes serving the business well? Is there an opportunity to consolidate common functions across the Business Areas / Lines?
5. What competitors are posing a threat to the business and what are those threats? What agencies in other governmental organizations are doing better and, in effect, posing a threat?
6. What are the strengths and weaknesses of the company's key competitors? If your business is a State or Local Government, what are the strengths and weaknesses of the adjacent States or Local Governments?
7. What are the company's / agency's strengths and weaknesses in the market place?
8. Is the organization structured to execute current plans and proposed investments? What is the operational readiness of the business / agency to execute current plans?
9. Does the business have the necessary skills and people resources given present goals and objectives? Does the business / agency have the capacity and physical resources needed to achieve present objectives?
10. What is the company's market share compared to the total market and compared to the top three competitors?
11. Does the business have the financial resources needed to achieve current goals and objectives?
12. For businesses that are competing for market share, does the business have exclusive contracts that provide a marketplace advantage?
13. Is the business an innovator in the marketplace and what patents does the business have in place?

Whether you have Agents / Apprentices or good old-fashioned architects (people), these questions need to be asked and answered and then the Architecture, business, and Strategic Plan (Goals, Objectives, and Investments) need to be adjusted accordingly. The adjustments to the Architecture may include the outsourcing of a Business Area, a re-organization, an Acquisition, Business Process Re-engineering (BPR), or some minor Business Process Improvement (BPI).

COMPETITIVE ANALYSIS

One can formulate a strategic plan without considering what others are doing, but strategic plans are more effective and informed when created with an understanding of what others in the same space are trying to achieve and how they are going about getting the job done. This applies to both product and services companies as well as governmental agencies and authorities. In the case of governmental bodies, it is actually easier because they tend to be less competitive and more open to sharing.

Candidate Apprentices under the Competitive Analysis Agent are:

1. Goals and Objectives Apprentice
2. Strategies Apprentice where a Strategy is an approach for achieving a particular Goal
3. Assumptions Apprentice
4. Capabilities Apprentice
5. Business / Product Line Apprentice
6. Mergers and Acquisitions Apprentice
7. Competitor Strengths Apprentice
8. Competitor Weaknesses Apprentice

Apprentices in this space deal with questions like these:

1. What business / product lines do the top competitors have that your business does not have? Should the business have similar product lines? If not, why not?
2. Are competitors more profitable?
3. Are competitors more efficient? What is the expense to revenue ratio for each of our top ten competitors?
4. What capabilities do competitors have that your company does not have?
5. What capabilities are competitors outsourcing?
6. What Cloud based and Software as a Service (SaaS) solutions are competitors using and at what cost? Are competitors gaining a competitive advantage as a result?
7. What are the goals and objectives of our top ten competitors?
8. What strategies are our competitors employing to achieve their goals?
9. What assumptions are our competitors making about the industry / market?
10. What mergers and acquisitions are taking place within the industry?

As you can see from the questions being asked, Competitive Analysis is a form of SWOT Analysis in that it delves into the Strengths and Weaknesses of ones' competitors. The Competitive Analysis also considers the Opportunities that competitors are tracking, and things that competitors consider Threats. In effect, one's Competitive Analysis can be viewed as an analysis of your competitor's SWOT.

PEST ANALYSIS

A PEST Analysis entails looking at political, economic, social, and technological factors outside of the business that may affect goals and objectives. Depending on the nature of the business, one might be looking at the political, economic, social, and technological factors within another country or geography. If your business is based in and does business only in the United States, you may still need to perform a PEST Analysis. For example, your architects / executives may be looking at the impact of Federal Regulations or Regulations being issued by State and Local Governments. The regulations may impact your Business Lines, Business Areas, or both.

The obvious Apprentice candidates are:

1. Political Apprentice
2. Economic Apprentice
3. Social Apprentice, and
4. Technology Apprentice

Questions that these Apprentices deal with are:

1. What new Federal or country Laws and Regulations exist that potentially impact the business?
2. What new State and Local Government Regulations exist and impact my business?
3. What is the Political stability of the Country that we are in or would like to do business in?
4. What is the risk of military invasion?
5. Is the legal framework for contract enforcement a strong one in the target country?
6. What levels of Intellectual property protection are available in the country?
7. What trade regulations and tariffs are in place within the country and are they an impediment to our business?
8. Do we have favored trading partners in the country?
9. Are there pricing regulations that constrain the opportunity?
10. Are tax rates conducive and are there tax incentives that help?
11. Is there wage legislation in place that negatively impact the opportunity?

12. Are there mandatory benefits that make employment exorbitant and impact profitability?
13. Are there Industrial safety regulations in place that will affect overhead and profitability?
14. What type of economic system is practiced and does that system affect the market and company?
15. Is there government intervention in the target region / country?
16. What are the comparative advantages of the proposed country over other countries?
17. What are exchange rates like and what is the stability of currency in the proposed country?
18. How efficient are the financial markets in the country? How quickly can the company affect a change in the marketplace?
19. Does the region / country have suitable Infrastructure conducive to the business?
20. What is the skill level of work force in the region / country being considered?
21. What are the Labor costs compared to other countries that the business operates in?
22. What is the stage and status of the economy (prosperity, recession, recovery)?
23. What is the economic growth rate of the country?
24. What is the typical discretionary income and spend in this country?
25. What is the unemployment rate?
26. What is the Inflation rate?
27. What are the Interest rates for the various types of money to be borrowed?
28. What level of education has the majority of the population achieved?
29. What is the entrepreneurial spirit of the country / geography?
30. Are the people environmentally conscious?
31. Are the people health conscious?
32. What are the leisure interests in this country / geography?
33. What recent technological developments have come from this geography and are they applicable to our business?
34. What is the proposed expense to revenue ratio for doing business in this country / geography?
35. What is the rate of technological innovation and circulation / distribution?
36. Should we be using Cloud Computing and the services of a Cloud Service Provider? In which countries?
37. What portions of our application portfolio should be in the Cloud?
38. What Mobile applications should we have?

39. What Software should we be using as a Service (SaaS)?

The outcome and output of a PEST Assessment is the cost and risk associated with a particular architecture and doing business in or supporting the chosen country / geography. This is relevant to federal level governments and Agencies that may operate in countries outside native boundaries.

SCENARIO ANALYSIS AND PLANNING

Traditional approaches to Strategic Planning emphasize past trends, the history of the business, and incremental improvements to the architecture. Scenario Planning is an alternative approach which is forward-looking and results in more significant changes to the architecture. Scenario Planning challenges planners to think about the future and to think out of the box. This form of analysis and planning considers a focused set of scenarios around (A) where the market and competitors[135] might be heading, (B) how competitors intend on navigating the market and (C) how competitors intend on getting to where they want to be. Scenario Planning considers political and social factors associated with the chosen scenarios. As a result, some of the aforementioned analyses, like PEST Analysis, applies to Scenario Analysis and Planning as well.

Regardless of the approach, the outcome and output are the same: a new architecture which by definition includes a new set of goals, objectives, and strategies for achieving the goals. The architects assure that objectives are actionable and that the necessary investment plans and budget are in place to support the architecture and build.

Bear in mind that each scenario may result in a different architecture so care should be taken on the number of scenarios considered and one should ultimately choose one scenario to go after and invest in given the level of effort and cost associated with changing the architecture and retooling the business.

---

135 Government agencies have competitors in the form of other agencies, and citizens have a choice to live and work, in the case of the US, in other States.

PART IV – CASE STUDIES

STATE GOVERNMENT

BACKGROUND

Considering Architecture purely as an IT matter is evident in one of our very own U.S. State Governments where, the State placed the Architecture and Engineering Program within the newly formed IT Agency[136]. Within that Agency, the Architecture and Engineering Program was placed in the Office of the Chief Technology Officer (CTO). The creation of this centralized IT agency was one of many initiatives outlined by a committee supporting the Governor. The agency was formed by consolidating all IT resources throughout the other agencies. After consolidating the people, the agency built out a modern data center and proceeded to migrate agency Applications to the new data center.

The Acting CIO at the time signed out a memorandum that the CTO was to establish an Architecture for the State. Building on this memorandum, the architecture team wrote into policy that the scope was the State and the

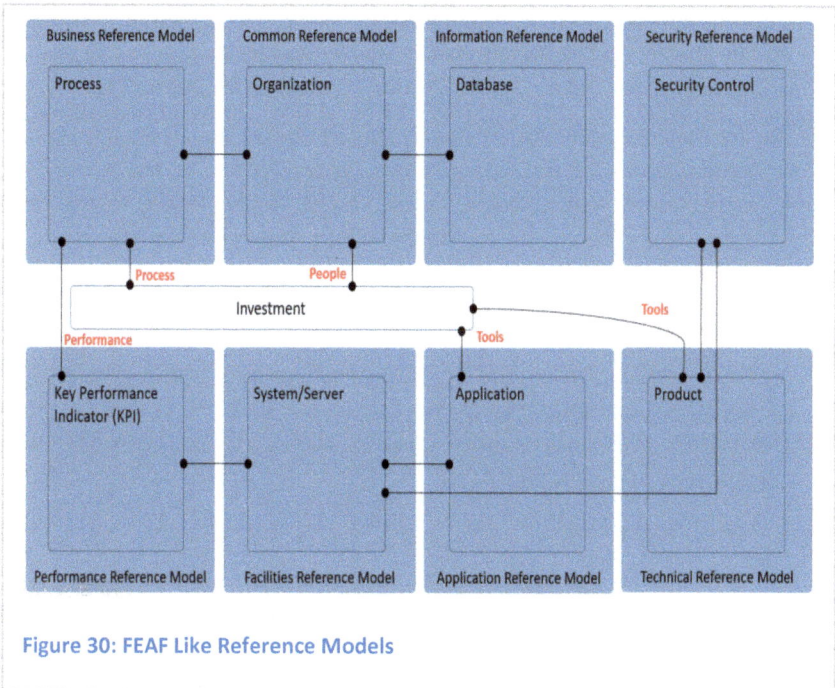

Figure 30: FEAF Like Reference Models

---

136 Within State Governments the ideal place for an EA Program is in the Department / Office of Management and Budget (D/OMB) because they hold the purse strings for all the Agencies and they are not biased towards IT.

approach was to build out FEAF-like Reference Models that document State Business Operations including the Business of IT within the State. Those reference models are depicted in Figure 30: FEAF Like Reference Models. The intention was to use those reference models to inform both the IT Strategic Plan and the State budget at large.

In addition to consolidating the IT infrastructure, the State consolidated CIO organizations. Previously, each Agency had its' own CIO. The number of CIO's was effectively cut in half and all CIO's were now responsible for multiple Agency's and reported to the Deputy Commissioner of this newly formed IT Agency. The CTO reported to the Commissioner of this IT Agency where the Commissioner held the title of State Chief Information Officer (CIO).

APPROACH TAKEN

The approach was more or less a Crawl, Walk, and then Run approach were by crawl the Agency meant, start with spreadsheets and general-purpose drawing tools. By walk they meant, get an Architecture Repository up and running. And by run the team meant to delve into being a service provider and emphasizing the higher order uses of Architecture. The one higher order use turned out to be Application / System Rationalization.

Because the Agency had little Architecture[137] and because the architecture they did have was IT detail locked in WORD documents, the starting step was to establish a set of business focused FEAF-like Reference Models. That business focus was on Capabilities but given the size of and budget for the architecture and engineering team and the fact that the organization was IT focused, the initial products were **(A)** the Application / System inventory, **(B)** the inventory of software Products that were used to create or required to run the Applications / Systems, and **(C)** the inventory of Business Capabilities that those Applications / Systems automated. The team applied the rules of three: three artifacts / artifact inventories with correlations between them:

- o Capabilities
- o Applications / Systems mapped to the Capabilities they automated

---

[137] The architecture that this client had in place was limited to informal documents at the application level. No frameworks, methods, or tools were employed. The documents were office suite documents.

- o Products with part number detail, mapped to the Applications / Systems that they enabled

With the development of the Reference Models under way and with an Architecture Board (AB) in place, the team began discussions around the consolidation of architects under the Director of Architecture and Engineering and the Architecture and Engineering Program as a service provider. The plan was to have the Architecture and Engineering Program provision architecture and engineering services to the new Deputy CIO's. The Architecture and Engineering Program was to provide the following services:

1. **Zoning and Planning Services** - to assist Agency's in establishing the "Governor's View of Business Operations" and the identification of other consolidation opportunities

2. **Architecture Services** – to Architect Business Capabilities and establish business cases for outsourcing certain Capabilities (including App Dev)

3. **Engineering Services** – to assure that the necessary engineering detail was in the Architecture and the Configuration Management Database

4. **Tools** – offering Architecture and Engineering tools through the Service Catalog and assuring that one set of tools were used for the gathering of Architecture and Engineering data

5. **Education and Training** – to assure that all architects and engineers understood exactly how the frameworks, methods, and tools were to be used.

Finally, the Director of Architecture and Engineering and the supporting architecture and engineering team embarked on a mini communications and marketing campaign. The emphasis was on the importance of focusing on State Business Operations, business performance, and the higher order uses of Architecture. Those higher order uses included the development of the IT Strategic Plan and the IT Budget. The marketing campaign also included information about the "Application / System Rationalization" service that the organization offered to the Agency's.

CHALLENGES ENCOUNTERED

The primary challenges for the Architecture and Engineering Program and the Director of Architecture and Engineering were the lack of executive backing from the CIO that replaced the Acting CIO. There was also a lackluster enforcement of the policy that this new CIO himself signed out. Other challenges included:

1. Lack of funding and nominal staffing under the Director of Architecture and Engineering
2. Insufficient communications and marketing, within the IT Agency and outside the Agency
3. Lack of funding for Education and Training
4. A separate and distinct management / governance system that did not include the Architecture
5. Nominal buy-in from the CTO's peers
6. Isolating the Architecture and Engineering Team
7. Emphasis on Service Management and the service catalog
8. An abundance of informal architecture
9. The Architecture was viewed by most in the Agency as the Application inventory.

Generally, this IT Agency relegated itself to being an Application Development shop and Operations group. They fielded requests from the agencies for Applications, they purchased software and built Applications / Systems, they built out supporting infrastructure, and then deployed and maintained those Applications / Systems.

DELIVERABLES PROVIDED

The architecture team started with a general-purpose data and knowledge management tool which at the time was called Enterprise Elements[138]. Enterprise Elements (INQUISIENT today) served as the Architecture Repository for storing and sharing information comprising nine Reference Models. The repository also stored architectural details for each capability. The Reference Models and repository housed the Building Blocks of that Enterprise. Ultimately, the reference models included:

1. **A Business Reference Model (BRM)** – the inventory of capabilities, services, and processes
2. **A Performance Reference Model (PRM)** – the inventory of key performance indicators
3. **A Service Component Reference Model (SCRM)** – inventory of business and IT services

---

138 The product and company are now referred to as INQUISIENT®. More information about the product and company can be found on the company website at: https://inquisient.com/

4. **An Application Reference Model (ARM)** – having the inventory of Applications / Systems
5. **The Technical Reference Model (TRM)** – inventory of hardware and software products[139]
6. **Data / Information Reference Model (IRM)** – inventory of data store / databases
7. **Security Reference Model (SRM)** – holding the security policies and assessments[140]
8. **Facilities Reference Model (FRM)** – the inventory of all data centers
9. **A Common Reference Model (CRM)** – for key organizational and person data[141]

These reference models contained the basic information required for managing IT investments, Application / System portfolio management, Application / System Rationalization, understanding the scope of each capability, and general reporting.

The Architecture and Engineering Program delivered a tool environment as depicted in *Figure 20: Depiction of the basic tool environment*. The environment contained:

1. A general purpose and comprehensive modeling tool called UNICOM® System Architect®[142].
2. Microsoft® VISIO® to accommodate the culture and knowledge base
3. Enterprise ERWIN® for Data Modeling

The general-purpose modeling tool (SA) was integrated with the Architecture Repository. Raw data residing in the general-purpose modeling tool was configured to facilitate the flow of architecture and engineering data into the Architecture Repository. A subset of that data

---

139 This product information went into the architecture first, once placed into production some of that data was transferred to the State's Service Management System.

140 As an example, one application assessment comprised of 26 questions about each application was maintained in the repository so that the organization could establish a graphical "Security Lens" and report out via a heat map as to where the problem areas were.

141 This information was used for, among other things, reporting out on skills and skill deficiencies

142 UNICOM System Architect - https://teamblue.unicomsi.com/products/system-architect/

would later flow from the Architecture Repository to the client's ITIL based Configuration Management Database (CMDB).

BEST PRACTICES APPLIED

Setting aside the issues associated with the placement of the program and the day to day issues associated with operations of the tool environment, the architecture and engineering team established a broad yet thin view of the business / government in the form of nine reference models. This was referred to as "*A Governor's View of Business Operations*"). The team also provided limited architecture and engineering services that enabled the organization to deep dive on any one capability.

The Architecture team also applied the Federal Enterprise Architecture Framework (FEAF) and the Practical Guide to Federal Enterprise Architecture[143] as Best Practices. Using guidance from the Practical Guide, the architecture and engineering team:

1. Established the Architecture Policy
2. Established a matrix organization of lead architects form each Business Line
3. Provisioned services to the Business Lines
4. Provided Quality Assurance
5. Established the necessary tool environment
6. Established leadership in the form of an Architecture Board

The above listed aspects of the Architecture and Engineering Program comprise the organizations "*Common Architecture Approach*" and Architecture and Engineering service offering.

The Director of Architecture and Engineering directly drove an "Application Rationalization" effort using the architecture. This effort applied a Gartner® Best Practice for Application / System Portfolio Management. The Gartner® engagement team was able to directly leverage the data in the Architecture Repository, The Architecture team in turn configured the State's Architecture Repository so that the Application / System Assessment data and results were stored in perpetuity. Like the portfolio management example presented in section *A Portfolio*

---

143 The Practical Guide to Federal Enterprise Architecture (GAO-10-846G) https://www.gao.gov/assets/590/588407.pdf provides guidance to Federal Agencies in initiating, developing, using, and maintaining an Enterprise Architecture (EA). It offers an end-to-end process to initiate, implement, and sustain an EA program, and describes the necessary roles and associated responsibilities for a successful EA program.

Management Example, for the IT Community, this Gartner® practice enables the Business to categorize their Applications / Systems so that they fall into one of four categories and based on numeric ratings the Applications / Systems are depicted on a Gartner® like Quad chart. The model is referred to as the TIME model having these categories:

1. **T**olerate
2. **I**nvest
3. **M**igrate
4. **E**liminate

This practice was quite a success for the Director of Architecture and Engineering. He was able to get the practice in front of the CIO, he was able to get her support, and the Architecture team was now working directly with the CIO's and Agency's to assess their Application Portfolios and use the Architecture (Data) to drive the IT Budget. These efforts lead to adjustments in the budget for IT Application / System Modernization.

Public Company

Background

One of the authors supported a product and services company that leveraged Architecture concepts very early on. It was not long after the advent of the Worldwide Web (WWW) in 1990 and before the time that U.S. Federal Government enacted the Clinger Cohen Act (1996). New business models, including e-Commerce, were driving the need for transformation and the company was also heading straight on into y2k without a company-wide Application / System inventory. In addition to using their architecture to manage the y2k issue, the company used the architecture to manage the segue from a traditional sales models and a business partner sales model to e-Commerce.

Simultaneously, the company had embarked on a worldwide effort to consolidate data centers and to establish a common platform in those data centers for applications that were developed internally to support the business.

Approach Taken

The approach was a matrix management approach that brought people together from all legs of the company to restructure the business, to re-engineer business processes, and to deliver new supporting Applications / Systems company-wide. As an example, rather than having each Business Line own and manage its' own product sales system, there would be one product sales system that supported all Business Lines.

The company leveraged Integrated Product Development (IPD)[144] to manage their transformation. This included an Investment Review Board (IRB) and Integrated Portfolio Management Teams (IPMTs) operating under the auspices of the IRB. The IPMTs were established to manage related legs of the business and the corresponding portfolios of Applications / Systems. One of the Integrated Portfolio Management Teams (IPMT) was a company-wide Architecture Board (AB) which held a seat for an executive from each Business Area / Line. The approach was designed to break down the siloes that had formed. It was designed to take

---

144 See DoD Integrated Product and Process Development Handbook.
https://www.secnav.navy.mil/rda/onesource/documents/program%20assistance%20and%20tools/handbooks,%20guides%20and%20reports/page%203/ippdhdbk.pdf

a company-wide and customer-centric view of business operations and sales.

The focus was on the transformational initiatives that were required to segue into the new world of e-Business and e-Commerce. As an example, the Architecture Board (AB) chartered a team of people to investigate corporate / worldwide order management, billing, and invoicing. Simultaneously, the AB chartered teams looked at other related facets of the business, like Export Regulations and how they were handled worldwide.

CHALLENGES ENCOUNTERED

One of the challenges for this company was the overhead associated with the matrix management approach because each Business Area / Line had its' own IPMT and many of the same executives that sat on multiple IPMTs. The number of IPMT meetings became a burden to the executives.

A technical challenge was the company's attempt to take COTS Applications / Systems that were highly integrated and designed to support a business end-to-end (horizontally), and stand them up vertically to support individual Business Areas or business function. Interestingly, this challenge still exists today and the authors are dealing with the problem at a U.S. Federal Agency in 2019/2020.

DELIVERABLES PROVIDED

To its' credit, this company did not view the Architecture as an end in itself. They viewed the Architecture as a means to an end. Architecturally, the primary deliverables were the organizational changes to the business, the introduction of common processes, and the new applications / systems that the transformational projects purchased to modernize and to automate the business processes.

The primary written deliverable was what the company called their Corporate Blueprint. This blueprint was published on a yearly basis for all to view and use internally. Publishing was handled via the company Intranet. The company was quite successful in using the Corporate Blueprint to drive business value across the entire company and in transforming the business. This company was especially good at governing development of the Corporate Blueprint and the transformation.

A companion to the Corporate Blueprint was the inventory of Applications / Systems. This work product and approach to managing a portfolio of

Applications / Systems was introduced in Figure 26: Four categories formed using the two indicators. This company used two indicators to break the portfolio of Applications down into four categories. Those categories are depicted again here in *Figure 31: Categorizing Applications*. The categories are formed by the combinations of two indicators or Booleans. One indicator states if the Application / System is "Mission Critical" or not. The other indicator stated if the Application was "Strategic" or not. This resulted in the following truth table:

	Strategic	Mission Critical
Green (upper right quadrant)	True	True
Purple (Upper left quadrant)	False	True
Yellow (Lower right quadrant)	True	False
Orange (Lower left quadrant)	False	False

This Work Product was instrumental in driving a more disciplined approach to managing the portfolio of Applications / Systems. The approach and the chart depicted in *Figure 32: Projecting Application Portfolio Size* were institutionalized within this company by having periodic reviews with executives at the Business Area level where the executives were required

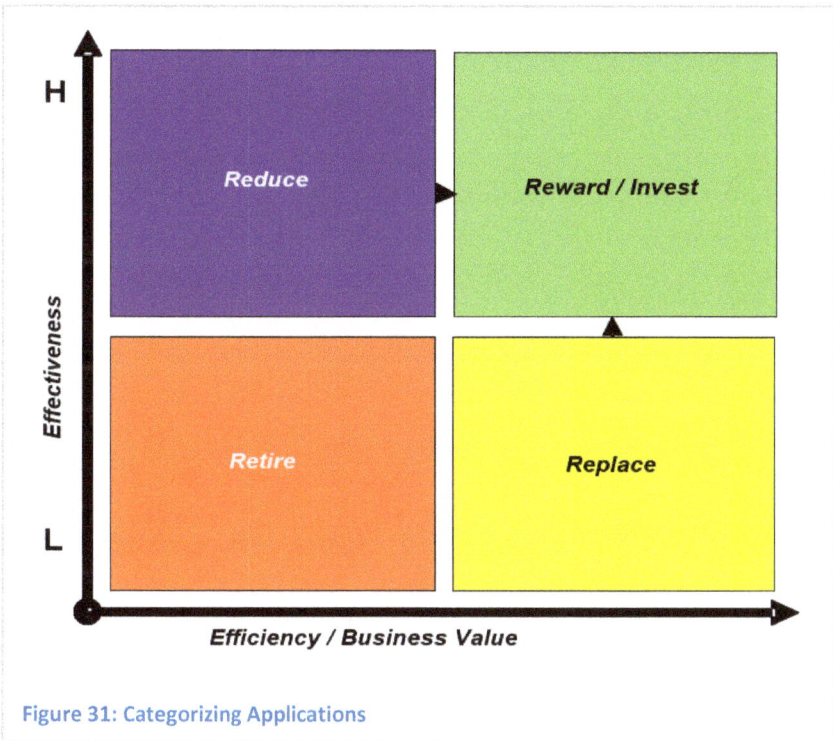

Figure 31: Categorizing Applications

to report out the numbers and show progress towards a more streamlined and modern portfolio of Applications / Systems.

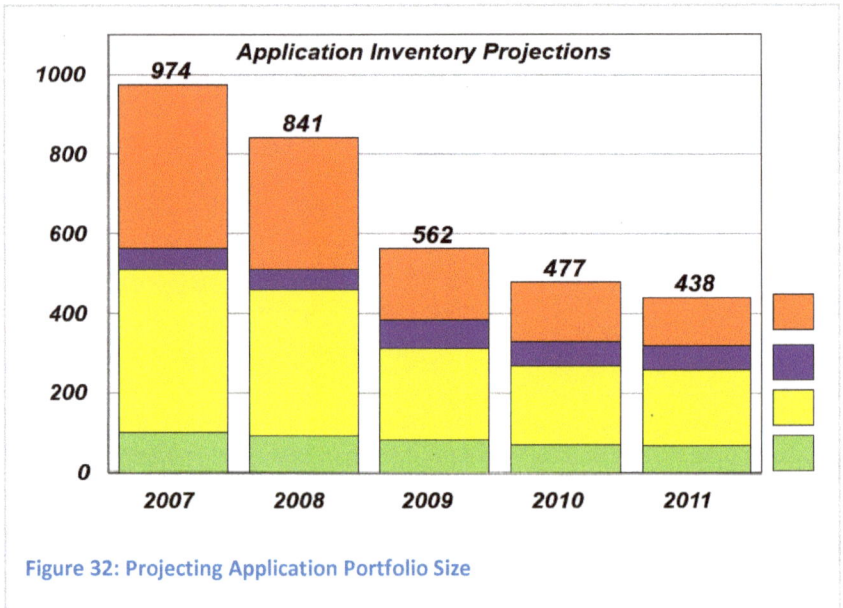

Figure 32: Projecting Application Portfolio Size

One additional Work Product was a bar chart on the status of the Application portfolio by calendar year. That bar chart is depicted in *Figure 32: Projecting Application Portfolio Size* where each bar in the chart is segmented to show the number of Applications / Systems in each category for that calendar year. This approach and the bar chart are simple and yet a great example of putting architecture data to use.

BEST PRACTICES APPLIED

This company is the source of many best practices. In this case, the most notable application of a best practice was the use of Integrated Product Development (IPD) to manage the business transformation. The IT portion of the transformation included Data Center Consolidation, GRID Computing, system virtualization, and a focus on the delivery of Commercial-off-the-shelf (COTS) Applications / Systems that supported the entire business worldwide.

FEDERAL AGENCY

BACKGROUND

Taking an architectural approach to IT modernization became a recognized best practice in U.S. Federal Government with the passage of the Clinger-Cohen Act in 1996. The Clinger-Cohen Act (1996) and more recent Office of Management and Budget (OMB) mandates require that agencies be accountable for technology expenditures. Having an Architecture to secure funding is part of that accountability.

This case study deals with a rather large Federal Agency and in particular, one of its' components that implements a broad spectrum of energy and environmental research and development (R&D). This Laboratory's portfolio includes R&D conducted through partnerships, cooperative research and development agreements, and financial assistance. It also included R&D conducted through contractual arrangements with universities and the private sector. The goal was to improve their technology planning at the enterprise level through the establishment and use of a Lab-wide Architecture. The Lab faced a simple yet challenging goal, to document current technology programs and define future technology development so that it could make better decisions about systems acquisition or development. The solution was an architecture enabled capital planning system for making budget decisions.

CHALLENGES

Both the Agency and the research lab had architectures, but there was little to no collaboration to assure that the architectures were aligned and supportive of one another. The Agency and client would have benefited from a federated approach and better coordination between the Agency and research lab. Federation aside, the client faced several challenges given its' size and the complexity of its' business operations. Focusing on the research lab alone, some key observations were:

- A significant number of Applications / Systems with overlapping with duplicative system functions
- Stove-piped systems that could not intercommunicate, were not reusable, and were costly to replace
- Systems did not support a coordinated set of processes that in turn support overall agency mission
- Data was not easily interchangeable and exchangeable
- Information was being captured in incompatible formats

- The information needed to build the architecture was inconsistent or unavailable
- IT governance was ad-hoc

While a federated approach may not have helped with some of the challenges listed, it does help with governance and ensuring that the architectures are aligned and put to use. One of the biggest challenges was the absence of an established Architecture and Engineering Methodology or approach to use Architecture and Engineering in support of organizational transformation.

APPROACH

The effort and approach focused on the use of the Architecture to translate business vision and strategy into the organizational transformation programs and information technology investments required to support current and future operations. The team employed a three-phase approach (shown in *Figure 33: Three Phase Approach*), designed to fill some gaps in the existing program, identify the transformative projects that were required, and then get those projects funded and executed.

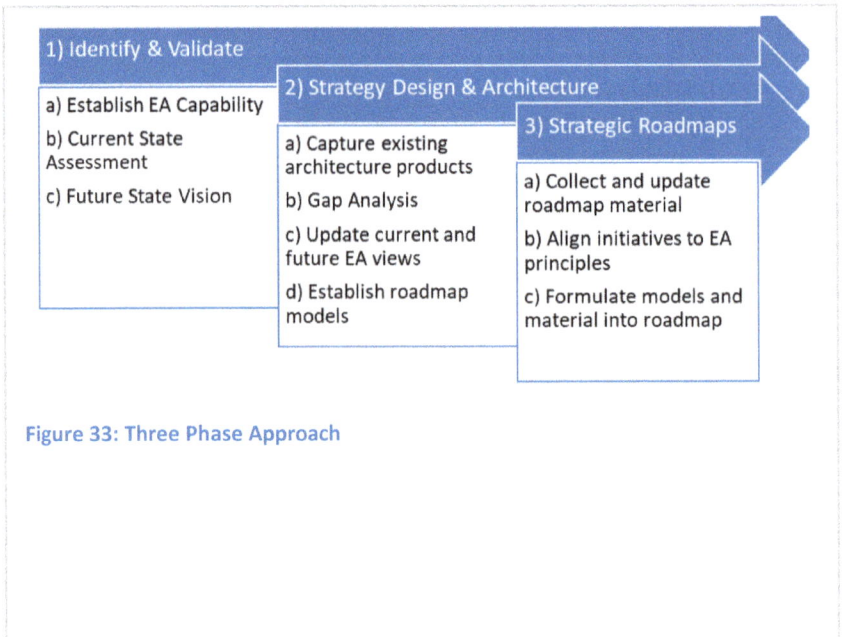

1) Identify & Validate

a) Establish EA Capability

b) Current State Assessment

c) Future State Vision

2) Strategy Design & Architecture

a) Capture existing architecture products

b) Gap Analysis

c) Update current and future EA views

d) Establish roadmap models

3) Strategic Roadmaps

a) Collect and update roadmap material

b) Align initiatives to EA principles

c) Formulate models and material into roadmap

Figure 33: Three Phase Approach

The phases and activities conducted within those phases are presented here in outline form:

Identify and Validate Phase:

- Architecture and Engineering Program Assessment – conducted executive interviews on both the client and program side and identified improvement opportunities
- Current State Architecture Assessment – developed the business model through a variety of document analyses, interviews, and systems analysis. Identified key processes and systems using a combination of strategic business and IT analytical views, and summarized the view of current business applications support
- Future State Vision – identified initial systems with overlapping capabilities, identified potential functional gaps in applications support, evaluated systems and identified merits of potential consolidation, and developed preliminary vision of future state business systems.

Strategy Design and Architecture Phase:

- Analyze needs – determined the appropriate architecture models, such as system interface description and capability alignment models
- Analyze current state – analysis of strategic goals and initiatives, business services and information flows, applications, infrastructure, security and privacy and standards
- Gap Analysis – performed analysis of gaps between current state and target state and an analysis of the existing investment initiatives to identify adjustments required to attain target start
- Update current and future views – using the abovementioned gap analysis, the team updated existing current state documentation, documented the necessary adjustments, planned the target state, and updated the Architecture repository

Strategic Roadmap Phase:

- Collect and update roadmap material – collected and updated non-architecture information such as: tasks, milestones, and timeframes for already initiated implementation projects
- Align initiatives to Architecture and Engineering principles – validated priority of investment initiatives and aligned Architecture and Engineering principles to reset priorities
- Formulate models and material into roadmap – obtained and generated the appropriate material and models to summarize the current state, future state and transition plan(s) of the strategic roadmap.

The approach was a "keep it simple" approach that was minimalistic but effective.

DELIVERABLES

As the architecture matured, it was used by the client to enable more consistent planning and decision-making. The Architecture Program helped to facilitate and support a common understanding of needs, helped formulate recommendations to meet those needs, and facilitated the development an action plan grounded in an integrated view of the systems and technology landscape.

The architecture team provided facilitation and integration (as depicted in *Figure 34: Operating Model*) to enable collaborative planning, and work with specialists and subject matter experts to formulate an appropriate action plan that was implementable given the financial, political, and organizational constraints of the research and development organization.

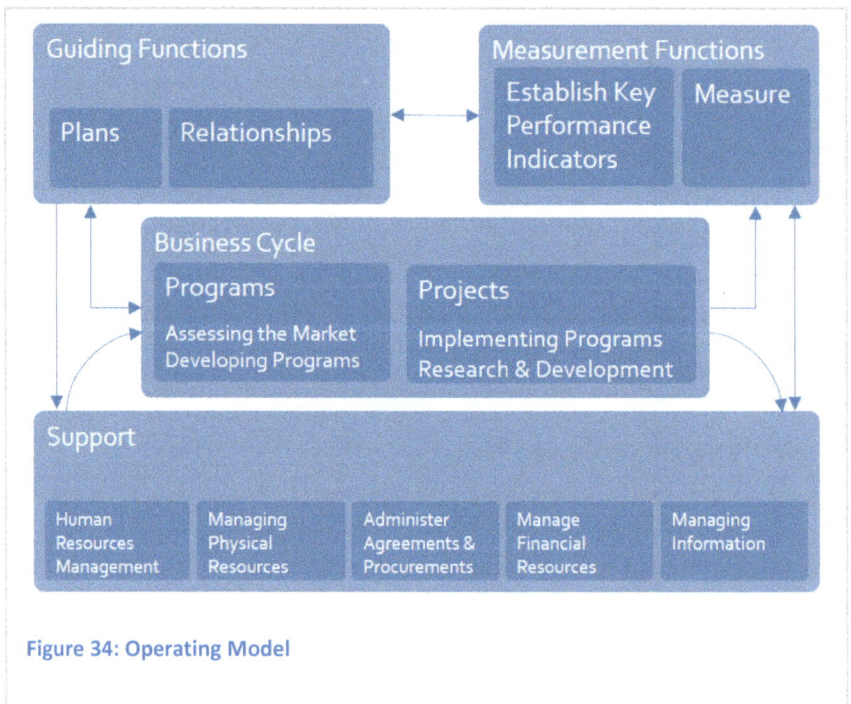

Figure 34: Operating Model

The architecture and engineering team played an important role in the investment, implementation, and performance measurement activities and decisions. While there was an architecture repository containing some of the details about recommended investments (see *Figure 35: Data Used* to *Generate Strategic Roadmap*), the following deliverables were established for this client to support the transformation process:

- **Business Strategy (Model)** – incorporated the Architecture and Engineering Operation Model shown in *Figure 34: Operating Model* to facilitate the understanding of the current and future state of client's system support. The client's transformation from current to future state allowed the organization to be more effective in accomplishing its mission. Through the transformation process, significant benefits were realized by moving from a poorly integrated state with little Governance and overlapping systems to a state with a comprehensive Governance process, tightly integrated enterprise-wide systems, and increased automation.
- **Architecture Principles** – architecture principles were used to reflect a level of consensus across the business which provided a basis for decision-making throughout all levels of the business. These principles also informed how the organization goes about fulfilling its mission.
- **System Interface Description** – Each of the client's systems were mapped to the capabilities of the client business model to provide an understanding of how many systems were supporting each function. System overlaps and gaps were identified and recorded as Findings and Recommendations.
- **Strategic Roadmap** – a Business Systems Roadmap was created by analyzing current business systems and the technical environment. Documenting and communicating changes to business systems among stakeholders is a key element the assessment report directly addresses.

The Strategic Roadmap was generated using the data as shown in *Figure 35: Data Used to Generate Strategic Roadmap*. The roadmap contained a detailed view of target transition dates and other milestones for each initiative.

BEST PRACTICES

The team applied the concept of business-focused and outcome driven architecture to create operational and strategic views of the business and technology that improve business operations, coordinate diverse initiatives, and accelerate the pace of change. This included an explicit alignment of Applications / Systems with Business Capabilities and being explicit about Gaps.

Another best practice applied is the *Practical Guide to Federal Enterprise Architecture* where the program acquired and maintained executive buy-in, established a cohesive architecture vision, and communicated with and educated stakeholders.

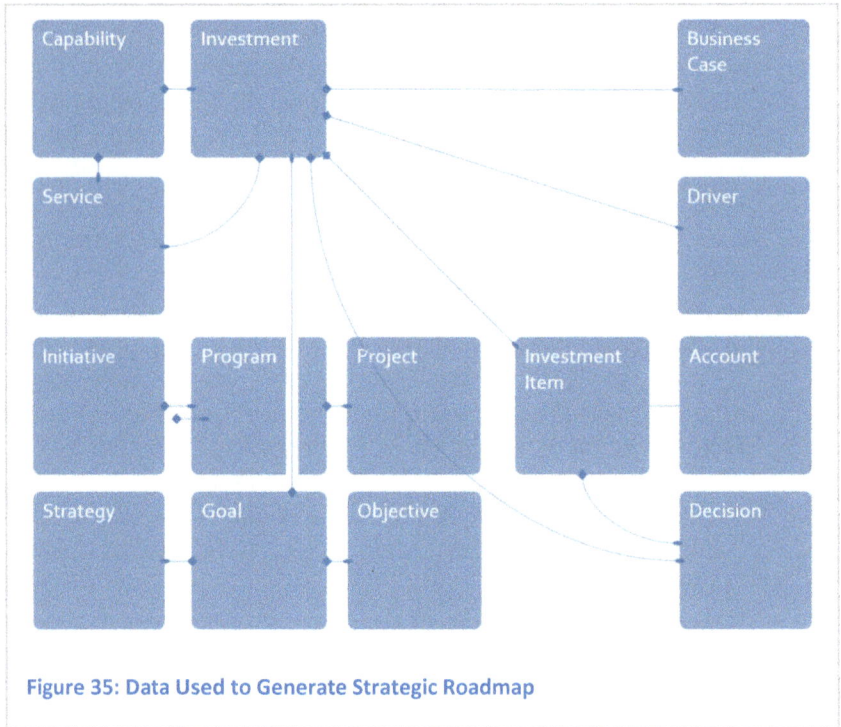

Figure 35: Data Used to Generate Strategic Roadmap

PART V – FOUNDATIONS

METHODS, LANGUAGES, AND NOTATIONS

In order to Zone the Business, Architect Capabilities, and in particular to Engineer DOTMLPF, one needs modeling Methods. These modeling methods must support all aspects of DOTMLPF and result in the creation of sound architecture and building blocks. Methods also enforce structure, syntax, and standards. To a certain extent, the application of methods to Zoning, Architecting, and Engineering is a quality assurance (QA) exercise conducted by the Engineers to assure that the Architect is doing more than just drawing pretty pictures. This form of quality assurance also minimizes the need for Independent Verification and Validation (IV&V) which can be costly.

> It is always amazing to encounter architects who think that they don't need architecture, and to observe architects that don't apply methods. The authors were engaged with one client running an architecture program and interestingly, there was no architecture describing what the organization / program did. There were no models, and conspicuously absent was a system wiring diagram. The team started to formalize the existing documentation which was not based on methods. One of the first up was the creation of a model to document the Systems / Applications and how they interoperated. To our amazement, the director of the architecture organization said "I don't think we need a system model".

Whether one is Zoning, Architecting, or Engineering, methods are applied to **(A)** create drawings that comply with an agreed to standard / notation, and **(B)** to assure that required data is captured. While Zoning the Business entails the creation of Reference Models and while those models are created without modeling tools (they are primarily declarative in nature), modeling does play a role because pictures are valuable even at this level. The old saying *"a picture is worth a thousand words"* rings true. Not just pretty pictures, but models drawn based on standards. This is where methods come in.

In addition to establishing standards and facilitating the creation of pictorials based on the standards, the methods and tools facilitate data gathering. When practiced, the methods lead to a sound set of blueprints that a builder can use for costing and construction. The Methods also result in data that is used by the business at large for, among other things, computing net-present value to support a business case. The important thing is that the data is designed to benefit the business at large as opposed to a single person to get him / her through their business day.

Methods also help minimize ambiguity. There should be no ambiguity and no question in the mind of the builder as to what the owner wants.

As depicted in *Figure 36: Methods and Tools are Foundational*, the Reference Models are fed and augmented by models or drawings created using methods and tools that implement and enforce those methods. Note that the line in this figure from "*Drawings based on Methods*" goes to the dashed lined that encircles the three disciplines: Zoning, Architecting, and Engineering. This is to emphasize that methods may be applied to create drawings in all three disciplines.

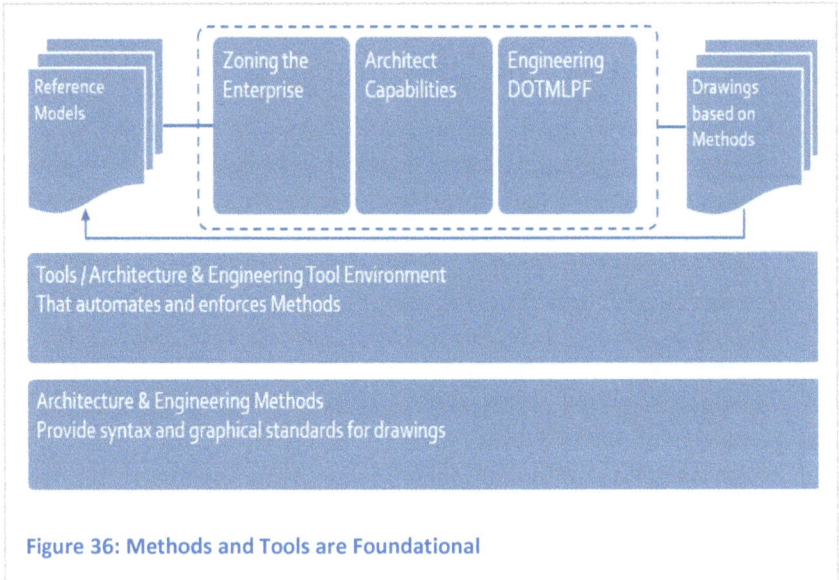

Figure 36: Methods and Tools are Foundational

At this stage in the game though, there are gaps and issues when it comes to Architecture and Engineering Methods. There are gaps without even introducing the concept of Engineering DOTMLPF. Gaps are partially due to a myopic view of the disciplines at play and, to a certain extent, people not acknowledging the inter-relationships between the disciplines and methods. An example of this is Business Analysts not fully understanding what an Architect does and not understanding some of the basic methods used to architect capabilities and to engineer DOTMLPF.

The need to look across the methods is apparent when applying IDEFo® and the more modern notation called the Business Process Modeling Notation or BPMN®. These are thought to be independent and mutually exclusive but, to the contrary, they complement one another. Among other things, the IDEFo® is used for process decomposition and the BMPN® for workflow modeling. In this example, one applies the IDEFo method first to document the constituent parts of one's processes that required for developing a BPMN-based process / workflow model. This includes the decomposition of Processes into Activities for a more refined understanding of <u>what</u> the business does; and second, task detail in the decomposition which is used to create the BPMN® based workflow models. These workflow models are then referred to as descriptions of <u>how</u> the business executes the respective processes.

While there are gaps in the methods, the DODAF does fill some of them, and certain other languages, and notations do help. At this point in time, the modeling methods and notations include:

- o Notations and methods that are implicit in the DODAF
- o IEEE Systems of Systems Engineering methods
- o IDEFo method for documenting the things that the business does
- o Business Process Model and Notation (BPMN) for workflows
- o Unified Modeling Language (UML) for modeling data and software
- o IDEF1X for data in relational database management systems[145]

If one is going to practice Architecture and Engineering then, depending on the Capability being engineered, one applies several and perhaps all the above methods, some in conjunction with one another.

The DOD understood the need to specify scenarios for when to apply methods. To that end they provided guidance in the DODAF 1.5 documentation in table form as depicted in *Figure 37: DODAF Guidance for the applicability of Diagrams*. The table guided both architects and engineers on what DODAF diagrams to use in certain scenarios. The table contains columns representing the Diagrams and rows representing scenarios. The intersecting cells provided guidance on the applicability of the Diagram given the intended use of the Architecture.

To reinforce the need for methods, the DODAF went on in in subsequent versions, to allow for a "Fit for Finish" approach which basically left it to the architect to decide what diagrams should be used and even what formats / tools. This has led to some architects and engineers foregoing the methods completely and actually attempting to practice their trade using spreadsheets.

Regarding gaps though, it makes sense that the DODAF fills certain gaps which are apparent when looking at the world through a DOTMLPF lens.

---

[145] Note that at this point in time modeling relational data is really not required because technology exists to generate relational models from object models.

This is because both the DODAF and the DOTMLPF framework come from the United States Department of Defense (DOD). Not all the gaps are filled though. For example, the DODAF does not have an Operation View (OV) diagram for documenting Curriculums and Courses which are required to be proficient in a Functional Areas of the business or with a particular Capability.

One's ability to Engineer DOTMLPF is covered for the most part, with the

		All View		Operational View (OV)							Systems Vi
		1	2	1	2	3	4	5	6	7	1	2	3	4	5	6
RECOMMENDED USES OF ARCHITECTURE:																
Planning, Programming, Budgeting Execution Process																
Capability Based Analysis for IT Investment Decisions		●	●	●	●	●	●	●	●	◉	●	◉	●	●	●	●
Modernization Planning and Technology Insertion/Evolution		●	●	◉	●	◉	◉	●	◉		●	◉	◉	◉	●	◉
Portfolio Management		●	●		●			●	◉		●			◉	●	
Joint Capabilities Integration and Development System																
JCIDS Analysis (FAA, FNA, FSA)		●	●	●	●	◉	◉	●	●		●	◉		◉	●	
ICD/CDD/CPD/CRD		●	●	●	●	●	●		●	●	●	◉	◉	●	●	●
Analysis of Alternatives (AoA)		●	●	●	●	◉		●	●		●	◉	◉	●	●	◉
Acquisition Process																
Acquisition Strategy		●	●	●	●	◉		●	◉		●	◉			●	
Information Support Plan		●	●	●	●	●		●	●		●			◉		●
System Design and Development		●	●		●	●		●	●	◉	●	●	●	●	●	●
Interoperability and Supportability of NSS and IT Systems		●	●	●	●	●	◉	●	◉	◉	●	◉	●	●		●
Integrated Test & Evaluation		●	●		●	●	◉	●	●	◉	●	●	●	●	●	●
Operations (Assessment, Planning, Execution, ...)																
Operations Planning & Execution		●	●	●	●	●	●	●	●	◉	●	●	◉	◉	●	●
CONOPS & TTP		●	●	●	●	●	●	●	●		●	◉	◉	◉	◉	
Communications Plans		●	●	●	●		◉	◉			●	●				
Exercise Planning & Execution		●	●	●	●	●	●	●	●		●	●	◉	◉	◉	◉
Organizational Design		●	●	●	●	●	●	●	●	◉	◉	◉			◉	
BPR/FPI		●	●	◉	●	●	●	●	●	●	◉					

● = Product is highly applicable
◉ = Product is often or partially applicable
▨ = Product is specifically addressed in policy
▨ = Product is required for an Integrated Architecture
blank = Product is usually not applicable

Figure 37: DODAF Guidance for the applicability of Diagrams

DODAF, the Unified Modeling Language® (UML®), the IDEF® methods, and the Business Process Modeling Notation® (BPMN®). The authors have filled in some of the gaps on their own. Here is the coverage of methods from a DOTMLPF perspective:

1. **D**octrine / Policy – modeling is covered by the DODAF
2. **O**rganization – modeling is covered by the DODAF
3. **T**raining – method gap closed by the authors
4. **M**ateriel in a business context includes:
    a. Processes – covered by IDEF0® and BPMN®

b. Software Applications / Systems – UML®

c. Physical systems – IEEE Systems of Systems and DODAF

5. **L**eadership – method gap closed by the authors
6. **P**ersonnel – method gap closed by the authors
7. **F**acilities– modeling is covered by the DODAF and certain methods gaps closed by the authors

A graphical representation of the various forms of modeling required for a complete Architecture and for fitting the DOTMLPF framework is depicted in *Figure 38: Forms of Modeling in the DOTMLPF World*. The upcoming sections provide an overview of these categories and the forms of modeling that fall within them.

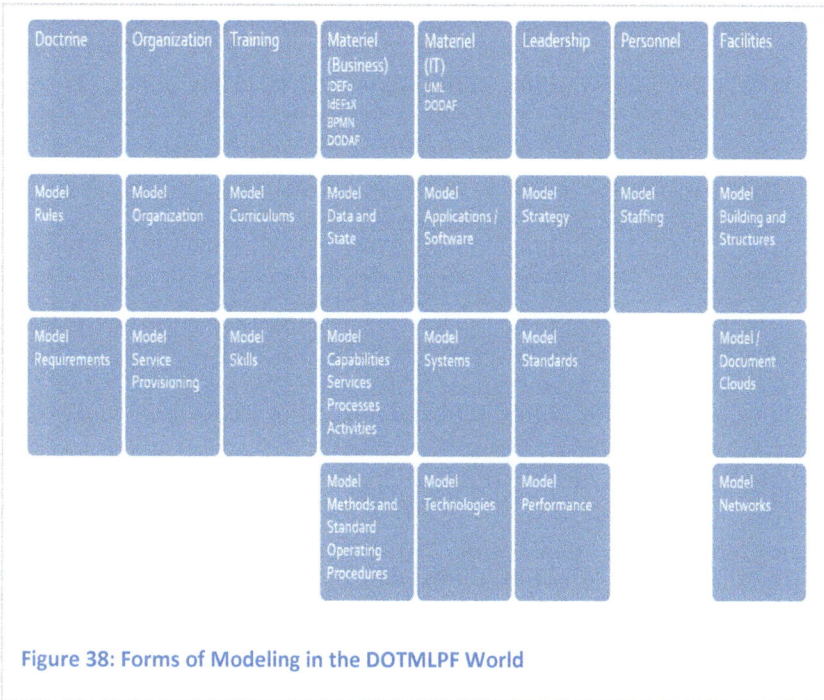

Doctrine	Organization	Training	Materiel (Business) IDEFo IdEFsX BPMN DODAF	Materiel (IT) UML DODAF	Leadership	Personnel	Facilities
Model Rules	Model Organization	Model Curriculums	Model Data and State	Model Applications / Software	Model Strategy	Model Staffing	Model Building and Structures
Model Requirements	Model Service Provisioning	Model Skills	Model Capabilities Services Processes Activities	Model Systems	Model Standards		Model / Document Clouds
			Model Methods and Standard Operating Procedures	Model Technologies	Model Performance		Model Networks

Figure 38: Forms of Modeling in the DOTMLPF World

In the remainder of this section, we introduce the key building blocks of a business with a focus on those that fit the DOTMLPF categories. This includes building blocks that we believe fill gaps. Examples of gap fillers include, building blocks required for modeling Training Curriculums, Leadership in the form of Strategic Plans and Management Systems, Personnel in the form of things like Skills and Staffing Plans, and Facilities to cover, in particular, Clouds.

DOCTRINE

Under the heading Doctrine we include building blocks like Laws, Regulations, Policies, Directives (LRPD), and Instructions. We do this bearing in mind that some of these may come from outside the business. Policies, in particular, may be created by the business in order to impose internal constraints on how something is done. In the case where the LRPD comes from outside the Business, the Architect has an obligation to record the LRPD by name and then, elsewhere in the Architecture, show where the constraints are imposed and what in the business is impacted by the LRPD.

Doctrine is defined as "*a stated principle of government policy*"[146]. The fact that it is typically associated with government policy is immaterial. What is important is the concept of principles, which by extension include (A) directives in the form of "thou shall" statements, and (B) expressions of need typically translated into "we need" statements. Both types of statements being applied to the organizations that need to come together to execute on and realize a mission in a concerted manner.

In stretching the definition, we have made accommodations to include Requirements and Specifications under this heading in the DOTMLPF framework. The word *Requirement*[147] itself is a general term used to refer to "needs" of the business, capability, or a system. With respect to information technology or systems, requirements are an expression of what systems / applications must do to support and automate business operations.

But requirements actually take on many forms. For instance, if a new business model comes about, then the business model at large may be viewed as a requirement. Similarly, Best Practices are large grained requirements. A business model is a business requirement while a best practice can be business related or technical. Broadly speaking, requirements are business or technical. Both can be stated textually and broken down to form a hierarchy of large and then small grained requirements. In all cases, each Requirement has a source which enables one to tie it back to some first order building block, like Best Practice. This enables one to answer the question: "Where did you get that Requirement

---

146 A definition can be found at https://www.merriam-webster.com/dictionary/doctrine
147 Note that a Requirement is an Element

from?". The forms of requirements that we cover here are depicted *Figure 39: Types of Requirements*:

There are some formalized methods for documenting requirements. As an example, a group referred to as the Usability Body of Knowledge[148]

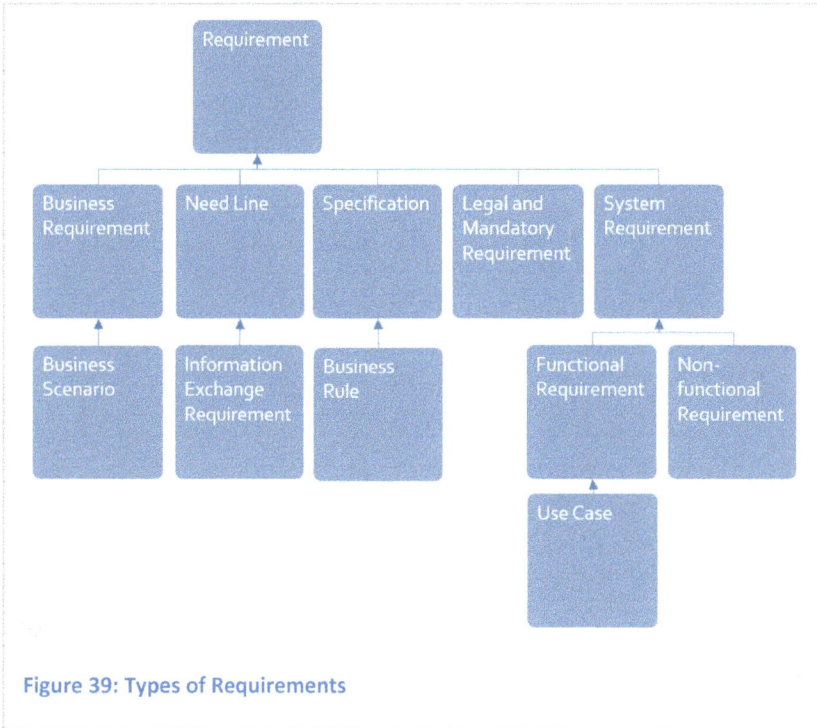

Figure 39: Types of Requirements

documents a method called *Affinity Diagramming*. With Affinity Diagramming, concepts written on cards are sorted into related groups and sub-groups. Given the original intent of Affinity Diagramming (to help diagnose complicated problems) it is ideally suited to documenting the requirements / needs associated with a new business capability.

We focus in now on the different forms of requirements: Legal and Mandatory Requirements, Business Requirements, and Information Exchange Requirements (IERs).

LEGAL AND MANDATORY REQUIREMENTS

In Engineering Legal and Mandatory Requirements (LRPD), one is recording the applicable Laws, Regulations, Policies, and Directives that

---

148 More information about the Usability Body of Knowledge can be found at
http://www.usabilitybok.org/

constrain the business and Capabilities. If those artifacts (LRPDs) are provided as a web page then one records the URL. If those artifacts are provided in file format then one attaches the file to the corresponding building block in the architecture. Using the source documents, one then breaks down the document into sections and paragraphs to have a more granular view of the Legal and Mandatory Requirements and Business Rules.

The DODAF has an implicit method for modeling legal and mandatory requirements. It comes in the form of the Operational View numbered 6a (OV-6a) for modeling Policies with embedded Business Rules. The DODAF refers to the model as an "Operational Rules Model" but generally, and as depicted in *Figure 40: Legal and Mandatory Requirements*, this includes Laws, Regulations, Policies, and Directives (LRPD) that house those Operational Rules. What is most important is the decomposition of those LRPDs into rules and requirements that need to be met by the business, systems, and people conducting business with and without those systems.

As depicted in *Figure 40: Legal and Mandatory Requirements*, a Legal and Mandatory Requirement refers back to an LRPD if so derived. Also depicted, are Business Rules which we consider Specifications as a descendant of Requirement.

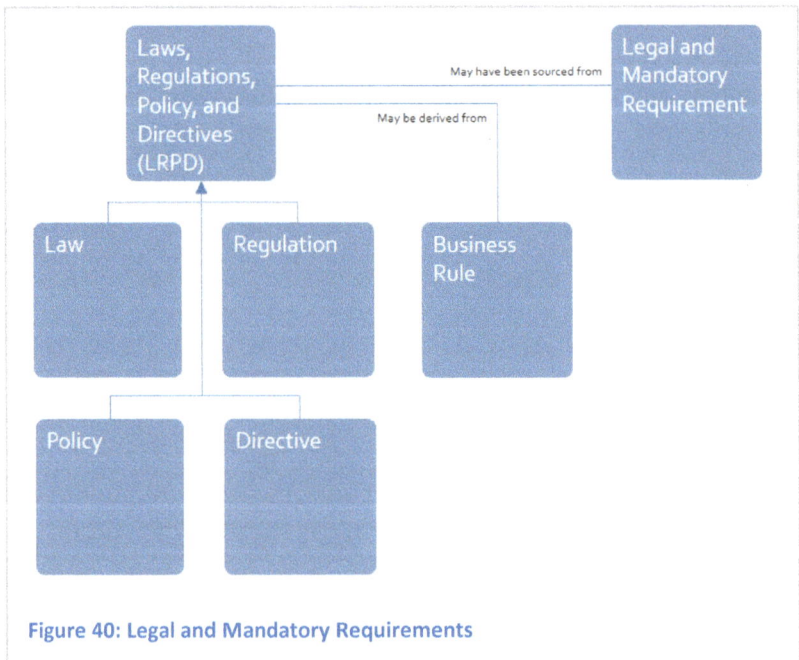

Figure 40: Legal and Mandatory Requirements

BUSINESS REQUIREMENTS

Business requirements are typically stated textually as large grained needs and then broken down into small grained statements of need. These are statements about what is needed in the Capabilities and the underlying Services that comprise each Capability. Business requirements also take the form of business scenarios which are descriptions about situations in the real world that the business must be capable of handling. Business scenarios have one or more triggering events and one or more possible outcomes. The triggers and outcomes ultimately manifest themselves visually in workflow models created using the Business Process Modeling Notation (BPMN). Said another way, a business scenario is a route through or mathematical subset of a workflow. In this respect, complex workflow models are viewed as an expression of requirements. They actually lean towards being a specification because they are prescribing how something should be done or how a scenario should unfold.

While the above-mentioned business scenarios can and should be found in the workflow models, it is better to start documenting them simply as an ordered pair of business events: a trigger and a preferred outcome. This can be done in matrix form where Business Events considered Triggers are the rows and the Business Events considered Outcomes are columns. An 'X' in any cell indicated that the trigger and outcome are paired. One can create a more elaborate data structure to representing what is in the cell. For instance, one might want to document the activity which is being triggered.

The scenarios alone, without all the sequencing found in the workflow model, are a better form of requirements because they are not prescriptive on how the scenario unfolds. The workflow models become prescriptive when one documents the tasks that get one from trigger to outcome and when one includes the logic associated with the execution or flow of those tasks.

To summarize, there are approximately four DODAF Operational Views that can be considered an expression of business requirements. The first is the Operational View number 2 (OV-2) which documents Information Exchange Requirements. The second model is a functional decomposition of operational activities, or OV-5a. This model is a statement of need in the form of an IDEF0 Activity Model. Each Activity in the model is an expression of what the business needs to do. The third is the Operational View (OV-6a) used for documenting Policies and Business Rules found in those Policies. The fourth is the workflow model or OV-6c.

INFORMATION EXCHANGE REQUIREMENTS

Implicit in the DODAF, Version 1.5 Operational View 2 (OV-2), is a method for modeling and documenting Information Exchange Requirements (IER's). As depicted in *Figure 41: Need for Information Exchange,* Operational Nodes and by extension businesses, government agencies, and organization within a business / agency are examples of the legal entities that exchange information. It follows then that they have Information Exchange Requirements (IERs).

Before modeling Information Exchange Requirements, one must first take a stab at Zoning the Business because it is in Zoning the Business that one identifies and creates many of the Operational Nodes that need to exchange information. Having said that, this method can be applied during the Zoning to provide some engineering detail including the Need Lines to

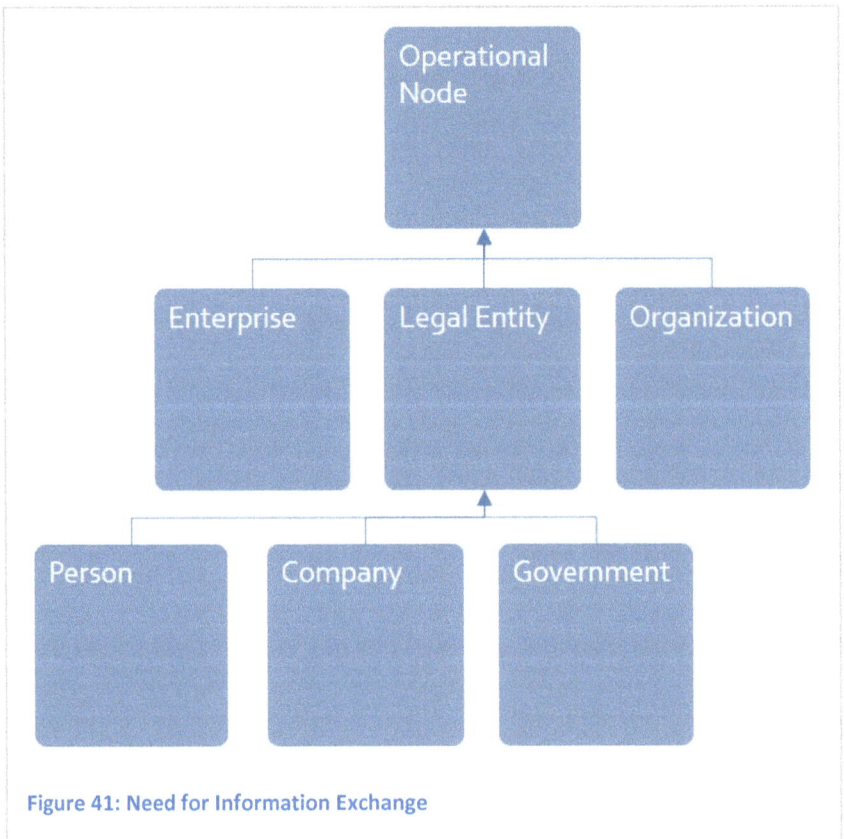

Figure 41: Need for Information Exchange

represent dependencies between the Operational Nodes. In any case, knowing the Operational Nodes is a pre-requisite.

To re-iterate, one does this form of Engineering at both the business and Capability levels: one does a bit of this engineering while Zoning the Business (while establishing a Planner's View of the Business) and then while Architecting a Capability (while establishing an Owner's View of the Capability). When one is doing this at the Capability Level, one should make sure that they are not contradicting something that was modeled at the corporate or business / enterprise level. As a matter of fact, the dependencies (Need Lines) and Information Exchange Requirements at these two levels should be aligned and complimentary. One way to do this is to stop at the Need Line level in the Planner's View and then get down to the Information Exchange Requirement level when one is architecting a capability.

To document these information exchange requirements with the DODAF version 1.5, one draws Operational Nodes which in the case of a business or government can represent organizational units. One then draws lines called *Need lines* connecting the Operational Nodes that need to exchange data. At this point one knows what operational nodes / organizational units are dependent on one another. Subsequently, one creates the list of *Information Exchange Requirements* associated with each need line. Please note that while the DODAF makes Need Lines directional, we do not. Need Lines are inherently bi-directional and it is the Information Exchange Requirements that have direction (are unidirectional). As an example, if there are two partners, A and B, then an IER expressed by partner A states that A needs something of B. On the same Need Line, partner B might have an Information Exchange Requirement on A.

To assure the quality of the Architecture and specifically to assure that Information Exchange Requirements are met, one creates and maintains a mapping of actual *Information Exchanges*[149] to the *Information Exchange Requirements.* There must be at least one Information Exchange that wholly satisfies each requirement, or there must be several that collectively satisfy an Information Exchange Requirement. Reports are run to identify Need Lines that do not have Information Exchange Requirements and Information Exchange Requirements that are not met.

Further down, in the workflow models, one also finds Messages and / or Data Objects attached to Business Events. Both need to be associated with Information Exchanges that are in turn associated with Information Exchange Requirements.

---

149 These Information Exchanges are found in the in the IDEF Activity Models which the DODAF refers to as the OV-5b.

ORGANIZATIONS

For modeling Organizations, we recommend using the method implicit in the UNICOM® System Architect® implementation of the DODAF OV-4. This method implements the very basics of an org chart where boxes represent Organizations and lines are either solid or dotted line reporting. Why make it any more complicated?

The value that the DODAF adds and the UNICOM® System Architect® supports, is the mapping of the Organizations to Operational Activities (things that the Organizations do). If you have Organizations in your org chart that are not mapped to Activities in your Activity Model (OV-5a), then you have a potential gap in your Activity Model, or you have organizations doing things that are not in the architecture. Conversely, if you have Activities in the Activity Model that aren't mapped to Organizations that perform the Activity, then you aren't doing things you said you were going to do.

As part of your Organization modeling effort, one can add and document Roles that each Organization should have in order to be successful. Bear in mind that the Roles are in turn related to Skills required for a Person to be successful in a Role. With both the Roles and Skills documented, the Architect can and should assess the current staff to identify gaps and then provide both Staffing and Training Plans.

Methodologically, we differentiate between certain logical and physical types of organizations. For example, a Legal Entity is a Person, a Company[150], or a Government. These are physical in nature. Things get more logical and less physical when one looks inside a Company or a Government and when modeling those parts of the organization structure we generally speak about organizational units. The organizational units of a company may include a division, a business line (Operating Unit), or a business area (Non-operating Unit). Within a Government one finds Bureaus, Sections, etc.

---

150 There are various types of companies: Corporations, Limited Liability Partnerships (LLP), Limited Liability Company's (LLC), etc.

As Legal Entities, Companies and Governments have a root organization which is then broken down into the above-mentioned organizational units.

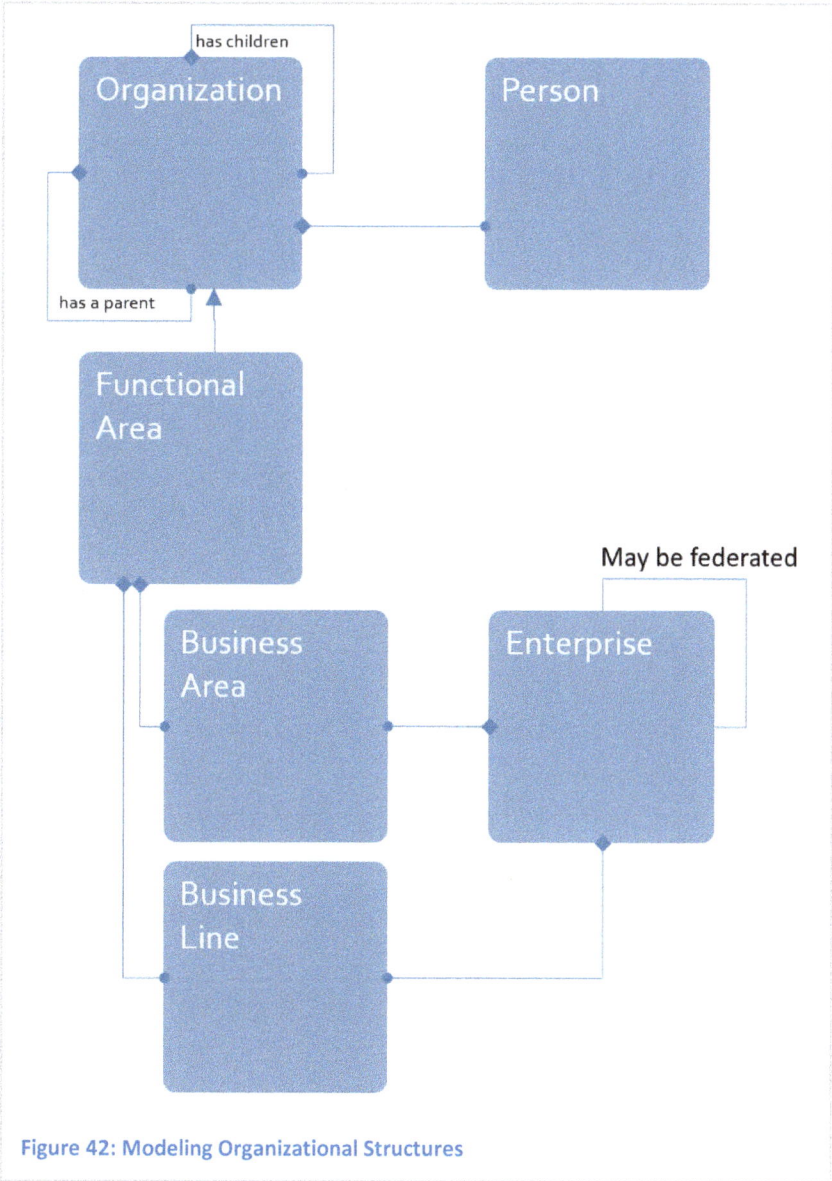

Figure 42: Modeling Organizational Structures

There is no legal substance to these organizational units. They are just logical groupings of Roles designed to realize a mission and deliver services. People are then assigned to the Roles in those organizational units.

Note that one should establish the Capability / Service taxonomy either as a pre-requisite or in parallel with the development of the Organizational Model. This is because at some point the Architect / Engineer must map Organizations to the Services they deliver or provision. A Capability / Service taxonomy should have been created in the Zoning of the Business where you broke the business down into Business Areas and Business Lines and then, for each Business Area / Line, documented the Capabilities of the Area / Line.

Having developed the Organization structure, check it against Best Practices and compare to your Competitors. Are your competitors doing more with less?

TRAINING

Curriculums are sets of courses designed to educate people in a particular discipline or practice. We believe that each Business Area and Line should have a Curriculum for educating people for that leg of the business.

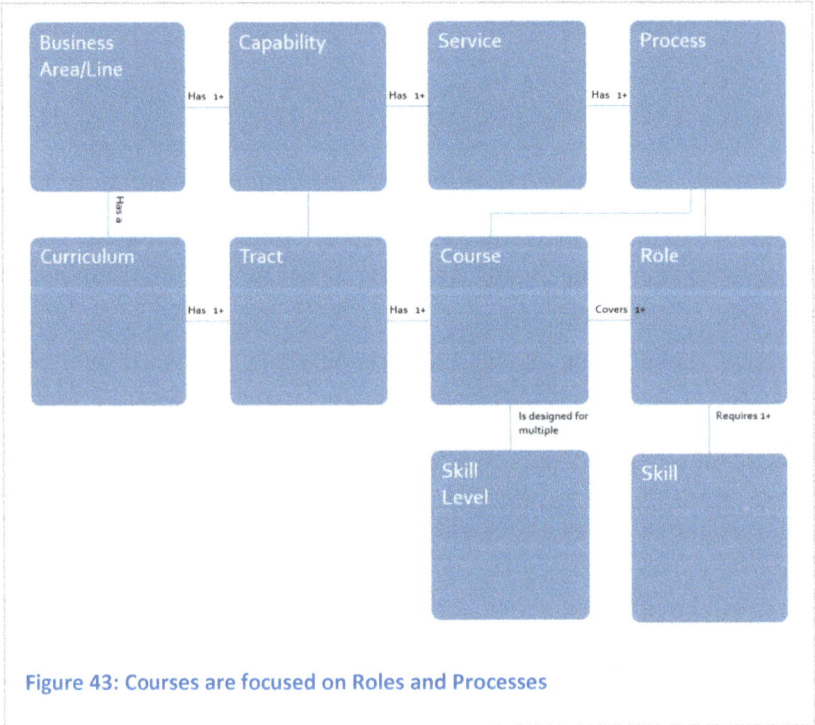

Figure 43: Courses are focused on Roles and Processes

Each of these Curriculums is comprised of Tracts that correspond to the Capabilities that comprise the Business Area / Line. Each Tract is, in turn, comprised of a set of Courses that provide training for people at the various skill levels. As depicted in *Figure 43: Courses are focused on Roles and Processes*, the Courses provide training for all associated Roles and all Skill Levels (Beginner, Novice, Intermediate, Advanced, Expert).

As depicted in *Figure 44: Curriculums, Tracts, and Courses*, the Courses are associated with a Process that comprise a Service, where the Service is germane to a Capability. For a company-wide view of the Courses, and Course coverage, one can maintain the list of all courses in the Performance Reference Model and then create a matrix where the columns are the Business Areas / Lines and the Rows are Services and the cells are the Courses are required. This sort of matrix can be created in a tool like UNICOM® System Architect®.

Most companies outsource training and leverage online training. Regardless, your Architecture should document Curriculums, Tracts, and Courses. The details for reach course may include the name and logistics of the company providing the course, whether it is on-line or not, a URL for

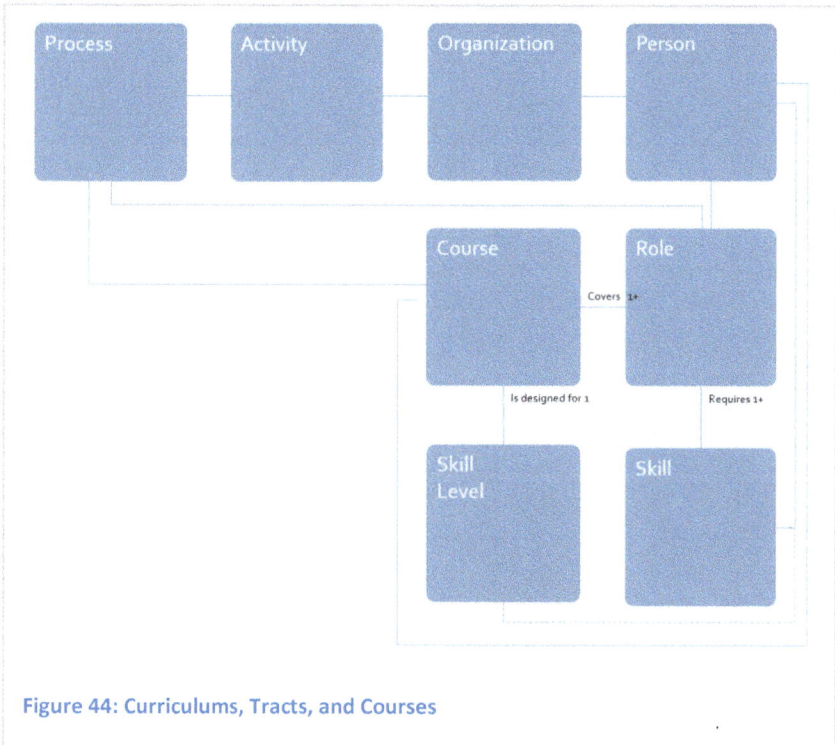

Figure 44: Curriculums, Tracts, and Courses

registering, etc.

While it isn't architecture, don't forget to monitor who is taking the courses and who has what skills. If your company / agency / business doesn't have a system for tracking who is signing up for courses and what skills people have, there is no reason why you can't place this sort of information in the Architecture Repository.

MATERIEL

Materiel is a word used primarily by military organizations in referring to the supplies and equipment used by an organization in order to conduct and execute its' mission. In the spirit of the DOTMLPF framework, we differentiate some physical infrastructure categorized under the heading Facilities and some found under the heading Materiel. Generally, facilities include the buildings, like office centers, retail space if applicable, data centers, and clouds. We also include physical infrastructure that is integral to the buildings, like and the electrical and network infrastructure. The Materiel sitting in the facilities includes physical infrastructure like printers, racks, uninterruptible power supplies, computers, specialized hardware systems and sub-systems. If the Materiel is an integral part of a facility then it is not considered separately and is just part of the facility.

For Architecture and Engineering purposes we consider Processes and tools that automate processes Materiel. We will cover the Processes now as part of a discussion about things that the business does.

MODELING WHAT THE BUSINESS DOES (WHAT YOU DO)

Generally speaking, Capabilities, Services, and Processes can all be considered tools and classified as Materiel. These are statements about what the business does. Modeling what the business does entail multiple

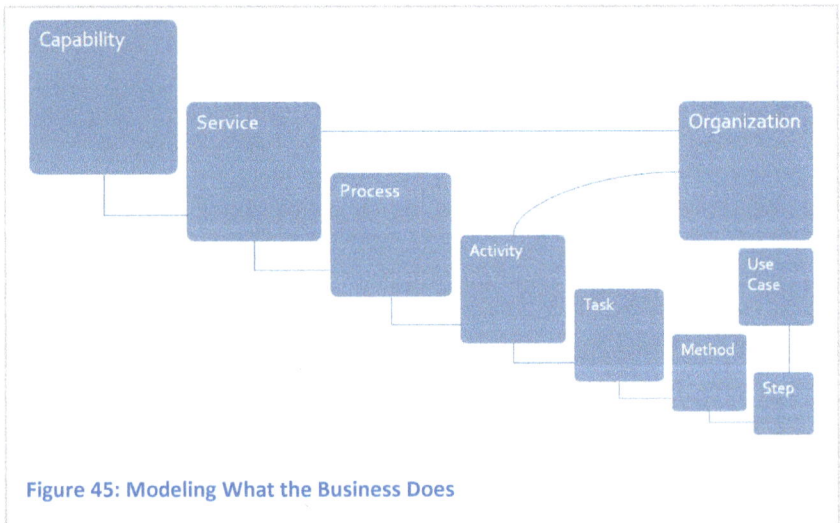

Figure 45: Modeling What the Business Does

building blocks and spans several methods. It starts with the creation of a Capability / Service Taxonomy and then continues with the creation of an IDEFo® based Process Taxonomy where processes are broken down into Activities and Activities into Task. The complete taxonomy is depicted in *Figure 45: Modeling What the Business Does*.

As stated by the owners of the IDEF®[151] modeling methods, the IDEFo® method is designed for modeling the Activities performed by an organization or system. IDEFo® enables the modeler to document what Activities are performed, decompose those activities into finer grained activities, and then document what is needed to perform those Activities. We do use IDEFo® but a variation of it. In IDEFo® one decomposes large grained activities into to smaller ones, and then decomposes those smaller Activities into yet smaller ones. In a traditional IDEFo® Activity Model, from the highest level of the model to the lowest level, it is Activities all the way down.

We do the same thing except we give the things at each level of decomposition a different name. We depict this in *Figure 45: Modeling What the Business Does*. As depicted, one decomposes Capabilities into Services. Then one documents and decomposes the Processes that are executed to automate the delivery of the Services. Those Processes are then broken down into Activities and Activities into Tasks. If needed, the final decomposition is of Tasks into Steps. Due to the many-to-many relationship between delivery Processes and Service being delivered, the Processes are related back to the Services through a matrix mapping.

Figure 45: Modeling What the Business Does also shows the relationship from Step to Use Case. While many people create Use Cases without documenting the Steps that comprise them, we do this to show the relationship and touch point between you IDEFo® Activity Models and your UML® based Software / System Models.

It is worth noting the two different relationships from Organization depicted in *Figure 45: Modeling What the Business Does*. Just as there is granularity in the building blocks that describe what you do, there is granularity in the organizations as well. You may find, and may want to establish a rule, that organizations at a certain level in the organization chart are assigned to deliver Services. For completeness, you need to assure that supporting Organizational Units are covering all the Activities that comprise the Processes which have been designed to deliver those

151 More information on IDEF® can be found at http://www.idef.com/idefo-function_modeling_method

Services. The relationships from Organization to Activity is achieved through a matrix. Obviously, you are looking for gaps: (A) Activities not performed by any Organizations, and Organizations that don't do anything (don't perform / are not mapped to an Activity).

There are two other models that fall under this heading but they are more focused on details that are required later and information flow. The models are what we call the Process Detail Diagram (OV-5b) and the Process Information Flow (OV-5c). For each Process in your Process Decomposition (OV-5a) you develop an OV-5b Diagram that documents the following:

1. Inputs in the form of Business Events that trigger the process along with an attached Data Object
2. Outputs which are also Business Events and may have Data Objects attached (Outcomes)
3. Policies that constrain or guide the execution of the Process
4. Applications / Systems that automate the Process. This can be done here or in your DODAF System View (SV-05) Diagram which is a matrix mapping of Processes / Activities to Systems that automate them
5. Roles required
6. Skills required
7. Courses required to mature the organization and to establish proficiency

This is all referred to as Process Detail, some of which is used later in the Workflow Modeling. After the process details are established one conducts an analysis of inputs (triggers) and outputs (outcomes). The analysis is focused on observing Process Outputs / Outcomes that are Inputs / Triggers to another Process. This analysis is done to create one or more Process Information Flow (OV-5c) Diagrams. The OV-5c Diagram makes this i/o and the connectivity explicit.

At this time one can and should map the *Information Exchanges* in the OV-5c Diagram to *Information Exchange Requirements* in the OV-2 Diagram. This is a quality assurance measure assuring that the Information Exchange Requirements have been addressed.

Note that all of the above-mentioned detail can be created in matrixes. For example, rather than creating graphical diagrams that show Skills attached to a Process, one can create a matrix of Skills to Processes that require them. Another example is a matrix of Roles to Processes they are associated with. With a matrix of this sort in place and a matrix mapping of Tasks to Roles that perform them, one can forgo swim lanes in the workflow models. This is extremely valuable because swim lanes can make for complex looking workflows. In these examples, the important thing is the data and the report that can be generated using that data.

MODELING WORKFLOWS (HOW YOU DO WHAT YOU DO)

We just finished talking about the Process Taxonomy and the parts of it as descriptions of what the business does, now we talk about how the business goes about executing the Processes. The Business Process Modeling Notation® is leveraged to model the flow of Tasks that comprise a Process. You may have noticed that we refer to this model as a workflow model. We do this to differentiate it from the process related models (OV-5a, b, and c Diagrams) that need to be developed before the workflow model is developed. These are, the Process Taxonomy (OV-5a), the Process Details Model (OV-5b), and the Process Information Flow (OV-5c). The Processes are first declared, defined, and broken down to the Task level and then a BPMN®-based workflow model is developed to document the sequence of the Tasks.

The BPMN®-based workflow models can be developed, one for each Process in your Process Taxonomy (OV-5a) or one for each Activity. In the latter case, the linkage between Activities is made explicit and apparent though Business Events as outcomes of one Activity that are triggers to another Activity. The drawback to working at the Activity level is the number of Activities and the number of workflow models. Working at the process level will result in fewer yet somewhat more complex workflow models.

The building blocks used to describe how a process is performed are depicted in *Figure 46: Elements of a Process Model or Workflow.* While we say that these are part of the workflow model, some originated in other models and are brought forward into the workflow model. They include; (A) the Data Objects which come from your OV-02 and then DIV-01 models, (B) Business Events as Triggers and Outcomes come from your Process Detail Models (OV-5b), (C) Tasks come from the Process Taxonomy (OV-5a), (D) Business Rules come from your Policy Models (OV-6a). In effect, all but the Sequence Flows, Gateways, and the Messages come from pre-requisite models.

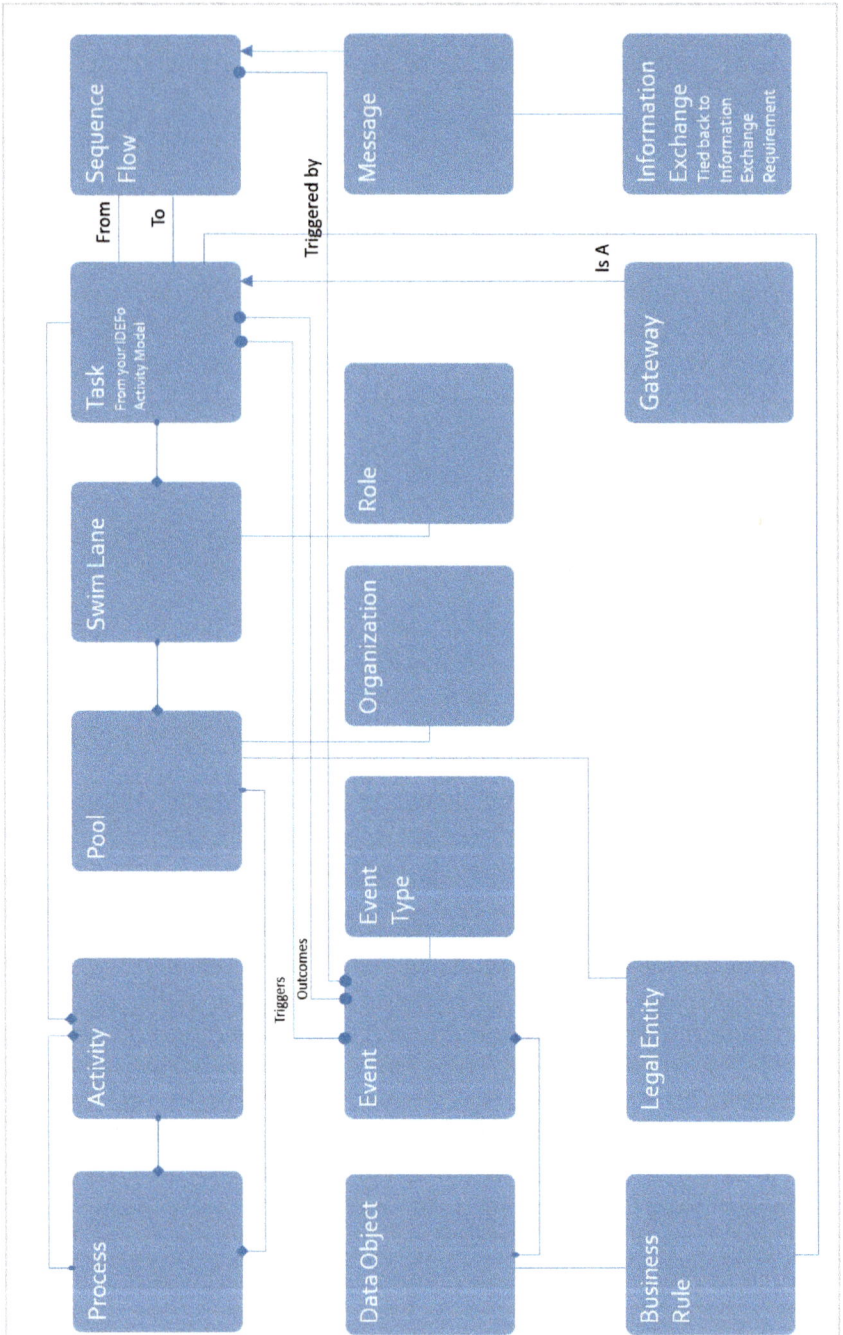

Figure 46: Elements of a Process Model or Workflow

MODELING DATA

We cover Data under the heading Materiel because your data is physical and a tool. Your Classes of Data, Entities, and Reports are also the jewels of your business; much more important than any System / Application. Whether you are modeling Data Objects in a workflow model, Classes of Data, or Entities, we are talking about tangible physical things that the business cannot operate without. With or without computers, businesses cannot operate without data.

There are three basic methods that one can use to model data, two of them being for Relational Data Modeling and one for Class or Object Modeling:

- o   IDEF1X® for Entity Relationship / Data Modeling
- o   ER – Entity Relationship Modeling
- o   The Unified Modeling Language® (UML®) for Object Modeling

For the most part, the two Entity Relationship Modeling methods vary in syntax only and given that tools are able to convert models from one type to the other, we cover only one method: IDEF1X®.

While we are covering IDEF1X®, we are not covering relational data modeling in depth as there are many books on this topic and relational data modeling happens to be one of the most mature[152] of the engineering disciplines. Additionally, there is detail that goes into complete entity relationship models that is of no concern at a corporate or agency level. As a matter of fact, much of that detail is germane to the Engineer and can remain in the engineering tools. That is, relational meta-data like keys, indexes, tables, and columns need not go in the Architecture Repository. And class meta-data like methods, method parameters, return values, etc. can stay in the engineering tool. Having stated the exclusions, it is important to note that Application Programming Interfaces (APIs) should be documented in the architecture and then pushed into an API Gateway[153] for day to day use. Similarly, XML

---

152 Having said that data modeling is a mature form of engineering does not guarantee success. In particular because data modelers and organizations in general tend to use different tools for modeling data than they use for modeling other aspects of a Capability. This leads to a loss in Referential Integrity and Trace-ability. Even if modelers are using the same tools, getting them to collaborate and getting them to establish proper trace-ability is always a challenge. Ergo the need for quality assurance and Independent Verification and Validation (IV&V)

153 For a description of an API Gateway, see this Wikipedia article on API Management: https://en.wikipedia.org/wiki/API_management

Schemas should be brought into the general-purpose architecture tool and the Architecture Repository.

The building blocks for both Object and Relational Data Modeling are depicted in *Figure 47: Elements for Modeling Data*. Note that a potential set of relationships between Class and Entity is excluded. Given the advent and maturity of Business Object Containers and the mapping of Object to Relational, this is a set of relationships that we don't cover here.

Also note the analogs in the Object and Relational worlds. In the far left of *Figure 47: Elements for Modeling Data* you see that Package in the Object world is analogous to Subject Area in the relational word. Continuing to the right of the figure, Class is analogous to Entity. And Class Properties are analogous to Entity Attributes.

Make special note of "Data Element" in this figure, where the two worlds come together. The Data Element is a powerful building block brought to market by the makers of System Architect®. Data Elements are reusable specifications of common bits of data. For example, one can define a Data Element called "Social Security Number". The engineer then uses the modeling tool to assign that Data Element to Classes and / or Entities that need it. Once assigned it becomes a named Attribute or Property of the Entity or Class. This enables the engineer to document details about social security number once, including meta-data stating that Social Security Number must be encrypted regardless of which Class or Entity houses a social security number. With Data Elements and the assignment of them to Classes and Entities, the architect is able to ask the architecture, "Where, throughout the business, do we store Social Security Number?".

The intention of Data Elements is the get the architects above the programming and language level. The architects should not be speaking about Booleans or VARCHAR, and BLOB or CLOB. Business people don't care about that form of specification.

In addition to creating Data Elements, one creates Data Domains to categorize them. In the example of social security number one creates a Data Domain called Personal Identifiable Information (PII) and then documents the Data Elements that comprise the domain:

- o Social Security Number
- o First Name
- o Middle Name (same as first)
- o Etc.

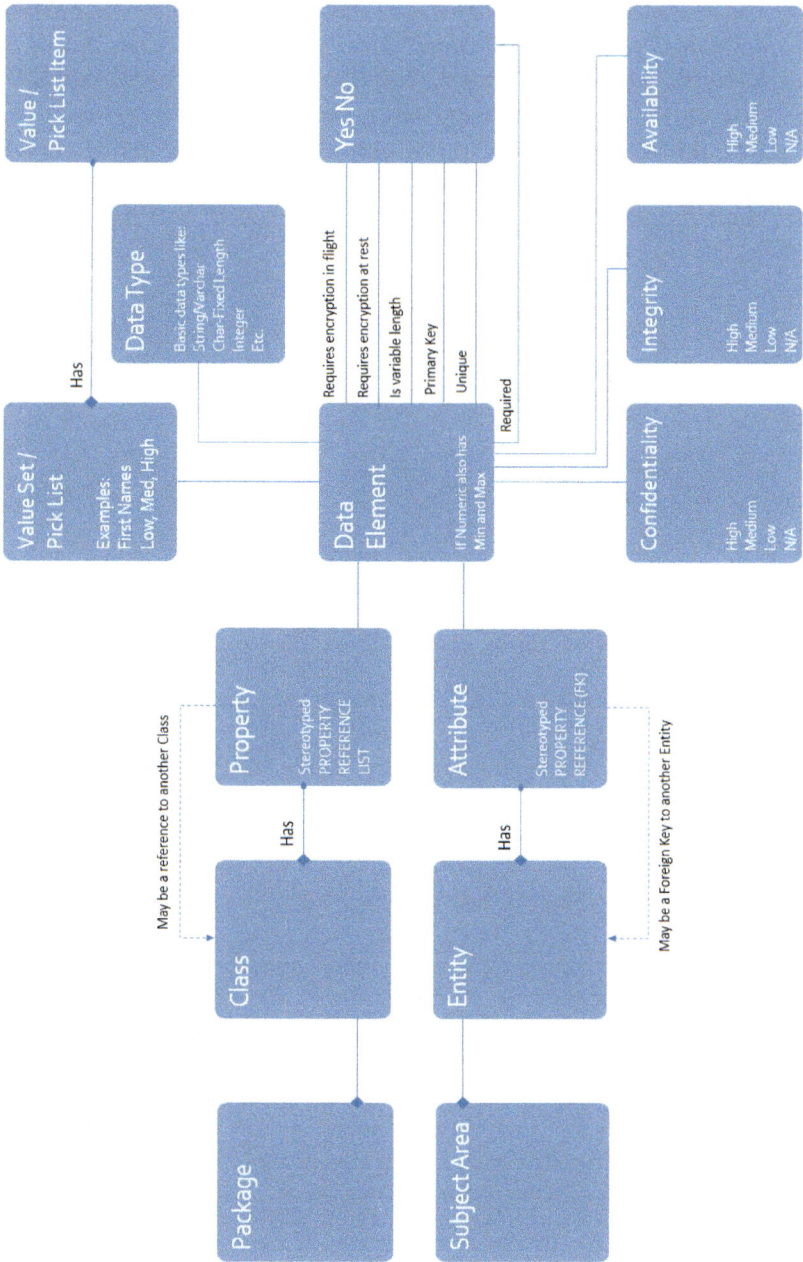

Figure 47: Elements for Modeling Data

OBJECT MODELING

The Unified Modeling Language® enables one to model both data (Objects) and function[154] in one fell swoop. This is referred to as Class or Object Modeling where Class is meant to mean Class of Object or Class of Data. Given the state of technology today, and while we cover the use of IDEF1X® for relational data modeling, we recommend Class / Object Modeling over any form of relational data modeling. This is because the Object to Relational Mappings that have been establish are very sound and the modern

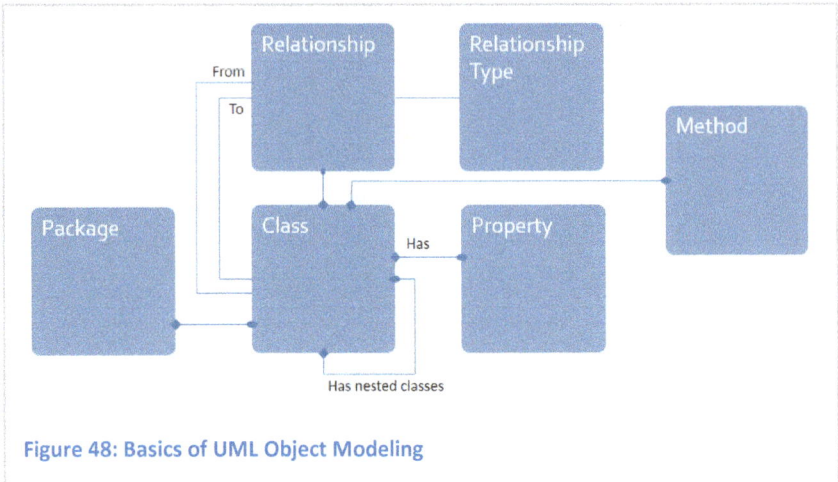

Figure 48: Basics of UML Object Modeling

middleware is able to generate the corresponding relational database structure from the Object Models. This is the case with both J2EE and Microsoft dot Net specifications and the platforms that implement those specifications. There are also some very important features of, and advantages to, Object Modeling which include:

- o A more powerful form of Inheritance (specialization / generalization) relationship
- o Nested Classes
- o Boundary Objects
- o Encapsulation of data and function / methods

In addition to the abovementioned advantages, the UML Class / Object Modeling allows for more concise models.

---

154 Functions are sometimes referred to as methods, not to be confused with Method or Methodology.

Entity Relationship Modeling

IDEF1X® is a method for designing relational database structures or schemas. A schema is a single integrated definition of data in that is not biased toward any single system or application that will use the data. The constituent parts of an IDEF1X® model include, but are not limited to, Entities, Relationships between Entities, Attributes of the Entities, and details about each Attribute like length and data type.

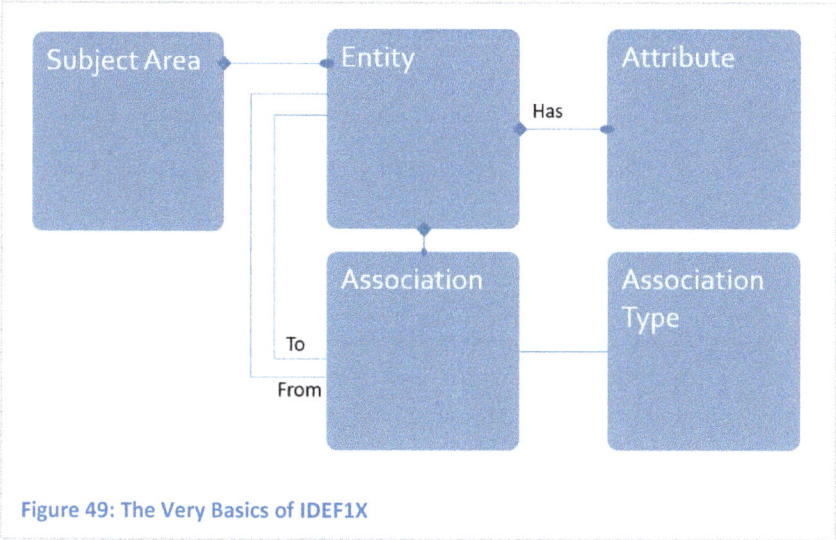

Figure 49: The Very Basics of IDEF1X

Without getting into the details of relational data model, we describe this using an example. The example considered is the modeling of "Person" data. In our example, "Person" is said to be an Entity in the model where Person has "First name" and "Last name" as Attributes. The IDEF1X® based entity relationship model is then used to create tables with columns in a relational databased so that, in this example, a list of people can be maintained.

IDEF1X® may be used at the corporate or enterprise level to document company-wide common data for subject areas like "Legal Entities" which includes public and private companies / corporations, people, and governmental bodies.

MODELING CUSTOM SOFTWARE / APPLICATIONS

UNIFIED MODELING LANGUAGE® FOR MODELING SOFTWARE SYSTEMS

The Unified Modeling Language® is a general-purpose modeling language used in the field of software engineering. UML® provides a standard way to visualize the design of a System / Application. The creation of UML® was originally motivated by the desire to standardize the disparate notational systems and approaches to software design.

In 1997 UML® was adopted as a standard by the Object Management Group®) and has been managed by this organization since that time. In 2005 UML® was also published by the International Organization for Standardization (ISO) as an approved ISO standard.

The UML® is leveraged for software design to include the modeling of data. It is designed to get one from concept to deployment through the following set of artifacts:

- Use Case Diagrams that describe what the Application / System shall do (Specifications)
- Class Diagrams that describe the classes of data and, components of the Application / System as objects
- Package Diagrams that depict the software Packages comprising the system and the relationships between those packages. Package Diagrams enable one to provide a top-down view of the software design
- Object Diagrams that enable the engineers to create examples of things modeled in the Class Diagrams.
- Sequence Diagrams that describe the conversations between the piece parts of an Application / System
- State Diagrams that describe the various Status States that an instance of a Class might be in and the valid Status State Transitions
- Component Diagrams depicting the physical and deployable constructs (Components) of a software design and what interfaces exist between them.
- Deployment Models that describe how the Application / System is to be packaged and deployed

UML® Version 2 includes a diagram for modeling Activities but given our use and coverage of IDEF0®, Activity Modeling in UML® would duplicate what is done with IDEF0 in the related DODAF Diagrams.

TRADITIONAL APPLICATIONS MODELING

Traditionally, Applications were monolithic in that the Application handled the interaction with the user, contained embedded business logic, and handled the storage of data all in one program. At the time, Applications were generally said to have Modules and / or Components. While the Applications were monolithic, they always had the basic concept of a Presentation Layer, Business Logic Layer, and Data Layer. This was even true in the days of 3270-based Mainframe Applications / Systems. These were referred to as 3-Tier systems and the concept became more formal and evident with the advent of what the industry called the "Model View

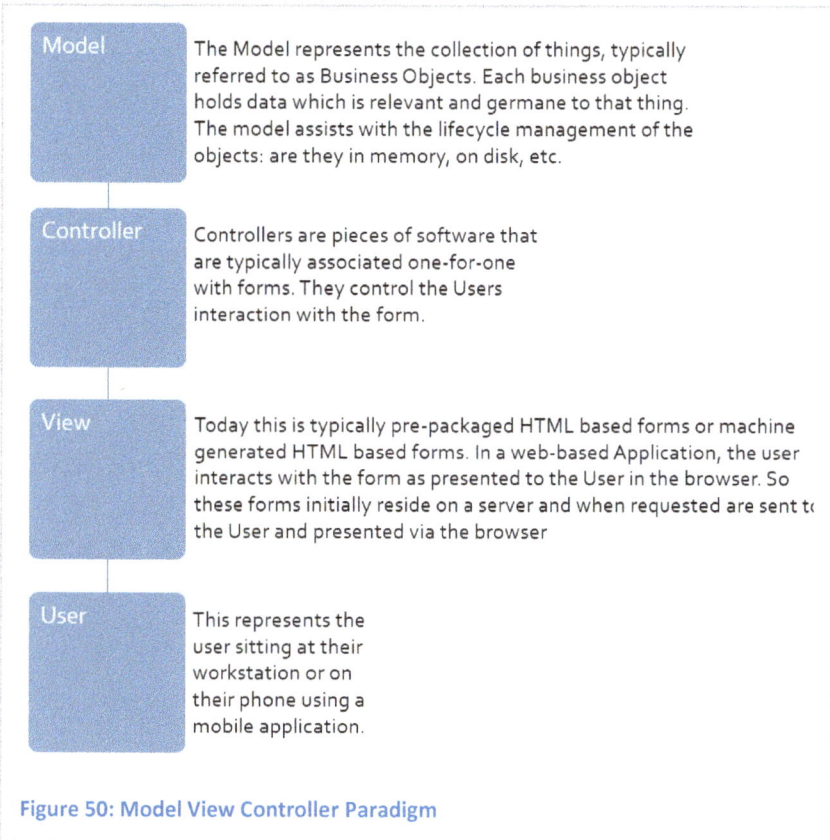

Model
The Model represents the collection of things, typically referred to as Business Objects. Each business object holds data which is relevant and germane to that thing. The model assists with the lifecycle management of the objects: are they in memory, on disk, etc.

Controller
Controllers are pieces of software that are typically associated one-for-one with forms. They control the Users interaction with the form.

View
Today this is typically pre-packaged HTML based forms or machine generated HTML based forms. In a web-based Application, the user interacts with the form as presented to the User in the browser. So these forms initially reside on a server and when requested are sent to the User and presented via the browser

User
This represents the user sitting at their workstation or on their phone using a mobile application.

Figure 50: Model View Controller Paradigm

Controller (MVC)" paradigm depicted in *Figure 50: Model View Controller Paradigm*.

While the Model View Controller paradigm persisted, and is widely used today, the number of Tiers increased and the Applications / Systems are said to be n-Tiered. Additional Tiers like a "Business Rules" Tier were added.

These concepts are all prevalent today in Web and Phone based Applications where Forms are packaged using HTML / XHTML, etc., where there are objects or components that control the interaction with the user at the browser or phone app, and in memory business objects whose lifecycle is managed on behalf of the Application / System. Distributed computing and pervasive networks also added value and some complexity by enabling engineers to spread these layers across Servers and Clusters of Servers.

The model depicted in *Figure 51: Applications/Modules and Application Instances* shows the building blocks comprising an Application. Note that the figure depicts both, the information that engineers need to have in the Architecture Repository, and the related information that IT operations needs in the IT Configuration Management Database (CMDB).

Having mentioned both the Architecture Repository and Configuration Management Database, this is a good time to dispel a misconception. Some have asserted the Architecture is a subset of the ITIL/CMDB. We respectfully disagree and view the CMDB being the IT portion of the Architecture that is needed for day to day operations of the IT environment. This is changing a little as industry segues from the concept of Information Technology Information Library (ITIL) ® to the concept of Service Management where the primary focus is still IT but emphasizes the use of Software as a Service. With this emphasis there is more discussion around services.

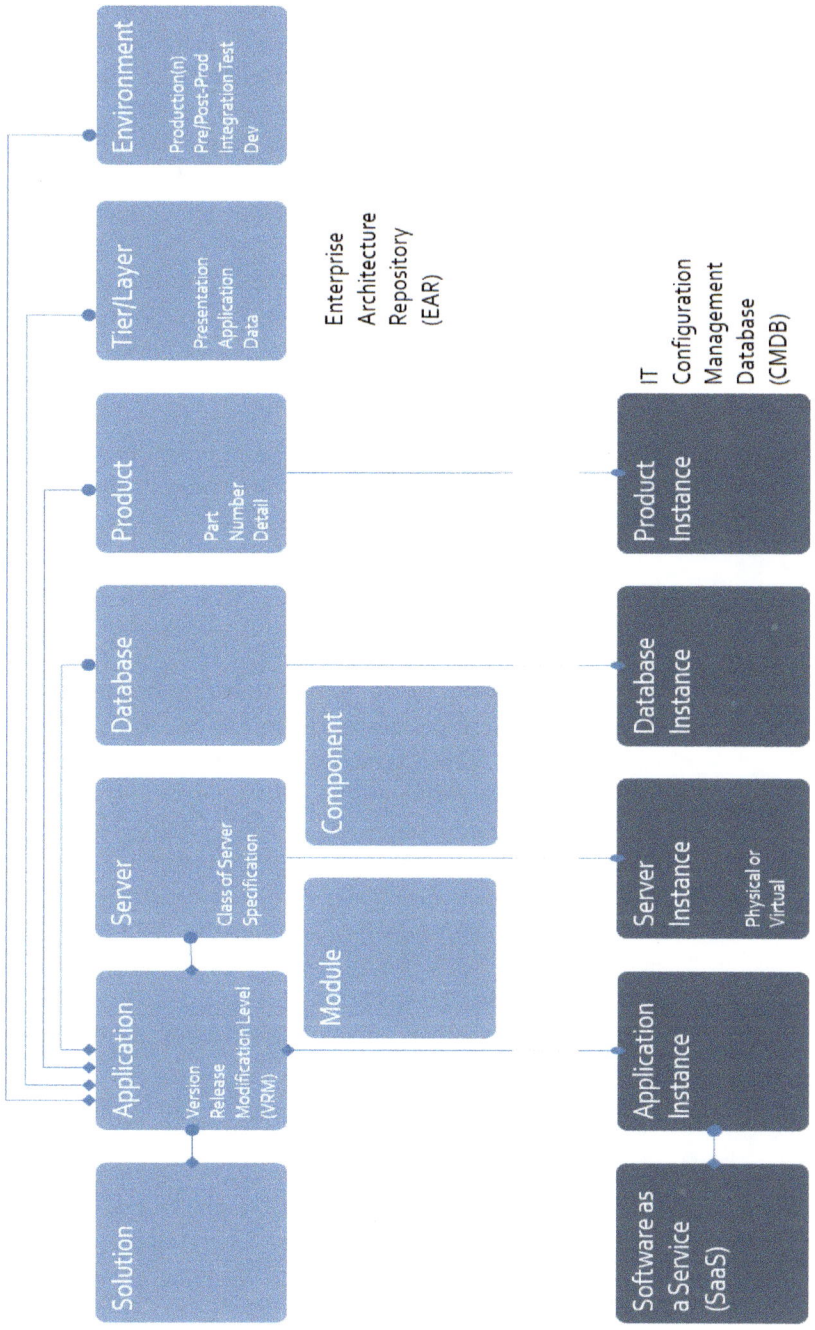

Figure 51: Applications/Modules and Application Instances

Here is a partial list of some of the things Engineers need to document about the Application:

1. **Business Solution** that the Application may be supporting or a part of. Map the Application to Business Solutions. This enables some level of Application portfolio management where the Business Solution is viewed by IT as an IT portfolio. This is a form of Zoning where the solution areas may be synonymous with the Business Areas and Lines.

2. **Classes of Servers that are required** – these are Server specifications for sizing and estimating purposes. They are also used by the operations team when to build out the Server Instances. In addition to documenting the classes of servers, the engineers document how many instances are required and where they need to be located. This is done whether one has a dedicated data center or using a Cloud Service Provider.

3. **Databases** that the Application / System either owns or uses. The engineers should maintain an inventory of databases, a mapping of databases to applications, and a Create, Read, Update, Delete (CRUD) matrix of Databases and Entities. **Create a Data Model** for each Database owned by the Application / System

4. **Products** with part number detail. These are the hardware and software products that are being used to develop, test, and run the Application. This is the equivalent of a Window and Door Schedule in building architecture, part number detail and cost information are both required. Be sure to know, by part number, what you have and what the associated costs are.

5. **Tiers / Layers** that comprise the Application is required. Document the tiers and the security enclave that each tier resides in.

6. **List of the Environments** that the Application needs with an emphasis on multiple Production environments if the Application has multiple.

7. **List the hosting Facilities** for the Application / System Instances where Clouds are considered Facilities that host Applications / Systems. It is inappropriate to just say, "my application is in the Cloud". It is best to be specific and say which Cloud because there are many cloud service providers and many clouds.

The engineering necessarily includes information required for Application Portfolio Management, details required by operations, and information needed later for capacity planning. Some of the basics are:

1. Name
2. Acronym
3. Business Description
4. Business Owner, this is a person so don't write "Many" or "Various", put the name of a person.
5. Owning Organization (can default to Organization that the Business Owner is a member of)
6. IT Owner (Person)
7. Subject Matter Expert (SME) (Person)
8. Developed By (Legal Entity) – this applies if the application is a Commercial-off-the-shelf or Government-off-the-shelf Application. Otherwise record the Organization within the Business that developed the Application
9. Is failover available (YESNO)?
10. Is the Application Mobile Accessible (YESNO)?
11. List of Reference Documentation (may be URLs)
12. Disaster Recovery Plan (Attachment)
13. System Security Plan (Attachment)
14. Internal, Public Facing, or both – derived from count of internal users and count of external users
15. Count of Internal Users (at inception and then to date)
16. Count of External Users (at inception and then to date)
17. List of Organizations that are using the Application (combined list of internal Organizations and external Legal Entities)
18. COTS / GOTS / Custom Indicator
19. List of Interfaces (other Applications / Systems that the Application / System interoperates with)
20. List of Application Programming Interfaces (APIs) published and available
21. List of Releases (Versions, Releases, Modification Levels)

Certain reports that Owners need rely on the relationship from Application to Database and the detail about the Data Elements that reside in the Database. Examples include:

1. Does the Application deal with Payment Card Information (PCI)?
2. Does the Application deal with Protected Health Information (PHI)?
3. Does the Application deal with Personally Identifiable Information (PII)?
4. What are the levels of data Confidentiality, Integrity, and Availability (CIA)?

Many people seem to misinterpret the guidance on Confidentiality, Integrity, and Availability. They seem view these as attributes of an Application / System whereas they are attributes of Data Elements. The CIA for an Application / System is derived then, from the data that the Application / System accesses and provides access to:

o   The CIA of Entity is the Max(C), Max(I), and Max(A) of all Data Elements / Attributes in the Entity,
o   The CIA of a Database is the Max(C), Max(I), and Max(A) of all Entities in the Database and the
o   The CIA of an Application / System is the Max(C), Max(I), and Max(A) of all Databases that it accesses.

Keep in mind that a certain amount of Application / System information needs to be gathered even for purchased Applications / Systems. Whether you purchased the Application / System and installed it in your own data center or are using the Application / System as a Service (SaaS), the business needs to know the basics of their Architecture and they need to verify from a legal point of view that the provider has designs / blueprints. The blueprints should actually reside in escrow.

MODELING SYSTEMS

It is rare today that systems are purely physical. Physical systems, like cars, are typically a combination of hardware and software. Included here are, (A) Systems that combine hardware and software, (B) Systems of Systems as defined by the IEEE, and (C) physical assets like Trucks and the Fleets that the Trucks comprise. In the Military world then, system includes aircraft, tanks, ships, etc. and things like mobile data centers.

The things that Accountants consider fixed assets[155] are split across two DOTMLPF categories: Materiel and Facilities. It isn't a hard and fast rule but, the authors placed things like Networks and Clouds, in the Facilities category. This in spite of the fact that they are descendants of System of Systems, which is in the Materiel category.

Throughout this discussion on methods, and generally in our approach to defining the building blocks of a business, we have stayed away from abstractions. We made a conscious effort to define building blocks that are intuitive and real to people. This discussion about physical systems is a departure because there are just too many types of physical system to deal

---

155 A description of fixed assets can be found at
   https://en.wikipedia.org/wiki/Fixed_asset

with. Our abstractions then are depicted in *Figure 52: Elements for Modeling Systems*. It is up to the Engineers to create types or stereotypes and make it clear through the stereotypes as to what the System or Sub-system is. The three exceptions to this rule are Facility, Network, and Cloud which we elaborate on in the section *Facilities and Clouds*. Given their potential complexity and the need to be explicit, Facilities, Networks, and Cloud are descendants of System of Systems.

Not only is there a high degree of abstraction in this systems model, there is a high degree of recursion. That is, Systems may contain other Systems and because Sub-system is a descendant of System it inherits the ability to contain Systems. Similarly, both may contain System Components.

Note the ability to relate one or more Applications with a System and through inheritance with a Sub-system. This accommodates the ability to model physical Systems that have Applications, or generally speaking software, associated with them.

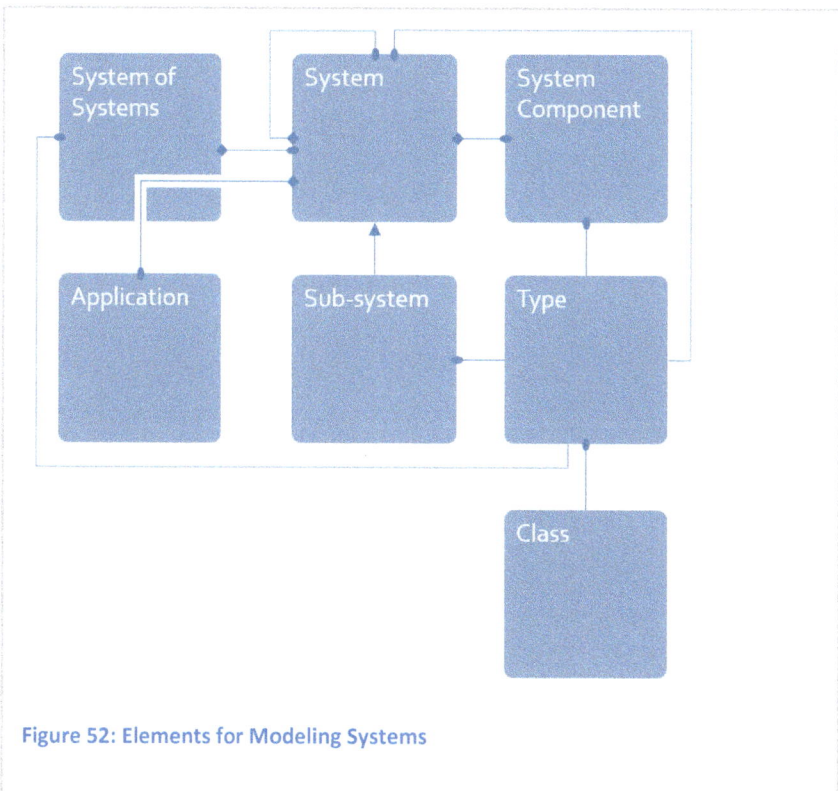

Figure 52: Elements for Modeling Systems

LEADERSHIP

It might seem odd that Leadership is engineered but it doesn't hurt to have engineers involved as they can assure that executive vision is well-documented and that the Strategic Plans, Visions, Goals, Objectives, and performance expectations are documented in perpetuity. Strategic Plan and its' related building blocks are not the only ones that fall under this category though. Leadership includes the establishment of and documentation for all Business Models in play. We cover each of these here in this section starting with Strategic Plans.

MODELING STRATEGIC PLANS

Engineers assure that leadership related building blocks are sound, not just for the current leadership team but the ones that follow as well. In the case where the business is a government, the Architecture and embedded Strategic Plans are handed off from administration to administration. In the case of a company, the Architecture and Plans are handed off from one leadership team to the next and, perhaps, the Board of Directors wants to know that there is continuity.

This "handoff" is an important point, especially for those practicing in the government space. Contracts change fairly often and it is important to be able to pick up where the incumbent left off. Many times, this isn't possible because the architecture is in poor condition and lacks quality.

As depicted in *Figure 53: Leadership includes Goals and Objectives,* the baton being handed off includes the building blocks shown and modeling / documenting Strategic Plans necessitates:

- Strategic Plan itself as a first order business object
- Documenting the time period that each Strategic Plan covers: "from" and "to" Fiscal Years
- The creation of Goals for each Organization in the Business. We advise the establishment of Goals down to the Service Provider level in your Organization, so this includes Business Areas / Lines, Organizations that own Capabilities, and then the sub-Organizations that own the Services that comprise each Capability. These Service providers should have Goals. It is below this level in the organization structure that one focuses on concrete and actionable Objectives that comprise the Goals.
- An effort must be made to assure semantic alignment of the Goals in the organizational hierarchy

- The Creation of a Strategy for each Goal. The Strategy describes the approach to be taken and how you will achieve the Goal.
- For each Objective, document target performance improvements. Each of these is a Key Performance Indicator (KPI).
- Document the Initiatives to be launched and Investments to be made at the Goal Level. Document the Programs within the Initiatives that are required to realize Objectives and assure that each Objective has an owner across these Programs
- Document the Projects within the Programs that will be responsible for working on the specific performance improvements. Be agile on this front by using your process taxonomy as a means of breaking work down into Sprints and User Stories. This form of agility applies whether one is building software or purchasing Commercial-off-the-shelf (COTS) systems.

Also, under the heading Leadership we find the following building blocks:

- Merger, Acquisition, Divestiture where leadership on both sides of these transactions assures that an Architecture is in place and having the Architecture facilitates a timely transaction. Once a merger or acquisition has taken place, the architecture is used to integrate the two businesses (if that is the plan).
- Assessments, like Competitor, Management, SWOT, and PEST Assessments, all fall under this heading. The leadership team leverages these to adjust the Architecture and to make decisions to merge, acquire, and divest.
- Issues, Weaknesses, Gaps, Findings, Recommendations, etc. The Owners and Architects make investment recommendations to eliminate things like Gaps. Good leaders are not afraid of issues, they acknowledge them and tackle them head, and they place the issues in the architecture.
- Principles which the leadership team adheres to and supports. Along the same lines, good Leadership encourages Questions, documenting Answers, Reasons, Rationale, etc.
- Best Practices and Maturity Models as best practices. A good leadership team monitors maturity. They don't ask for a Maturity Model to be established and then ignore it. A good Leadership team considers Architecture itself as a Best Practice and they have a related Principle that states "Architect First"

While Directives and Policies are included under the heading Doctrine, they are a matter of leadership as well. Good Leadership assures that Laws and Regulations are documented and enforced.

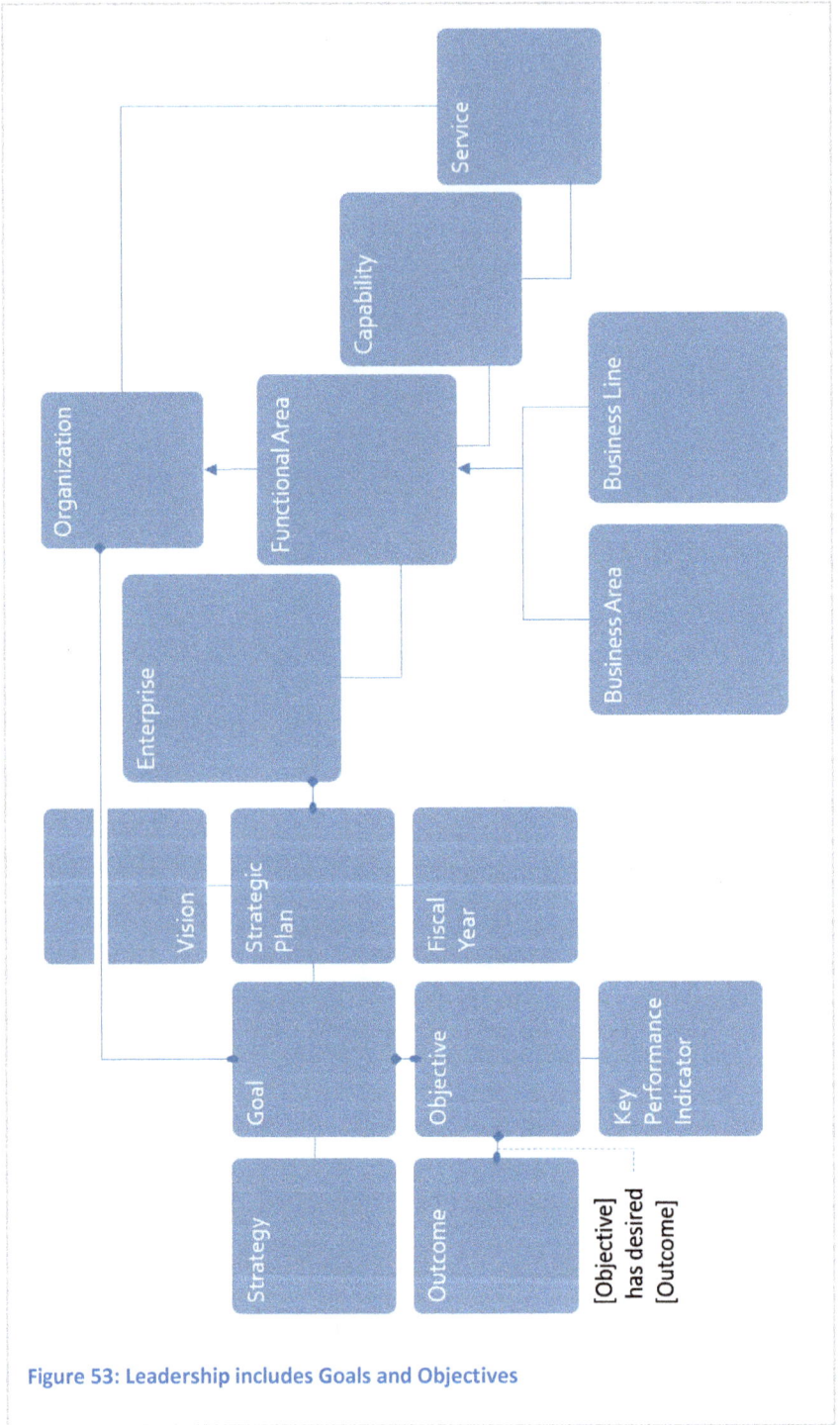

Figure 53: Leadership includes Goals and Objectives

Thankfully, there is a book that presents a Method for documenting and modeling Business or Operating Models. To our liking, the book starts with a definition. According the book, *"Business Model Generation"*[156], *a Business Model describes the rationale behind how an organization creates, delivers, and captures value.* Given our discussion about the structure of a business, this particularly relevant to Business Lines because they are customer facing, they deal with different customer segments each having different wants and needs. The Business Lines are responsible for profit and loss which is a form of value generation. Each Business Line then, may have a distinct Business Model, multiple Lines may share a Business Model, and if a Line is large enough and very diverse, it may have multiple Business Models.

In *Figure 54: The piece parts of a Business Model* we've broken the Rule of Three[157] but we get the conversation going with this view of some of the building blocks of a Business Model. The primary piece parts are those directly related to Business Model as depicted in the upper left-hand corner of *Figure 54: The piece parts of a Business Model*. They include:

- The Communities being served
- The business Activities required to address the needs of the Communities
- Channels that are employed to get your product / service to market. The Worldwide Web is an example of a Channel
- Partnerships that are required
- Contracts that are needed (sometimes these are exclusive)

Note that some of the building blocks are not directly related to the Business Model as they are contextual. For example, the below list of building blocks exists in the context of the relationship to a Community being served:

- Products and Services / Programs that are offered to address Community needs
- Value Propositions for each Product / Service being offered
- Industry / market gaps that are filled
- Vision
- Cost

---

156 Business Model Generation, by Alexander Osterwalder and Yves Pigneur 2010
157 The Rule of Three is a writing principle suggesting that a trio of events or characters is more effective than other numbers

Also note that there are other related building blocks that are key to a holistic Architecture:

- Processes that the Activities comprise
- Organizations that are in involved in the delivery of Product and / or Services
- Roles
- Skills
- Training Courses
- Etc.

While it is not Architecture per se, we acknowledge authors Osterwalder and Pigneur for their use of the term Customer Relationship and we've depicted such an artifact in *Figure 54: The piece parts of a Business Model*. Customer Relationships are managed once the Business Model has been established and Products / Services have been entered into the Market. They are typically managed in a Customer Relationship Management (CRM) System. From an Architecture point of view, we see Opportunity as the means of modeling and describing Customer Relationships and also Revenue Streams which are both part of what Osterwalder and Pigneur call "*The Business Model Canvas*". *We view* their *Business Model Canvas* is equivalent of our Drawings / Diagrams / Models.

Customer relationships and feedback are key then for documenting changes to the architecture that might be needed.

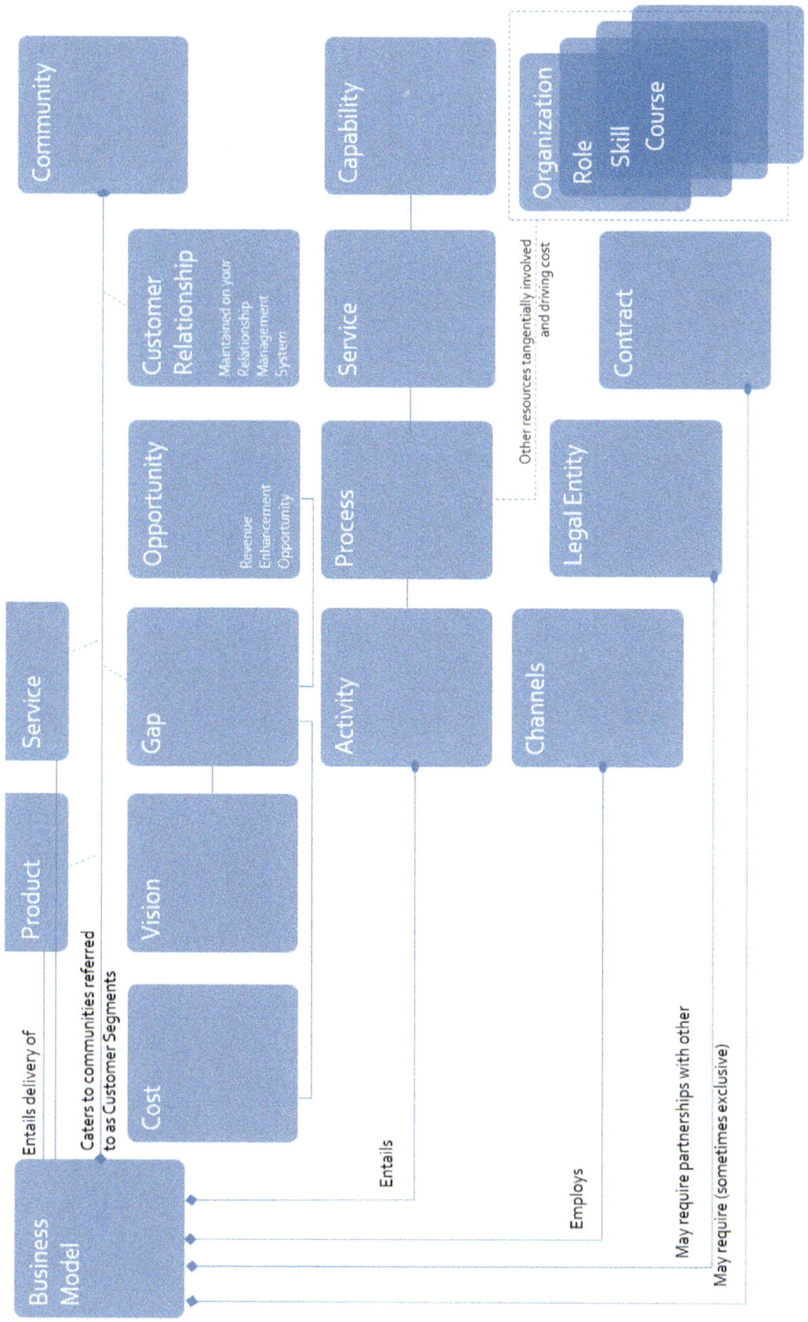

Figure 54: The piece parts of a Business Model

PERSONNEL

Personnel is not modeled, but person information is certainly foundational and staffing plans are key to a successful architecture. Having said that, included under this section of the DOTMLPF framework is a focus on Skills, Skills assessments, and then Staffing Plans by Roles. This is done in conjunction with models created under the headings Organization, Training, and Materiel as those sections of the framework include Organizations that comprise the business, Courses that are designed for people filling a particular Role, and which Organizations are performing the Activities.

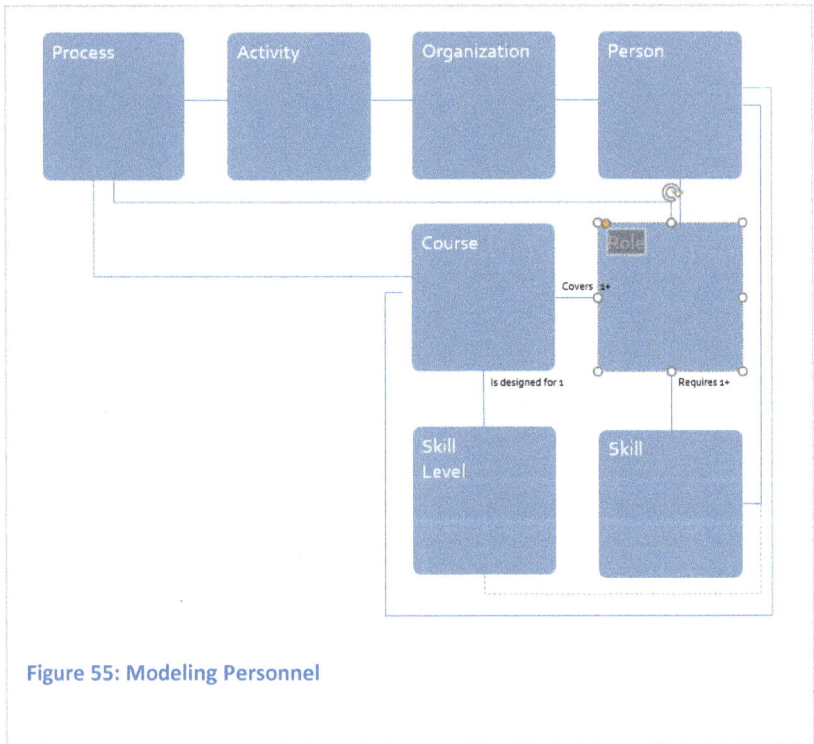

Figure 55: Modeling Personnel

Back to Personnel, one documents Skills required for all the Roles that comprise your Business Processes and then documenting the skills of the people in the organization to determine the gap / fit. With a Browser-based Architecture Repository in place it is easy for the business to conduct Skills surveys and pull that information directly into the Architecture.

Skill Levels are required here and in the Training section of the DOTMLPF framework because one needs to know that they can train people at all levels including the expert level.

Given that one now has a sense of the staffing gap / fit, one documents staffing plans by Role to show when needed Roles and Skills are acquired and when gaps are closed. Documenting staffing plans by Role means that one has a matrix in the Architecture where the Roles are rows in the matrix, key Milestones are columns, and the cells document the number of people required in that Role by that Milestone. To facilitate this and to avoid duplicating data, the Architecture needs to be integrated with the directory that the business has for person and organization data.

FACILITIES AND CLOUDS

Generally, this category in the DOTMLPF framework includes physical assets like data centers, offices, manufacturing facilities, retail centers, distribution centers, etc. It also includes things like HVAC[158] systems, Power Systems, Satellites, Networks, and other Infrastructure like Cloud Computing Infrastructure. Not that all of these things, and in particular buildings, need to be modeled, but they do need to be documented. They need to be documented so that one has a complete understanding of Cost and they need to be documented in support of other Methods that rely on their being in the Architecture. For example, data centers and Computing Clouds are treated as Facilities because, in the Architecture, one needs to document where Applications / System instances physically reside. An Application / System at a particular Facility is referred to as an Application / System Instance.

Note in *Figure 56: Modeling Facilities, Clouds, and Networks* how Clouds manifest themselves in an Architecture; they are both Facilities and a System of Systems. Also note that Facilities, Clouds, and Networks are descendants of System of Systems. This enables the business to document these Systems of Systems in detail.

With respect to Cloud Computing, the business needs to acknowledge that they might be using multiple Clouds and that a Cloud is basically a Data Center housing IT and running their Applications / Systems. As a Data Center, each Cloud is a place where a System / Application Instance might reside.

---

158 HVAC is Heating, Ventilation, and Air-Conditioning

If the Cloud is owned by a Cloud Service Provider (CSP) then it is a Black Box to the business and nothing more needs to be done aside from listing the Cloud as a Facility. On the other hand, if the Cloud is a Private Cloud that the business owns, then it is also a System of Systems and the business needs to document the composition of that Cloud. In effect, the business now has a Cloud Computing Capability and they need to Architect the Capability and Engineer the underlying DOTMLPF. They also should have a Service Management Capability to systematically manage the Cloud and its' constituent parts.

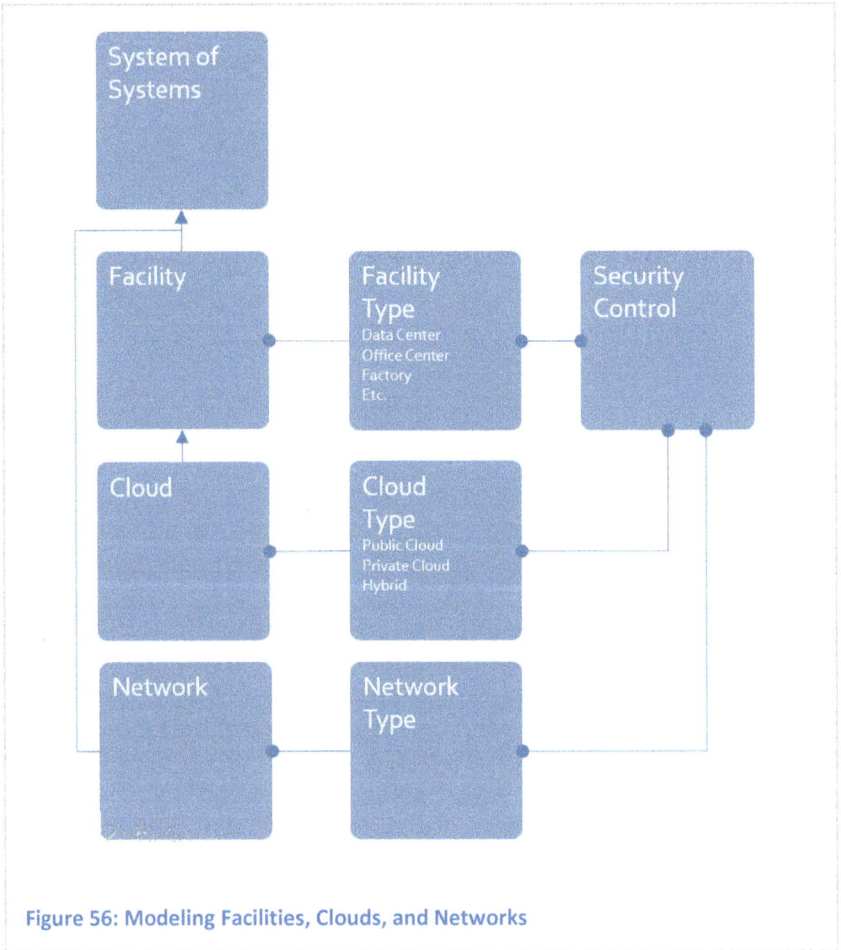

Figure 56: Modeling Facilities, Clouds, and Networks

Before discussing Buildings, Clouds, and Networks individually, note that Security Controls are created for and apply to Facility Types, Cloud Types, and Network Types. By extension, those Security Controls apply to the respective Facilities, Clouds, etc. that fall into those categories. Those Security Controls then, apply to the Systems / Applications instances that reside at those Facilities. Bear in mind here that the Security Controls are applied to the Instance and not the Application / System itself because if a System / Application has Instances at two different Facilities and they are different types of Facilities, then the Security Controls may be different.

BUILDINGS / FACILITIES

As very large grained Activities, Capabilities may include dedicated and special purpose buildings / structures. In Architecting a Capability then, one may be constructing, acquiring, and / or leasing buildings. It is immaterial as to whether they are purchased, built, or leased. What is important is that these assets have cost contributing to the Net-present Value of the Capability and also the life expectancy of the Capability.

In some cases, these assets are merely listed for reference and costing purposes and they are treated as "Black Boxes" whose content and structure you need not know about. Having said that, it does behoove the business to attach blueprints or floor plans to the appropriate records in the Architecture. We love products like Microsoft® SharePoint® but we advocate keeping this key information co-located in the Architecture. If the files containing the detail must remain in another system, hopefully that system is web-based and the files have URL's that can be placed within the Architecture.

CLOUDS

Before we start this discussion on Clouds, we'd like to make an important point about "The Cloud". People speak about "the Cloud" as though there is one and only one Cloud, when in fact there are many. As a matter of fact, each Cloud Service Provider may have multiple Clouds. In speaking of "The Cloud" then, we hope that you mean the assembly of Clouds that are provided by the various Cloud Service Providers (CSP)[159]. Another important point to make about Clouds is that there are three basic types of Clouds each with different Security Controls:

- Private Clouds
- Public Clouds
- Hybrid Clouds

As depicted in *Figure 56: Modeling Facilities, Clouds, and Networks* Clouds are both Facilities and Systems of Systems. Being descendants of Facility

---

159 Oracle, Microsoft, Google, and Amazon are some of the Cloud Service Providers that one commonly hears about today

enables you to list them as Facilities for reference purposes (a place where some of your Applications / Systems reside). Having them as descendants of "System of Systems" enables you to detail the composition of the Cloud. For the recipe on how to model and construct Systems and "Systems of Systems", we refer you back to *Figure 52: Elements for Modeling Systems*.

NETWORKS

Networks fall under the heading of Facilities because we consider networks to be infrastructure and because they are so foundational. In their most fundamental form, networks are named collections of Network Nodes and Network Links that interconnect the Network Nodes.

Most people speak of Network Nodes as Facilities or locations in the Network, but Network Nodes are really networking devices (assets given their cost) that reside at the Facilities. This is depicted in *Figure 57: Modeling Networks* where we show Network Nodes and Facilities as two distinct building blocks and where we show a Network Node residing at a Facility. Also shown in this figure are Network Links that have From and To Network Nodes. Enclave is also a building block and a named Network might be broken down into Enclaves, where a Node may be part of one of those Enclaves.

While we have the concept of Enclaves and provide the ability to break down a single named network into multiple Enclaves, some networks are designed and built so that each Enclave is a separate and distinct named Network. The structure depicted in *Figure 57: Modeling Networks* supports either approach.

At times, architects and engineers create drawings of the Local Area Networks (LAN) within a building. Under certain circumstances this may be required but generally, you may consider those local area networks as part of the Facility and to a large extent, the Facility is a Black Box.

Bear in mind that today networks are designed as business-wide assets that all organizations and all IT Applications / Systems are able to use. The point here is that the networks are, for the most part, independent of the Capability. Having said this, there are exceptions. For example, the Intelligence Community and an Emergency Communications and 911 Capability may require dedicated networks that are modeled by the owning organization.

In our model, Network Operations Centers (NOC) are Facilities that have one or more Network Nodes.

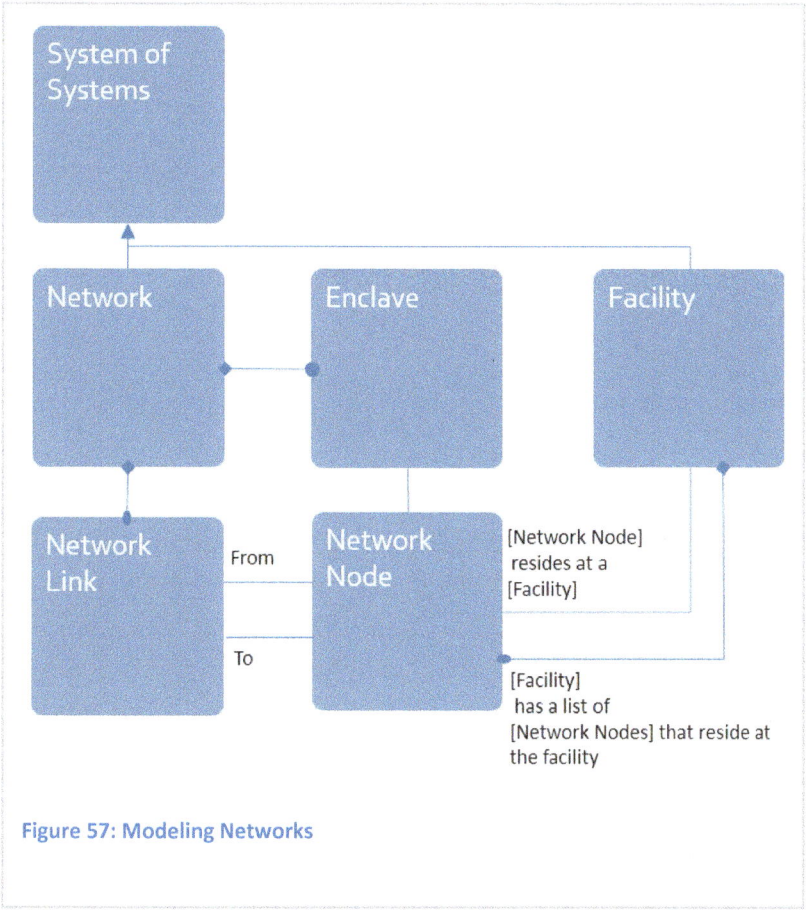

Figure 57: Modeling Networks

MATHEMATICAL FOUNDATIONS

In this world of Business Architecture and Engineering that we've been discussing, it is important to understand that the Business itself and many of the building blocks of the business are mathematical graphs. That is, they are a set of things (nodes), and a set of ordered pairs of those things (arcs). An unconstrained graph may contain any building block and the creator of the graph may inter-connect any of those building blocks with arcs. It is like your computer desktop, where you may place things represented by icons on the desktop but you now have the added ability to draw lines connecting the things / icons. Some graphs are special though insofar as there may be content restrictions and there may be rules about what can be connected.

With this idea, that the Business is a Graph, in mind and with (A) a sound meta-model that describes the Building Blocks, and (B) metadata that describes what can be connected to what, then one can mathematically determine if the business is complete and structurally sound. One can also mathematically compare businesses. Examples of Building Blocks or Elements that are graphs include, but are not limited to:

- **The Business** – is a graph whose Nodes are Building Blocks and whose Arcs are Bindings. One binds the Building Blocks of a Business in accordance with the Model being used as a guide
- **A Model** – is a graph whose Nodes are Classes and whose Arcs are Relationships between Classes. Models exist to guide the Architecture and Engineering of a business. You may be dealing with multiple businesses each having been documented using a different Model
- A **Process** is also a Graph but the Nodes are Activities and arcs are Information Flows between Activities.
- **An Activity** – is a graph whose Nodes are Tasks and whose Arcs are Sequence Flows from one Task to another. In this case and in the case of Process, the Sequence Flow as an Arc has an added attribute: Sequence Flows know what Business Event triggers the flow
- **A Subject Area** - is a graph whose Nodes are Entities and whose Arcs are Associations (relationships) between Entities
- **A Network** – is a graph whose Nodes are "Network Nodes" and whose Arcs are "Network Links".
- **Etc**.

While this might be a simple concept to grasp, most people (including most Architects), don't know graph theory or the benefits of graph theory to this form of Architecture and Engineering. It is our intent then, to try to simplify this topic and eventually commoditize this form of Architecture and Engineering so people that don't know Graph Theory can play without becoming a Mathematician first. An example of this is using Graph Theory to add one graph to another (take the Union of two graphs). This is intuitively valuable when you are dealing with a Merger or an Acquisition. Of course, both businesses need an Architecture. Think about the money saved during the Merger or Acquisition and the analysis that the unified Architecture facilitates.

The authors have used tools like THINKMAP® and D3JS© to create pictorial representations of certain graphs within the business. One great example is a THINKMAP®-based graph that one of the authors created for a well-known Federally Funded Research and Development Corporation (FFRDC). The FFRDC was asked to provide a graphic depiction of an Agency's Financial Management Systems. This Agency used the term System so that is what we will call them. The repository containing the inventory of Systems included some important "classification" and "time" data like which Systems were considered legacy and data about when the legacy Systems would be retired and removed from the IT landscape. The Agency in question was a Federation of four Agency's, each with their own Financial Management Systems numbering in the hundreds. Using THINKMAP® to display the graph of Systems and then using a feature of THINKMAP® to take the viewer though time, the architects were able to show pictorially how the System landscape was getting simplified over time and how the number of Systems was going down. The team also discovered and showed some interesting holes in the Architecture and Transition Plan. For instance, there were numerous Systems classified as "interim" that never went away. There were also numerous "Legacy" Systems that had no replacement. Clearly one could have generated a text report to show interim and legacy Systems that had no replacement and / or sunset date but no one thought to create such a query until the THINKMAP® based pictorial showed that this situation existed and needed to be addressed.

While some purpose-built graphs like the one just discussed are important, the architect should also have a general-purpose tool that enables them to look at the business at large and then pick a Building Block as the center and focus. Pick a building block like a "Capability". Pick the "Financial Management" Capability and take a look at all the things related to it.

You may find that many graph-based visualizations have so many nodes that they provide no valuable. To help out, the graph / tool needs to let you filter in two ways. First, the tool needs to let you specify how many nodes away from the chosen node to display. Do you want "1-away", "2-away", etc.? The other filter enables you to specify what elements you want to see. For instance, you may be looking at a Capability but you don't want to see the hundreds of Business Rules.

In addition to understanding the basics of graphs, there is also the matter of understanding some of the mathematics behind performance measurement. Presenting Measurements from history data entails averaging of historical numbers. While there are three types of Averages we are speaking of the Arithmetic Mean. This is the type of average that most people are familiar with, one adds up a set of numbers and then divides by the count of numbers in the set to get the Mean. While this is the most accurate and least misleading, one does need to be careful, especially with successive averaging that one might do to get (as an example) the CMM® rating of a Capability. Remember that in this example, one must successively Average the CMM® ratings of the Processes and then Services. A CMM® rating of a Capability might appear to be low but that doesn't mean that all the Services being provided are provided poorly and have a bad rating. There might be one Service as provisioned by one Organizational Unit that is pulling the rating down. In looking at a rating of this type then, one might see a bad number but one has to drill down to see what is causing the rating to be low.

Another example that is intuitive is your grades in school. Everyone is familiar with a "Grade Point Average". One might be pretty much a straight A student but with a single failure average comes down.

That's enough mathematics for now, we may explore this subject further in a sequel. This may include some of the mathematics behind determining the completeness of the methods.

PART VI – CLOSING

KEY TAKEAWAYS

A laxed form of architecture and engineering are pervasive in business and government today. Tremendous value can be gleaned from the practice if coordinated, and formalized. This book documents the key components of such a practice. They include Doctrine, Organization, Training, Materiel, Leadership, Personnel, and Facilities (DOTMLPF). This framework is a best practice within the defense industry. The authors have leveraged the DOTMLPF framework to adjust and unify (integrate) existing architecture and engineering frameworks.

The components of a successful architecture and engineering endeavor are typically minimized or overlooked. As a result, architecture and engineering efforts fail and get a bad rap. In fact, more than 66% of Architecture Initiatives fail.[160] But failure is not inevitable. Your business can avoid the pitfalls and failure by leveraging the lessons learned and the guidance provided below:

1. **Don't compromise ingredients:** Each ingredient and building block discussed is considered a critical success factor. Compromising on ingredients may compromise your success. Some of the ingredients discussed, like Organization, entails some organizational change. For instance, certain executive officers that do not report to the Chief Architect and operate without frameworks and methods will require some education and training.

   Establish the DOTMLPF required for your business to architect and engineer. And remember, it isn't one person reporting to your CTO. Architecture is like a Swiss Army knife with many features to it and planning IT is just one of those features.

2. **Too much planning, too little doing:** Avoid spending too much time planning and modeling in too much detail. Architects in the business and IT worlds are sometimes accused of living in an "Ivory Tower" and being completely removed from the realities of the business and real world. Make sure your architecture is aligned with the realities of your organization's business and budget. Establish a Planner's View of the Business that executives and business folks understand, appreciate, and use on a day to day basis. Assure that the IT is fit for your business purposes and use the architecture to assure that the IT is affordable.

---

160 Jonathan Broer, Rotterdam University, commissioned by IDS Scheer, summer 2008

Make sure that the architecture is being put to use and that meaningful reports are generated and used by the business. This includes but is not limited to, your annual business plan, your IT strategic plan, and your draft budget.

3. **Trying to model everything:** Do not try to model everything and for every eventuality. You cannot anticipate all the disruptive events that will influence your business. Ten years ago, who would have predicted the invention of the Smart Phone and iPad and the influence it has had on how we consume media and on business operations?

   By simplifying your Architecture and Engineering models and focusing on your capabilities, you remain flexible enough to react to unexpected events and trends. When it comes to Zoning your Business, you need to ask yourself, which problem you are going to solve and starting from there you can identify the data you will need to obtain and maintain. For example, if you want to identify which applications to invest in or divest according to their technical and functional suitability, you will need to collect information on the Applications / Systems and rate their technical and functional fit.

   Do not collect data without a good reason as the more detail you have in your inventory, the harder it will be to assure its quality. There is always a trade-off: if you want a deep and detailed model, you must compromise on how up-to-date your data is and how much effort you have to invest to maintain it.

   Think carefully about your use cases and which reports you really need. Start with the one or two important use cases and collect the necessary information for them. This could be Application / System rationalization. You can always consider adding more use cases later as your Architecture and Engineering practice becomes better established.

4. **Solving problems on the wrong level:** Getting too caught up in complex technical detail or spending all your time on high-level strategic models is not useful. Focus on doing "just enough" Architecture and Engineering "just in time" (Gartner®)[161] to achieve early results that are supported by your executive and management teams. Don't overcomplicate your work; focus on a small group of

---

161 Gartner® asserted that organizations can cut software costs by 30 percent using three best practices. 2016-07-19 http://www.gartner.com/newsroom/id/3382317

clear objectives, and measure and track success. It is important to keep the right perspective. Being too far removed from the realities of your organization may lead to negative outcomes.

One example of an Architecture having too broad an overview with a disregard for business details was the application rationalization project of a national justice business to save costs. Among the measures identified by the architecture and engineering team was the replacement of a parcel tracking application by a web-based system. They had already finalized the planning and allocated the budget, when the state level leadership pointed out, that the handheld devices used by the logistics drivers in some regions were incapable of running a web browser.

5. **No tool or the wrong tool for the job:** It makes sense to introduce an Architecture and Engineering tool early on – workarounds that are not purpose-built like spreadsheets and drawing/presentation tools create more work in the long run, as they soon reach their limitations. Missing quality assurance mechanisms create problems over time and lead to significant expenditure for troubleshooting.

   Find an Architecture and Engineering tool that is easy to keep up-to-date, fosters communication and collaboration across the Business, one which makes it simple to share information and extract meaningful reports that are meaningful to the business community. Use a tool that is highly configurable so that the tool adjusts to the needs of your business.

   Leverage tools that enable the business to focus on the data and enables lay people to enter that data. There are tools that are browser-based and highly configurable. This makes the architecture visible, accessible, and understandable (VAU) across your business or agency.

6. **Focusing too much on the past and the current state:** Most Architecture and Engineering Initiatives fail right at the starting gate by focusing too much on the current state. Pick a time not too far out in the future state and establish the architecture for that point in time. It will soon be your current state.

7. **Agility is achieved using Architecture and Engineering detail:** it is through the architecture that one becomes agile. We touched on this in our discussion about the elimination of "supplier rediscovery" in the section on *Supplier management* and *Putting the Architecture to Use* on

page 102. There is no "fast path to enlightenment" and there is no need to rush the job. Robert Louis Stevenson said it well in "Treasure Island". He said, through the voice of Long John Silver:

"Why, how many ships, think ye, now, have I seen laid aboard? And how many brisk lads drying in the sun of Execution Dock?", cried Silver, "and all for this same hurry and hurry and hurry. ... I've seen a thing or two at sea, I have. If you would on'y lay your course, and a p'int to windward, you would ride in carriages, you would."

Be agile, with architecture, and without compromising the integrity of your architecture or the business that it describes.

In a nutshell, we are talking about your ability to handle Strategic Planning and transformative initiatives in a systematic way. Your planning and resulting success in the market are worth the discipline and investment. We are in the midst of a digital revolution; it is in the midst of this revolution that you might take a moment to Architect and Engineer the business and future state, and to establish the Architecture as the heart and brain of your business.

CONCLUSION

This book treats the Architecture Reference Models and Capability Blueprints as living things whose lifespan goes well beyond the construction of the Organizations, Processes, and Systems they document. The Architecture and tools are used throughout the fiscal and calendar year and throughout the lifecycle of the business to understand what was built and how well the business is operating. We view the Architecture of your business as the heart and brain of the business.

We started with the assertion that Architecture is discretionary and today, there are no legal and mandatory requirements for Architecture and Engineering in the private sector. In the government arena, the US Federal Government's Clinger-Cohen Act requires each Federal Agency to leverage Architecture and Engineering for IT modernization. We've made a case for why architecture is important, why it should focus more on the business, and why it should be non-discretionary. Venture Capitalist can help on this front as they make investments in start-up companies. If the investment is significant enough, they can require a certain amount of architecture, a bit more than one normally includes in a business plan.

The Clinger-Cohen Act has set a precedent for legislation and perhaps it is legislation that will eliminate some of the pitfalls discussed. After all, it is legal and mandatory requirements in the construction world that provides the benefits that stem from having Blueprints for the construction of a house or building complex. Industry and companies that comprise the marketplace would benefit from having a Reference Models for the Business and Blueprints for each Capability.

The Sarbanes-Oxley Act[162] of 2002 was a step in the right direction but it fell short in that it does not require companies of a certain size have Architecture. We believe that it is through legislation that companies will be more successful with Architecture and Engineering. The idea of having legislation introduces the question as to when a business should have a set of blueprints. A company just starting out, with the intention of growing organically, may not be able to afford a full set of Reference Models and detailed blueprints for each Capability. Today one can pick a house style and buy a set of blueprints out of a catalog. Business and industry need to get to the same level of maturity. One should be able to pick a business model and buy a corresponding set of blueprints. Companies that are

---

162 H.R.3763 - Sarbanes-Oxley Act of 2002, https://www.congress.gov/bill/107th-congress/house-bill/3763

providing Services and Software as a Service (SaaS) should have blueprints for the Capabilities and Applications / Systems being provisioned.

High-performing organizations tend to develop Architecture and institutionalize the Architecture at both levels discussed; they use it on a daily basis. As an example, an organization may make assertions in the architecture about performance measures that need to be taken and monitored. A high-performing organization then takes measurements and compares them with expectations. While this information was traditionally programmed into point solutions, it can be centralized in the Architecture. In engineering terms, the Architecture is a "Closed Loop System" that follows through on its' assertions. The Architecture sends information out to the extremities of the business and it expects responses. This information is then used by the business to monitor health. In a high-performing organization this closed loop operates in near real time.

The Architecture also delegates certain analyses and monitoring to "Intelligent Agents". These Agents provide insight into recurring situations and how they were dealt with in the past. The Agents maintain the questions posed in the past about certain political and market conditions and they store information about how those conditions were met. These Agents maintain this knowledge in perpetuity for newcomers to the business.

The Building Blocks represent your business in its totality. The Building Blocks and the related data are designed to be used by the business and by business people for business reasons. While there are Information Technology Building Blocks, we emphasize stage setting with Building Blocks like Business Areas / Lines and the associated Goals, Objectives, Process, and Weakness.

Architecture of the business enables the Information Technology people to do what they do best: design and build Systems / Applications that automate business operations. The information technology groups within your organization can apply the practices outlined here to build Systems / Applications[163] that (A) address business needs, and (B) appeal to their clients as they attempt to understand that changing business and IT worlds.

To void controversy and certain political issues, you may euphemize the terms and you may eliminate the 'E' word, the 'A' word, and the 'F' word from your business. Regardless, we urge you to be systematic, apply

---

163 The IT can be Cloud or Data Center based and mobile as well.

methods, and be complete in documenting how your business is structured today and where it is going. We urge you to look at the DOTMLPF of your business. We urge you to take both traditional and scenario-based approaches to strategic planning. And to assure your agility and reduce risk, we urge you to maintain this information in perpetuity.

We challenge everyone in the business world to embrace the planning and architecture metaphor and to be as fastidious as the engineers from the world of building architecture. This includes things like "part number detail"[164] of the building blocks and the associated products purchased to build them. After all, the business needs this information and part number detail to be successful in the DevOps[165]. Be as fastidious as LEGO® Designers. If LEGO Designers can create blueprints for complex and operational LEGO models, and if those same designers can create instructions that young adults and children are able to follow to build the model, then why can't the architects and engineers in the business world do the same for the construction of a business or a governmental agency? It can be done.

---

164 Engineers handling the Information Technology portion of the Architecture are notorious for referring to products loosely and not understanding the need for part number detail.
165 A basic description of DevOps can be found at https://en.wikipedia.org/wiki/DevOps

www.ingramcontent.com/pod-product-compliance
Lightning Source LLC
Chambersburg PA
CBHW040851210326
41597CB00029B/4799